Unearthing Indian Land

Unearthing Indian Land

Living with the Legacies of Allotment

KRISTIN T. RUPPEL

The University of Arizona Press   Tucson

The University of Arizona Press
©2008 The Arizona Board of Regents
All rights reserved

www.uapress.arizona.edu

Library of Congress Cataloging-in-Publication Data
Ruppel, Kristin T.
    Unearthing Indian land : living with the legacies of allotment /
    Kristin T. Ruppel.
        p. cm.
    Includes bibliographical references and index.
ISBN 978-0-8165-2711-3 (pbk. : alk. paper)
        1. Indians of North America—Land tenure. 2. Indians of North
America—Government relations. 3. Indian allotments—Law and
legislation—United States. 4. United States—Ethnic relations. I. Title.
E98.L3R87   2008
323.1197—dc22   2008032916

Publication of this book is made possible in part by the proceeds of a
permanent endowment created with the assistance of a Challenge Grant
from the National Endowment for the Humanities, a federal agency.

16 15 14 13 12 11   7 6 5 4 3 2

Contents

Illustrations

Preface and Acknowledgments

Two weeks before I received the first proof of this book—when it was too late to change much of anything but typos—the following headline appeared in the *Blackfoot* (Idaho) *Morning News*: "Competitive bidding now the rule for Fort Hall [Indian Reservation] land leases" (see Emily Hone, 9/4/2008 at http://www.am-news.com/content/view/85475/1/).

Why was this news? Anywhere else but in and around Indian country, competitive bidding has *always* been the rule. Google it. News is made when government entities *fail* to provide for competitive bidding processes, not when they actually follow protocols long set out in federal, tribal, state, county, municipal, or business regulatory codes across the country, including the federal code called "Indians" (*Code of Federal Regulations, Title 25*), the Bureau of Indian Affairs' bible when it comes to the leasing of Indian lands.

The *Morning News* article began, "Farmers who lease land on the Fort Hall Indian Reservation found last week there's a new way of doing business there." For reasons explored in this book, the fact that there is now a new way of doing business on reservations like Fort Hall is a testament to the work of Indian landowner activists and advocates from allotted reservations everywhere. I'll leave the intricacies of "Indian land" and "allotment" for the book. Here, I want to state that the strides described in the following pages have been exceeded since the book went to press—even accounting for the backslides. The point is that, in their "performance of territoriality" (see the end of chapter 3), Indian landowners are changing the rules of the game. This is something I wish to celebrate and acknowledge. By doing so, I also acknowledge that the process, democratic as it is, is long, messy, and difficult.

viii   PREFACE AND ACKNOWLEDGMENTS

Acknowledgments

In the spirit of giving the proper credit and none of the blame, the people and institutions I have to thank for helping to make this book a reality are many. Foremost among them: allottees and advocates Ernee and Steve Werelus, Helen Sanders, Sally Willett, Theresa Carmody, Howard Belodoff, Patty and Roy Dan, LaNada (Boyer) War Jack, Alvin "Gus" James, Willie Preacher, Walter Nevada, Louise and Alfred Navo, Arlene Ortiz, Louida Unger, Frank Papse Sr., Alene Menta, Aletha Wetchie, Sam Hernandez, and (last but far from least) Drusilla Gould; professors and scholars Frank Pommersheim, Nan Rothschild, Nancy Bonvillain, and especially Teri Hall, Nick DeGenova, Val Daniel, and Simon Ortiz; freelance editor Jeff Lockridge and the good folks at the University of Arizona Press; the anthropology departments at Columbia University and Idaho State University, and my home department of Native American Studies at Montana State University; and, of course, my wonderful family. I wish that the words "thank you" could actually express what I wish to say to these most generous people.

Unearthing Indian Land

Introduction

"It's the same old problem," says 71-year-old Shoshone-Bannock land-owner and activist Ernestine "Ernee" Broncho Werelus. "Nobody down here on the reservations knows what's going on until it's too late. There's nobody around to explain the new laws to the people."[1]

Ernee is talking about section 207 of the Indian Land Consolidation Act of 1983, the first piece of general legislation to confront the huge and growing problem of fractionating Indian land ownership. Known as the "2 percent rule," section 207 authorized the secretary of the interior to take interests of 2 percent or less in reservation land allotments held by individual Indian landowners, and give those interests to the tribe upon the passing of the landowner.[2] The individual Indian landowners were neither warned that this would happen nor compensated when it did.

Twice, in 1987 and again in 1997, the United States Supreme Court struck down the 2 percent rule.[3] The Court said in no uncertain terms that section 207 amounted to an unconstitutional taking of private property interests. But before the Court rulings could have their intended effects, thousands of individual Indian landowners (not to mention their potential heirs) had lost their land.

When people began hearing stories from other landowners that the land interests they expected to inherit from recently deceased relatives had been taken, they went to the Bureau of Indian Affairs for help. There, Ernee says, they were told not to worry because they owned only "a teaspoonful" of land, anyway. She pulls out her calculator and continues: "Say I had a 2 percent interest in a 40-acre allotment. That's almost an acre. And they call it a spoonful of dirt!"

The amounts and descriptions of these small fractional interests in Indian land vary, from a spoonful to a shovelful. But the underlying message is always the same: "You don't own enough land to care about."

The conquest of Western America shapes the present as dramati-
cally—and sometimes as perilously—as the old mines shape the moun-
tainsides. To live with that legacy, contemporary Americans ought to
be well informed and well warned about the connections between past
and present. But here the peculiar status of Western American history
has posed an obstacle to understanding. Americans are left to stumble
over—and sometimes into—those connections, caught off guard by the
continued vitality of issues widely believed to be dead.
—Patricia Limerick, *The Legacy of Conquest*

A decade ago, while doing research on what I thought would become a
doctoral project on the ethnoecology of Shoshone-Bannocks in southeastern Idaho, I stumbled over—and into—one of those connections between
past and present that Professor Limerick warns us about. I was not "well
informed." In fact, until Ernee Werelus began to teach me about the
fractionation of allotted Indian trust lands, I had never given a moment's
thought to how American Indians own land except in the abstract terms
of my academic training: hunter-gatherers, systems of indigenous land
tenure, the tragedy of the commons. The smattering of American history I'd received in high school and college hadn't made much of the
General Allotment Act of 1887 (Dawes Act), even though this one single
piece of legislation helped to pave the way west for my homesteader great
grandparents and tens of thousands of other land-hungry whites. All I
knew was that the reservation was a different world from the one I'd grown
up in, and I didn't really know why. When Ernee introduced me to the
weird, tangled legacy of Indian land, I was, in Professor Limerick's words,
"caught off guard." I wondered somewhat angrily, much as my students
do when they learn about it today, "Why didn't I know this?"

What began, then, as an attempt to answer that question by way of
postcolonial and anthropological critiques has evolved into what I hope is
also a more grounded exploration of how "to live with that legacy"—into
an ethnography, not of a people, but of the colonial project that is Indian
land. It thus explores how the conditions for a truly post- or decolonized
future can be created and, more important, how those conditions are
being rediscovered in the ongoing (re-)creation of Indian land by the
landowners themselves.[4] Becoming "well informed and well warned"

gave me a place to start. From there, I began to understand that the connections themselves are the vital presence, buried in this case beneath the sometimes deadening weight of law and bureaucracy.

Unearthing "Indian Land"

From the perspective of federal Indian law, "Indian land" is a legal term, and refers to land held in trust for American Indian individuals and tribes by the United States federal government. From the perspectives of individual Indian landowners and tribes, it may also be much more than this, as I hope to show. But it is at least this.

Originally created as a means of recognizing "aboriginal title" (itself a creation of medieval European jurisprudence) and the "Indian right of occupancy," the legal structure "Indian land" eventually became a tool of U.S. hegemony, first through various treaty arrangements and allotment acts, and then through the General Allotment Act of 1887. In its attempt to destroy indigenous forms of government and community, the United States imposed its own rules of private property on indigenous people by dividing treaty lands among individual American Indians. The result was a massive transfer of land from Indian into white hands. This was followed by humanitarian advocacy for an indefinite extension of the 25-year period (specified under the original act) during which Indian allotments would be held in trust by the United States. In this way, it was thought that Indian landowners newly "emancipated" from the assumed evils of communal land ownership (never adequately defined; see "Marshall, 'Discovery,' and the 'Domestic Dependent Nations'" in chapter 1) would have time to familiarize themselves with the legal complexities of private land ownership and capital.

Most notably, Indian allottees would be kept from selling their allotments until it could be proven that they were competent to provide for themselves in ways appropriate to white-male-Christian American citizenship.[5] For a variety of reasons to be discussed in subsequent chapters, the trusteeship of the United States over Indian land allotments quickly became a permanent feature of the federal-Indian relationship, writing nineteenth-century notions of inherent racial "difference" into the structures and superstructure of federal Indian law.[6]

Throughout, the relational aspect of Indian land as place — the mother earth of indigenous philosophies — was interred beneath the alienating aspect of Indian land as object, as land in "severalty."[7]

❧

> Every time we come together . . . we have to sit back and try to give some kind of a history, background — why we are the way we are.
> —Comment heard during a "Community Relations" public forum, Pocatello, Idaho[8]

As I learned, the overarching and daily presence of federal Indian legal structures (like Indian land) seldom enters into non-Indian equations of why Indians are "the way [they] are." Yet these equations, for lack of some rather imposing variables, continue to yield up one-dimensional constructions of reservation Indians as the irredeemable Other, the victims of inevitable "conquest," and the "unfortunate" members of "an imploding culture" (as one non-Indian acquaintance put it). Such simplistic anthems of unavoidable ruin fit the "scriptures of dominance" that Gerald Vizenor (1994, 4) refers to as the "manifest manners" of Manifest Destiny. Whether romantic or tragic, they mark "the absence of tribal realities not the sources of a presence" (14).

As an absence as well as a presence, Indian land is a colonial invention, a colonizing tool, the product of an imposed "guardianship" under which indigenous people were forced into peculiar modes of private land tenure and inheritance. As such, it should come as no surprise that this invention was entirely foreign to Native American experience. Its peculiarity is redoubled by the fact that it was in many ways foreign even to the experience of the colonizers. To this day, the abiding strangeness of Indian land, for Indians as well as non-Indians, helps to make the internal colonization of the United States an "anti-place" of immense proportions.[9]

To illustrate one aspect of what I mean by "anti-place," the majority of Shoshone-Bannock Tribal members on the Fort Hall Indian Reservation own Indian land, also referred to as "trust land." However, many of them would be unable to show you — in anything but the most general terms — where their land is located. Some might be able to tell you how much land they own, more or less. Others would have to dig out a Bureau of Indian Affairs (BIA) report that renders property interests in ridiculously drawn out simple fractions, more recently rendered in their ridiculously drawn out decimal equivalents. Because of this fractionation of Indian land interests and the resulting difficulty of finding agreement among the numerous co-owners of any given allotment, almost all of the individually and tribally owned land here is leased out by the BIA to non-Indians. And Fort Hall is hardly unique. This is a circumstance common to every reservation that underwent allotment.

Hardly a new phenomenon, the loss of land among American Indians reached stunning proportions decades ago with the practice of allotment (under the General Allotment Act), which began in earnest around the turn of the twentieth century. But the loss that people have suffered *since* allotment—alienation from their land—is a predicament of exponentially growing proportions, one euphemistically referred to as "inheritance of tenancy in common," or fractionation.

The story of Indian land is a story of the smothering of earth as person beneath the bureaucratic weight and economic utilitarianism of earth as property, a contrivance of colonial design. My unearthing of Indian land thus recounts a story of assimilation and alienation. As told by some tribal members on allotted reservations, it is partly about controlling land as a resource, about making a living. But it is also about being and belonging—about maintaining the self as an aspect of the land, not simply as a possessor.

"It's a legal term," I said. Frowning, she looked away. "I mean, it's not only that," I added, trying to convince her that I understood something about the differences between us: I, a 30-something white woman of Norwegian-German descent whose ancestors came over and headed west a mere four generations ago; and she, a 40-something Shoshone-Bannock woman whose ancestors have, for all practical purposes, always been here.

I grasped for a connection: "I mean, it was the *mother earth* kind of Indian land before it was ever this Euro-American legal thing called 'Indian land.' Now it's just both . . . " I responded to the mental shifts evident in her scowl with some verbal shifts of my own. Indian land of the legal kind was "simply" an imposition of Euro-American assumptions about property, culture, and belonging laid out on top of her Indian land, her mother earth, in the United States' quest to "civilize" the Indian.

But the fact is, the term "Indian land" is highly charged, carrying with it a history of takings and mistakes, with consequences both intended and unintended. Its legal reality now lies there, heaved over mother earth like a wet blanket.

Her expression softened as she caught my meaning, but the sense of difference remained: the sense that for Indians the land is kin first—it is *Indian*—before it is an object, a legal entity of foreign (i.e., white) persuasion. For whites, on the other hand, the land is an object first: it is property in a world of properties. Although, for some whites, land might come to signify family, a person in a world of persons, even for them, this is something they acknowledge, not something they *know*.

And so the connections are made, just that quickly and almost as imperceptibly—marked perhaps by a scowl—between idealized definitions of land and distinctions of self. Who we are depends not only on where we come from, but also on how we come: on how we make that journey from place to person and back again. We take the journey for granted until we come up against someone for whom it is different. Then suddenly the connections we've made are revealed, as are the gaps they presuppose in our perceptions and conceptions.[10] In other contexts, like the one that follows, the connections remain hidden.

As I was writing the foregoing account, I received a phone call from Ernee Werelus, the person to whom I am most indebted for the information and insights recorded in this study. At one point in our conversation, she began to describe the "schooling" she had recently been providing for one of her nephews on the subject of Indian "blood quantum" (a colonial-era scheme for measuring an individual's racial identity according to the fractional inheritance of blood from parents of different races). Ernee has been a vociferous opponent of the repeated attempts by one faction to establish a one-quarter blood quantum for Shoshone-Bannock tribal membership (membership at Fort Hall is currently based on descent and residence). She argued that blood quantum is another of the federal government's ploys to "get rid of Indians." Its logical end, she explained, is extinction (whether by fact of law or biology) of the people and, by default, of the government's responsibilities in Indian land, which itself will then disappear. As soon as Indian land ownership passes to a non-Indian, or, as soon as its owner is newly *declared* a "non-Indian" because of some new definition or blood quantum rule, the land passes out of the federal trust.[11] The government gets rid of Indians and Indian land in one fell swoop.

As Ernee's argument reveals, within the hegemonic structure of Indian land, land and Indian are (re)identified with one another, but legally, in terms that simultaneously echo and mock ancient customary relations by threatening to neutralize the identification of person and place once and for all. Hence her exasperation when she described her nephew, "trying to explain this to the people at the last [landowner] meeting, why we shouldn't vote for blood quantum. And everyone just sits there wondering why he's talking about blood quantum and land loss in the same breath. . . . They just don't see the links!"[12]

This may be so because, in U.S. legal traditions, the "links" between Indian land and Indian have taken a somewhat longer time to construct than the definitions of land and self we pull out at a moment's notice in order to explain ourselves to each other. The introduction of Indian land by the 1887 General Allotment Act precipitated a system that demarcates property and person alike, subtly erecting boundaries between Indian and non-Indian, and not only (or necessarily) between distinct individuals, but also between and among the many identities that may be present in any given individual. One of the aims of *Unearthing Indian Land* is to expose the virulent habits of culture and society beneath this particular kind of anti-place.

At this juncture, it is important to touch on a key contradiction inherent in the federal Indian trust. Because the trust was set up so that Indian land would pass from one generation to the next as undivided interests (inheritance of tenancy in common), the allotted land itself remains physically undivided even though title to every square inch of it has been divided (fractionated) among exponentially increasing numbers of heirs.

Such a contradictory arrangement—imposition of a divided, *almost* private property right to undivided land—has preserved the Indian land base more or less intact at the expense of diminishing the individual land-owners' ability to interact with their land in meaningful ways.[13] With few exceptions, allotted Indian lands are fractionated and under control of the BIA, as trustee, or the tribe, where they have been easily appropriated to the interests of non-Indian, and often corporate, land users.[14] The consequences of fractionation are immense, indeed immeasurable when considered against the diversity of peoples whose single most unifying national symbol is a "passionate attachment to the land" (Jones 1982, 54).[15]

To fit Indian land and the individual Indian landowner into the context of (post)colonialism, chapter 1 presents a standard history of the United States' colonial civilizing strategies. The 1887 allotment of private land and the federal Indian trust were supposed to create "individuals" and "citizens" and to destroy the "tribal mass." In exploring what kind of individuals and citizens were created, chapter 2 examines the effects of the Indian Land Consolidation Act (ILCA) and its ongoing amendments, other key developments in the hegemonic history of Indian land, and Indian landowner advocacy in the context of related national movements, where the individual is positioned against both tribe and tradition before political and legal advocates, Congress, and the courts.

Chapter 3 presents the evolving citizenship of Indian landowners through the stories of how they affected the passage of federal Indian laws since the 1950s. Chapter 4 describes Indian land ownership both locally and nationally as, at once, a political, economic, cultural, and spiritual pursuit.

Much of the contemporary writing emanating from the West, and especially from the intermontane West, has engaged the notion of place as an emblem of personhood in the western United States. Chapter 5 brings the narrative full circle by sketching implacement and misplacement beyond the borders of the reservation, discussing U.S. Indian land ownership in the context of local and national indigenous movements, their staying power, and competing powers of interpretation. Chapter 6, the final chapter, represents my earliest attempts to capture a sense of the (mis)placed in the region of Pocatello, Fort Hall, and the Lemhi Valley, and of the face-to-face encounters I have experienced there. As such, its style is more personal than that of the other chapters.

CHAPTER 1

Nations In(di)visible

one nation, indivisible
—Francis Bellamy, 1892

Just five years before Francis Bellamy wrote the oath that would become a symbol, albeit a contested one, of American national unity, the U.S. Congress passed a bill—the General Allotment Act—that would, as it turns out, guarantee disarray in perpetuity for hundreds of thousands of American Indians and their heirs. Several hundred years of European legal and philosophical deliberation over the meanings of empire, conquest, colonization, property, and sovereignty preceded and mostly reinforced that guarantee.

Terra Nullius: By Virtue of Nothing

In these first moments in the story law tells us—in its assertion of *terra nullius*—we see the central role played by abstraction and theory in western law and culture: the world is conceived, and *acted upon*, as if reality can simply be conjured up in whatever form suits the desire of the powerful at the moment.
—Dara Culhane, *The Pleasure of the Crown*[1]

The entire purport of any symbol [convention] consists in the total of all general modes of rational conduct which, conditional upon all possible circumstances and desires, would ensue upon the acceptance of the symbol.
—C. S. Peirce, 1910[2]

Created in 1722 by memorandum of the Privy Council of Great Britain, the legal structure *terra nullius*, literally, "no one's land," extended the reach of the Crown across abstract space and time. It did so by virtue of nothing other than British imperial law and expertise in legitimizing violence, an expertise gained during its "indiscriminate slaying and expropriation" of the Irish, its next of kin (Canny 1973, 583; see also Culhane 1998, 37–57).[3] *Terra nullius* immediately became part of the "general modes of rational conduct" as established fact—as it is still sometimes presented today—and was applied with abandon under the "doctrine of discovery."[4] In Britain's competition with Spain and, to a greater extent, France over North America's purportedly wide-open spaces, the doctrine of discovery and its twin "doctrine of conquest" conveniently gave the Crown two alternatives in staking its claims. On the one hand, if the "discovered" lands were free of human inhabitants, the Crown could immediately establish British colonial law under the doctrine of discovery. On the other, if the discovered lands were found to be inhabited, the Crown could lay claim to colonial sovereignty through the use of military force, treaty, or both under the doctrine of conquest. The not-so-subtle twist in the actual application of the doctrines was that the definition of what counted for a human was conveniently Eurocentric. Especially where the balance of power had tipped in the colonizers' favor, non-Christian (i.e., all) natives could simply be categorized as "infidel" and, as such, unworthy of being counted as "inhabitants."[5] Indeed, they could be defined into oblivion.[6] Eventually, agriculture, private property, and profit would all be linked to the Christian standard. But with Britain's sixteenth-century racialization of the Irish as precedent, laws were early in place to facilitate that century's actual as well as legal disappearances of non-Christian, non-agriculturalist (and, later, noncapitalist) peoples wherever they were found.[7]

The historical growth of these imperial assertions is well known, as are the consequences that ensued in the colonial practices of exploitation, domination, and genocide in the Americas and elsewhere. The overweening "rationality" of these practices became especially pronounced in the development of Indian land laws in the United States. For one rather obvious example, European imperial assertions and assumptions about the "inferior" or "infidel" status of the "native" or Other meant that indigenous conceptions of property rights, especially to land, were ignored, patronized, diminished, or discounted by law (see Cronon 1983, 68).[8] And *terra nullius*, the prevailing symbol of the doctrine of discovery, which came to define humanness in terms of European land ownership, agriculture, and religion (Christianity), was codified. It is perpetuated through one of the founding cases of federal Indian law.[9]

Although the doctrine of discovery often provided a convenient justification for legally dispossessing Native people of lands and life, early colonial practices in North America were an odd mix. They were largely defined by competition among Europeans for Indian favor and by British imperial efforts to maintain the Crown's sovereignty over its English subjects. As long as there was an abundance of "empty" or "un-owned" land, "conquest" and colonization did not necessitate the assimilation of indigenous people—the goal of allotment.[10] For example, in its Royal Proclamation of 1763, the British Crown forbade white settlement west of the Appalachian watershed, and "formally reserved to the Indians 'all the Lands and Territories lying to the Westward'"(Bordewich 1996, 116). The king's declaration of a "clear line of demarcation" between Indians and whites was mostly ignored by white settlers, but it established ethnic separation—not assimilation—as a "keystone of government policy" (116). On the other hand, the same proclamation guaranteed the "protection of the Crown" over "Indian Nations or Tribes," effectively assimilating tribal nations wholesale with the Crown's claim to absolute sovereignty (cf. Culhane 1998, 54–56). This "protective" aspect of British imperial rule would become a central part of the United States' hegemonic discourse in Indian Country. But, since hegemonic systems develop unevenly over time, and are marked by the resistance as well as the complicity of the dominated, we should be able to discern the presence of a "counter-mythology" in Indian-white relations: a "different set of stories" emanating from the shocks and prods of "real things" encountered in North America, and productive of different beliefs (Williams 1997, 25).[11]

A Counter-Mythology

Contrary to British colonial assertions, *terra nullius*, discovery, and conquest were loosed upon diversely peopled and variously defended places.[12] Thus, as discovered people accommodated and opposed colonial presences, colonial settlers, depending on the need, became more or less attentive to the unfamiliar natural and cultural worlds they entered.

For instance, as Robert Williams (1997) argues, by quickly adapting precontact intertribal practices of negotiation and treaty making to the novel conditions and opportunities presented by the European newcomers, indigenous people actually facilitated much of Europe's early expansion. Using treaty documents from the Encounter era (seventeenth and eighteenth centuries), Williams describes the highly symbolic language of economic, political, and legal alliances that developed early on between Indians and whites (Williams 1997, 37). Unable to impose European principles of hierarchical and centralized authority wholesale, Encounter-era Europeans "had to learn of different language of diplomacy"(31–32). They had to conform their own negotiations in trade and survival to an indigenous language that had its own set of principles, symbolic gestures, metaphors, and rituals preadapted to the demands of negotiation and trade in a multicultural and multilingual society far more diverse than Europe's. Williams sums up the patterns discernible in the treaty dealings of Native nations with colonial powers across two hundred years:

> Indians can be witnessed inviting Europeans to make known the "good thoughts" of peace, to smoke the sacred pipe, to clear the path, to bury the hatchet, to link arms together and unite as one people, to eat out of the same bowl together, and to remove the clouds that blind the sun that shines peace on all people of the world. These and a host of other intricately related sets of recurring metaphors and sacred Indian rituals are part of a North American indigenous language of law and peace between different peoples that made diplomacy possible and effective on the multicultural frontiers of North America during the Encounter era. (Williams 1997, 36)

The cloud of European supremacy probably blinded most Europeans to the possibility of taking such sentiments seriously, as William Cronon (1983, 66) suggests in his reading of one of the earliest Indian deeds in American history. The deed represents a 1636 land transaction between William Pynchon's trading partnership, operated under the Massachusetts Bay Company, and a group of Indians from the Agawam village near present-day Springfield, Connecticut (66–68). Signed by thirteen Indians "for and in the name of al the other Indians" in the village including several named male and female "right owner[s]" of the land, the deed clearly states the Indians' understanding that they were selling use and occupancy rights to the land, and that they were *retaining* the *same* rights to themselves (66–67). Pynchon and his fellow settlers, on the other hand, interpreted the deed in starkly different terms, as their descendants do to this day.[13] Having been generally instructed by the Massachusetts Bay Company "'to make composition with such of the salvages as did pretend any title or lay clayme to any of the land' [the settlers presumed that] Indian rights were not real, but pretended, because the land had already been granted the company by the English Crown" (Cronon 1983, 68).[14] Deeds, like treaties, symbolized different underlying truths to their respective Indian and white interpreters, producing all manner of consequences and conflicts. For one, the double meanings embodied in these early land transactions resulted, from the Indian perspective, in sales of use rights for the same parcel to multiple purchasers who, from the white perspective, each thought they were buying a bounded piece of the land itself.[15] The ensuing confusion over land titles became an early justification for limiting both Indian and white land transactions to mediation by the British Crown and, later, the U.S. federal government. The irony of these restrictions was that, from the evidence at hand, early Indian land sales seldom pretended to be anything close to what the Crown and colonial governments were restricting: the physical alienation of abstractly delimited, bounded spaces. On the other hand, even after white land buyers came to recognize at least the existence of Indian principles of shared use rights in property, the old assumptions and settled beliefs in Anglo superiority prevailed in their dealings with "the natives," who, as the Massachusetts Bay Company told its agents, "wilbe willing to treat and compound with you upon very easie conditions" (Cronon 1983, 186n24).[16] For all that, Euro-American ethnocentrism and bad faith do not negate the forces embodied in a stubborn indigenous counter-mythology of mutual recognition, accommodation, and coexistence.

For example, in 1763, at the end of the Old World's Seven Years' War, Britain assumed that its victory over its European rivals gave it territorial rights in the New World. Individual Indians would again and again repudiate this assumption "in statements that were so widespread, numerous, and similar as to make it obvious that the Indians, in general, had a clear understanding of European concepts of territory and of how those concepts might affect them"(Jones 1982, 18–19; see also Smith 1997, 53). Dorothy Jones argues that, by the time Britain was induced to bow out of the North American picture, preexisting Indian diplomatic relations with the imperial powers—those early ones mapped by Williams (1997) above, as well as the somewhat later ones identified by Jones—would guarantee that the founding of the United States would be a contested one (Jones 1982, 169). In its evolving colonialism by treaty and statute, the young republic would sooner or later systematically and legally relieve American Indians of most of their land. Nevertheless, like its Old World predecessors, the United States would be forced to recognize and, to some extent, adjust its conduct to an alternative reality. Against assertions of total U.S. sovereignty and unilaterally imposed boundaries, Indian resistance was "so effective that the United States had to reverse itself. After 1786, the federal government began treaty negotiations anew on the basis of a recognition of Indian land rights and acquisition by purchase [as opposed to force]" (Jones 1982, 4). By the turn of the nineteenth century, power disparities between Indian nations and the United States were so great that the treaty relationship was only superficially one of negotiation. It had instead become a relationship of domination barely concealed by a thin veneer of diplomacy (185–186). Some would argue that, even in its earliest recognition of Indian land rights, the United States was always cynically motivated by greed and the eventual expropriation of all Indian lands. Yet the truth of this statement must not be allowed to obscure the fact that U.S. and colonial interests have consistently been undermined by the unintended effects of relationship. The indigenous counter-mythology asserted against Europe's imaginary *terra nullius* would create its own enduring terms of accord and discord.

Imagining the Nation Indivisible

> We cling tenaciously, not merely to believing, but to believing just what we do believe.
> —C. S. Peirce, from *The Fixation of Belief*, 1877

Treaty documents have recognized tribes' preexisting ("aboriginal," "original," or "natural") right to exist somewhere, but, as it turned out for many tribes, no place in particular. The ideal of inherent Indian sovereignty and peoplehood has been undermined and diminished with every step of the discovering sovereigns' march (Wilkinson 1987, 55). Chief Justice Marshall's three Supreme Court rulings, in 1823, 1831, and 1832, at first facilitated and then tried to counter the advance of dogmatic and authoritarian assertions of power over Indian nations. But, coming at what Rogers Smith calls the "high noon of the white republic" (Smith 1997, 197; see also 197–242), any sort of liberal interpretations Marshall might have advanced with regard to the treatment of Native peoples were swept aside by waves of entrepreneurial fervor that favored patriarchal white dominance, antifederalist sentiments, and white access to tribal lands.[17] Thus the federal Indian trust would rise from the troubled waters of conflicting civic ideologies, at a time when "racist, [white] nativist, and patriarchal views structured American political development and conflicts as fully as liberal republican ones" (Smith 1997, 199; see also Hoxie 2001). The indivisibility of the nation was an affair of the imagination, but it was also a matter of fact for those who stood outside the ideal (see discussion of the removal of the Lemhi Indians from Lemhi Valley, Idaho, in "The White Problem" in chapter 6).

Marshall, "Discovery," and the "Domestic Dependent Nations"

> [A]nd the character and religion of its inhabitants afforded an apology for considering them as a people over whom the superior genius of Europe might claim ascendancy. [. . .] Although we do not mean to engage in the defence of those principles which Europeans have applied to Indian title, they may, we think, find some excuse, if not justification, in the character and habits of the people whose rights have been wrested from them.
>
> —Chief Justice John Marshall, *Johnson v. M'Intosh*, 21 U.S. 543, 573, 589 (1823)

In 1823, Chief Justice John Marshall perpetuated the presumption that, from the government's perspective, Indian property rights in land are legitimized only by their incorporation into the legal structures of the "discovering sovereign." In a period when the United States was yet divided as a nation and subject to serious competition between state and federal sovereignties, the case of *Johnson v. M'Intosh* might have opened the gates to a disturbing undercurrent in the nation's already troubled image of itself by acknowledging the legitimacy of a third sovereignty. In its decision, however, the Marshall Court fell back on an imperial logic, one that Marshall upheld despite his qualms about it: "However extravagant the pretension of converting the discovery of an inhabited country into conquest may appear; if the principle has been asserted, it may, perhaps, be supported by reason." He went on to argue that, if this principle "has been asserted in the first instance, and afterwards sustained [and] if the property of the great mass of the community originates in it, it becomes the law of the land, and cannot be questioned" (*Johnson v. M'Intosh*, 591)[18]

As we will see, Marshall himself would later help to lay the groundwork for his own and others' interrogations of the principle. But, in *Johnson v. M'Intosh*, the Court was merely asked to decide which of two titles to the same piece of land was valid: the earlier title, representing the Peankeshaw and Illinois tribes' land transactions with non-Indians (predecessors to Johnson), or the later title, representing the federal government's post-treaty conveyance of the same land to a different non-Indian (M'Intosh). Writing for the Court, Marshall ended up departing from two long-established rules of common law, the one requiring that all individuals be treated equally before the law; the other recognizing the "first right" of the "first in time."[19] Under the common-law rules, Johnson should have won, and M'Intosh's title from the government ought to have been deemed invalid.[20] However, such a decision would have legitimized an Indian tribe's ability to dispose of its own land under U.S. law, thereby undermining the imperial and federal presumption of absolute sovereignty over lands that it had always claimed were "merely occupied" by Indians. In a decision that amounted to a loss for Indian land tenure and white land speculation alike, Marshall justified the Court's departures from its usual modes of conduct by relying on notions of racial difference based in the presumed "rights of the discoverer" over "heathens," over "fierce savages . . . whose subsistence was drawn chiefly from the forest," and so on (*Johnson v. M'Intosh*, 577, 590). And he thereby drew the distinction that still holds between the "occupancy" title of Indians and the "absolute" title of the United States by finding the origin of both in Europe's assertions of power based on the presumed subhumanity of "the native."[21]

Some contemporary Indian law scholars take Marshall's argument to task for its Eurocentric and racist premises and reject the doctrine of discovery as a "disabling certitude" (Carrillo 2002, 39; see also Williams

1990, 316–317, 325–326; Pommersheim 1995, 42–43, 106, 123).[22] Others, however, still tend unquestioningly to rely on and even to teach *Johnson v. M'Intosh* as an illustration of federal preeminence in property and the unqualified "naturalness" of private land ownership (see Carrillo 2002).

"Disabling" in a different sense is the Interior Department's requirement that any transaction involving Indian land be approved by the secretary, a rule bequeathed by one of Marshall's later opinions (*Cherokee Nation v. Georgia* [1831], described below) but still grounded in the certainty of Indian inferiority (for contemporary examples, see chapters 2–5). Indeed, for a variety of reasons, current regulations governing Indian land are markedly more detrimental to tribal sovereignty and autonomy than the laws of Marshall's time. Part of Marshall's argument in *Johnson v. M'Intosh* rests on the view that it was the tribe itself that had annulled its grant of title to Johnson by subsequently ceding the same territory to the United States by treaty. Under this argument, it was neither that the tribe was prevented from disposing of a portion of its lands nor that a private individual (whether Indian or not) was prevented from purchasing land from a tribe. Rather, it was that the buyer could purchase only "such a title as the Indian seller held," that is, "Indian title" (Getches, Wilkinson, and Williams 2005, 69). Marshall contended that such a grant would have "derive[d] its efficacy from their [the selling tribe's] will; and, if they choose to resume it, and make different disposition of the land, the Courts of the United States cannot interpose for the protection of the title. The person who purchases lands from the Indians, within their territory, incorporates himself with them, so far as respects the property purchased; holds their title under their protection, and subject to their laws" (*Johnson v. M'Intosh*, 593).

This seems a fair rendering of a tribe's national sovereignty. By way of analogy, simply because you're a U.S. citizen, you can't purchase land in Canada and have its title rendered under the laws of the United States. The upshot of Marshall's logic is that Indian title could not, in itself, alienate Indian land from Indian law unless, of course, it was first conveyed to the United States.

The crucial point to note here is that, in its earliest conception, transfer of property from tribes to any of the colonizing powers was to occur (according to the colonizing powers) only by military conquest or by treaty, that is, as the result of contact between two sovereign nations.[23] Indian lands certainly are still subject to the laws of the tribe in whose territory they are located—as well as to federal and, in some cases, state laws. However, the kind of autonomous Indian title to which Marshall referred was effectively eradicated under Allotment's imposition of "beneficial" title, which derives its "efficacy" from the will of the dominating sovereign.

~

> America, separated from Europe by a wide ocean, was inhabited by a distinct people, divided into separate nations, independent of each other and of the rest of the world, having institutions of their own, and governing themselves by their own laws. It is difficult to comprehend the proposition, that the inhabitants of either quarter of the globe could have rightful original claims of dominion over the inhabitants of the other, or over the lands they occupied; or that the discovery of either by the other should give the discoverer rights in the country discovered, which annulled the pre-existing rights of its ancient possessors.
> —Chief Justice John Marshall, *Worcester v. Georgia*, 31 U.S. 515, 542–543 (1832)

In the course of a turbulent decade, the Marshall Court decided three cases that would quickly become foundational to the shifting structures of federal Indian law: *Johnson v. M'Intosh* (1823), *Cherokee Nation v. Georgia* (1831), and *Worcester v. Georgia* (1832).[24] The second two cases occurred in the midst of heated debate in Congress, and desperation among Indians, over increasingly insistent calls by whites (including President Jackson) for Indian "removal" (see Clinton 2002, 136; Frickey 1990, 1228). Writing for the Court in all three cases, Marshall construed the Court's decisions in ways that have proven to be amazingly elastic, accommodating both assertions of American Indian peoplehood and restrictions of the same (see discussion below of allotment and the BIA's transformation of Marshall's notion of "dependency"). The elasticity of Marshall's interpretations may have something to do with changes in Marshall's thinking. In the years between *Johnson v. M'Intosh* and the other two cases in the trilogy, Marshall became increasingly troubled by state challenges to federal (particularly judicial) authority and vexed by the gross injustices being carried out against Indian people in the name of progress.[25]

In the opening lines of his opinion in *Cherokee Nation v. Georgia,* Marshall etched his concern: "If courts were permitted to indulge their sympathies, a case better calculated to excite them can scarcely be imagined" (*Cherokee Nation v. Georgia,* 30 U.S. 1, 15 [1831]) The Cherokee Nation had requested an injunction against the State of Georgia to halt its violation of Cherokee laws and its depredations of Cherokee lands and people. Lawyers hired by the Cherokees had argued that, under Article III, Section 2 of the Constitution, the tribe's status as a sovereign entity—essentially a foreign state—gave it recourse against the State of Georgia in the U.S. Supreme Court.[26] Marshall's answer, in which only one other justice concurred, was that the Cherokee Nation was indeed some kind of sovereign, but not a foreign one.[27] Instead, on strictly geographic grounds, he thought that tribes ought to be regarded as "domestic dependent nations [whose] relation to the United States resembles that of a ward to his guardian" (*Cherokee Nation v. Georgia,* 17). The triply divided Court ultimately refused to act as the tribunal either for assertions of Cherokee rights or for redress of Georgia's transgressions (*Cherokee Nation v. Georgia,* 20; see also Getches, Wilkinson, and Williams 2005, 110–111). Instead, the case was thrown out for lack of jurisdiction.

The Court's denial of the Cherokees' request for an injunction against Georgia seems to run contrary to Marshall's apparent concern. No order was issued to remedy the situation. Instead, Marshall went to some length to explain his reasoning in calling tribes "domestic dependent nations." As Robert Clinton contends, "dependency," for Marshall, "constituted a description of a relationship created by treaty in which the federal government owed the Cherokee certain obligations of protection. It was a source of Indian right!" (Clinton 2002, 141). Marshall placed blame on Congress and the executive for failing to uphold and enforce the United States' end of a bargain between sovereigns.[28] But, since "there was no order to enforce, there was no order to disobey" (Getches, Wilkinson, and Williams 2005, 112; see also Clinton 2002, 139–141; Johansen 2000, 99; Smith 1997, 237–240). In a political climate charged with Jacksonian racist state-centrism and contempt for treaties, Marshall's course of "judicial indirection" set down fundamental legal principles that could not be directly challenged. Indian nations, he declared, are sovereign entities under the protection of the federal government. Whether emanating from his own nascent federalism, a genuine concern for the tribes, or some mixture of the two, Marshall's ruling ended up laying the groundwork for his rather more direct support of tribal sovereignty in *Worcester v. Georgia* (18; see also Getches, Wilkinson, and Williams 2005, 112–113; Smith 1997, 197–242; Johansen 2000, 101–103; Clinton 2002, 140–141).

In *Worcester v. Georgia*, the ailing 77-year-old chief justice confronted Georgia's trespasses against the Cherokee Nation once more (Johansen 2000, 100). The question now before the Court was whether Georgia had the right to extend its powers over Samuel Worcester and Elizur Butler, two non-Indian missionaries residing with Cherokee permission on the Cherokee Reservation. As in *Cherokee Nation v. Georgia*, Georgia refused to appear.

This time, however, Marshall was unequivocal in his opinion for the majority. He finally abandoned the "extravagant and absurd" doctrine of discovery, the oldest principle in the colonial book, but he did so in favor of preemption among Europeans: "This was the exclusive right of purchasing such lands as the natives were willing to sell. The crown could not be understood to grant what the crown did not affect to claim; nor was it so understood" (*Worcester v. Georgia*, 545).[29]

Marshall argued that the Crown recognized tribes as nations "capable of maintaining relations of peace and war; of governing themselves, under [the Crown's] protection," even as the Crown, in turn, excluded other Europeans (548).

The chief justice then turned to the earliest treaties to argue for a tribal-federal relationship of "mutual consent" conducted in a "language of equality" between sovereigns. Thus he held: "The treaties and laws of the United States contemplate the Indian territory as completely separated from that of the states: and provide that all intercourse with them shall be carried on exclusively by the government of the union" (557). Not without sarcasm, Marshall maintained his contention that tribes are not foreign states, but are domestic nations dependent on the United States only for protection, which "does not imply the destruction of the protected" (552). In further explicating his position, he appropriated some of the language of Justice Smith Thompson's dissenting opinion in *Cherokee Nation v. Georgia* (53). Drawing especially on Thompson's discussion of the Swiss scholar Emmerich de Vattel's treatise (1758/2005) on international law, Marshall argued that "unequal alliances" between otherwise independent, self-governing, states do not necessarily bar the weaker state from inclusion among sovereigns" (*Worcester v Georgia*, 561; see also Williams 1990, 183n46; Clinton 2002, 140–141; Smith 1997, 237–238).[30] He thus declared that the "whole intercourse" between the Cherokee Nation and its rivals was "vested in the government of the United States." As such, Georgia's actions were "in direct hostility with treaties [and] equal hostility with the acts of Congress [and] also a violation of the acts which authorize the chief magistrate to exercise this authority [and furthermore], repugnant to the constitution, treaties, and laws of the United States" (*Worcester v. Georgia*, 561–562).

As suggested above, the Marshall Court trilogy (whose major findings are summarized in chapter 2) would ultimately provide a much-debated legal basis for the federal-Indian relationship. At the time, however, the Court's sweeping decision in *Worcester v. Georgia* was met with rejection by federal and state governments alike, and the Cherokee were removed to Indian Territory before Jackson was out of office (Smith 1997, 239; Getches, Wilkinson, and Williams 2005, 125). Furthermore, Marshall's lucid explanations of Indian national dependency on federal protections were utterly and deliberately misconstrued, giving way to the establishment of "a social and political control system in which Indians [as individuals] have been regarded legally as incompetents or children would be in other social and legal contexts" (Johansen 2000, 98).[31] And Marshall's unfortunate choice of analogy in *Cherokee Nation v. Georgia* (17)—that the tribal "relation to the United States resembles that of a ward to his guardian"—proved nothing short of devastating. Snapped up by Indian advocates and enemies alike, Marshall's terminology was to initiate a new mythology, soon to become policy. As Felix Cohen (1953/1960, 331–332) has written: "Under the reign of these magic words nothing Indian was safe. The Indian's hair was cut, his dances were forbidden, his oil lands, timber lands, and grazing lands were disposed of, by Indian agents and Indian Commissioners for whom the magic word 'wardship' always made up for lack of statutory authority." It would be another century before political, judicial and social misinterpretations of Marshall's rulings would begin to yield to the more egalitarian aspects of his arguments, and to the bleak everyday realities of manufactured and thus dominated tribal dependencies.[32]

The contemporary federal-Indian relationship owes much to Marshall's liberal nationalistic readings of colonial history (see Smith 1997, 238).[33] However, the genealogy of federal Indian law and of the modern "trust relationship"—grounded as it is in the Indian trust land of allotment—remains mixed. Federal Indian law is heir to an inherent indigenous autonomy that preexisted colonization, on the one hand, but also to the prejudices of its colonial pedigree, on the other.

From Treaties to Trust

Congress and the Supreme Court have ambivalently upheld Marshall's ruling that Indian nations are independent political communities having inherent rights of self-government within the boundaries of their reserved territories (Wilkinson 1987, chap. 3; Royster 1995, 3–4).[34] For the most part, Indian law scholars and advocates vigorously defend tribal rights and powers recognized through treaty with the United States as having been *reserved* by tribes, not given to them. They contend that tribal powers are both pre-constitutional and extra-constitutional.[35] As such, they are "measured initially by the sovereign authority that an Indian tribe exercised, or might theoretically have exercised, in a time so different from our own as to be beyond the power of most of us to articulate" (Wilkinson 1987, 62–63). The subsequent "measurement" of tribal powers, then, has depended on what the tribes agreed to by treaty with the United States. As tribes relinquished some of their lands in exchange for federal support and protection against the interests of states and land-hungry settlers, they also surrendered some of the powers inherent in their status as preexisting sovereigns. Why tribes acquiesced (where they were not coerced) reveals something of the counter-mythology typical to assertions of indigenous autonomy: that accommodation is not the same as capitulation.[36] As Charles Wilkinson (1987, 101) explains, the treaties represent the convergence of "tribal and federal interests [. . .] in one essential respect: Both sides wanted the tribes isolated. The tribes would be left alone to govern themselves in most respects but would receive federal protection against intrusions by outsiders and government support in the form of goods and services. Thus separation of tribes on the islands [i.e., reservations], [ostensibly] outside of the path of settlement, met the needs of both sets of negotiators."

Despite the early history of more and less authentic negotiation between tribal and federal sovereignties, and despite the Marshall Court's 1832 ruling emphasizing the tribes' preexisting rights to self-government, Congress put a stop to the United States' treaty making with Indian nations in 1871. With the General Allotment Act of 1887, the United States took its colonial assumption of entitlement to Indian lands one step further by declaring its executive authority to subdivide treaty lands under the rubric and rite of private property. As the culmination of the government's nineteenth-century strategies to assimilate Indian difference into the nation indivisible, allotment policies also had the support of a surprising array of the non-Indian public.

Writing two years before passage of the General Allotment Act, Cuban anti-imperialist writer José Martí reflected the ostensibly humanitarian, though still inegalitarian sentiments of the times leading up to allotment.[37] After attending a meeting of the influential, pro-allotment "Friends of the Indian" social-reform group at Lake Mohonk, New York, Martí described the Friends as "men and women of action [who] without a dissenting vote [. . .] recommended those practical reforms of simple justice that can change a grievous crowd of oppressed and restless men and women into a useful and picturesque element of American civilization" (Martí 1885/1975, 217, 223). Whether Indian people desired the "practical reforms of simple justice" the U.S. government was soon to inflict upon them was a question here left unasked, and one seldom broached by the Friends and other advocates of allotment. Rather, Indian people were to conform in whatever ways they were deemed capable of—that is, by being "useful and picturesque"—to the variously conceived grander project of American civilization.[38]

By this time, Indian individual and communal ties to particular places were being construed as "land ownership in common." This coupling of terms indicated an abiding Euro-American misapprehension of or, rather, indifference to the actual (felt) sentiments of place (see Jones 1982, 18–20, 83–86; Bobroff 2001). As Felix Cohen, the renowned human rights activist, legal scholar, and father of federal Indian law explained, quoting Delos Sacket Otis (1934/1973)—and other historical scholars agree—the Friends and other advocates of allotment had one overarching goal: to replace "tribal culture" with "white civilization" (Cohen 1942a/1971, 208; see also Rusco 2000; Hoxie 2001). The two ways of life thus conceived, the

Friends and others located the essential difference in conflicting notions of property (e.g., "common" versus "private"). But, in 1934, Otis would note for the *Congressional Record* that friends and enemies of allotment alike were unclear as to the details of the "Indian agricultural economy": "Both were prone to use the word 'communism' in a loose sense, in describing Indian enterprise. It was in the main an inaccurate term. What the allotment debaters meant by communism was that the title to land invariably vested in the tribe and the actual holding of the land was dependent on its use and occupancy. They also meant vaguely the cooperativeness and clannishness—the strong communal sense—of barbaric life, which allotment was calculated to disrupt" (Otis 1934/1973, 11; also quoted at length in Cohen 1942a/1971, 208).

The lack of understanding of—and interest in—Anglo-style private land ownership among most Indians and the ethnocentric, racist attitudes of most non-Indians all but guaranteed the cataclysmic loss of Indian lands wherever allotment took place (Brookings Institution 1928; Cohen 1942a/1971; Fey and McNickle 1959; Deloria and Lytle 1984; Nabokov 1999; Rusco 2000; Hoxie 2001). In Idaho, for example, the prevailing sentiment during the years following the ratification of the Fort Bridger Treaty of 1868, establishing a reservation for Shoshones and Bannocks, was that Indians simply had too much land (Madsen 1983/1996, 275).[39] Starting with 1.8 million acres of treaty land, the Shoshone-Bannock Reservation was reduced by a third through surveying "errors" and forced cessions by the turn of century (Madsen 1983/1996, 272–294). By the time allotment was completed at Fort Hall a decade later, the reservation had shrunk to less than 550,000 acres (Liljeblad 1972, 50–51).

The General Allotment Act

In 1887, Congress passed the General Allotment (Dawes) Act. The brainchild of both ill will and empathy toward American Indians, the Allotment Act made it possible for the federal government to divvy up treaty lands and to dole them out in prescribed units of usually 20, 80, and 160 acres to heads of households, individual Indian men, women, children, and orphans in what are still known as "allotments" (Cohen 1942a/1971, 218n22; Canby 2004, 20–23; Liljeblad 1972, 50). This particular arrangement was as pleasing to those who sincerely felt that private land ownership, along with Christianity, schooling, and profit making, could be the handmaiden of assimilation as it was to those who were just hungry for Indian lands, namely, those lands left over after all Indians had received their allotted share, and "fictitiously called 'surplus,'" according to John Collier, commissioner of Indian Affairs from 1933 to 1945 (see Cohen 1942a/1971, 216; see also Canby 2004, 20–23; Nabokov 1999, 232–237).

Under the Dawes Act, allotted Indian land was supposed to be held in trust by the federal government for a period of twenty-five years to give Indian people time, it was said, to master the rules and responsibilities of private land ownership. During this period, the government would hold absolute title to all allotted lands, while Indian landowners would hold beneficial or use title: in theory, they could benefit from the use of the land but they could not sell it. The government—and others interested either in assimilating Indian people or in keeping them confined to geographic and subsistence areas where they would be less and less likely to interact with or inconvenience the surrounding non-Indian population—surmised that "civilization" would thus swiftly occur under a regimen of private land ownership, farming, schooling, and religion. Instead, allotment usually resulted in frustration and worse. In Idaho, for example, historical accounts portray Shoshone and Bannock people actively resisting trading their usual practices of hunting, fishing, and gathering for the tedium of agricultural subsistence, especially when government supplies of seeds, farm implements, and stock were meager and often late in coming, and government agents were ineffectual or worse.[40] In a petition sent to the commissioner of Indian affairs in October 1895, Shoshone and Bannock tribal members first complained of an agent they would soon try to lynch: "Mr. Teter is afraid of us and we want no one that is afraid for he can do us no good. He carries a pistol and shot himself when he first came here. If he had been away from this agency and killed himself us Indians would have been accused of killing him. We cannot believe him he tells us so many lies"(see Madsen 1996, 309) In the same petition, they wrote: "Washington spent a lot of money for cattle. We know we were to get nice young cows, but in place of getting young cows, we got ones so old and poor they can hardly stand. Quite a number have no teeth and will be dead in the spring and our agent took them and said nothing" (303).

Competency

Ironically, it was the Indians who were required to prove "competency." The Burke Act of 1906 gave the secretary of interior the power to decide whether an Indian individual was ready for the "real" land ownership of fee title and, thus, for U.S. citizenship. For Indians deemed "competent" even prior to the end of the twenty-five-year transition period, a "certificate of competency" was issued, though it was not always clear by what criteria competency was measured (Nabokov 1999, 237). As with the allotment of private parcels among Indian individuals, some competency clauses were built into treaties long before allotment itself became a federal policy. In his chapter "Personal Rights and Liberties of Indians," Felix Cohen includes the following representative section of an 1864 treaty between the United States and the Chippewas, describing how the Indian agent should divide Indian allottees into two classes: "Those who are intelligent, and have sufficient education, and are qualified by business habits to prudently manage their affairs, shall be set down as 'competents,' and those who are uneducated, or unqualified in other respects to prudently manage their affairs, or who are of idle, wandering, or dissolute habits, and all orphans, shall be set down as 'those not so competent'" (Cohen 1942a/1971, 169). After allotment, the determination of competency proved a difficult administrative decision until Commissioner of Indian Affairs Cato Sells streamlined the policy in 1917 (169; see Sells 1917; Debo 1985, 314; Hoxie 2001, 181). Henceforth, competency would be indicated either by years of schooling or by blood: "Persons who were less than one-half Indian or who had graduated from a government school would receive fee patents immediately" (Hoxie 2001, 181). Historian Angie Debo (1985, 314) describes the process of "forced fee patenting" and its immediate aftermath:

> In 1920 a man who had headed competency commissions in several states explained their methods to a committee of the House of Representatives. They made a house-to-house canvass interviewing all the Indians owning restricted land and, disregarding their protests, ran them through the hopper in fifteen minutes to one-half hour for each. Asked what became of the Indian after his land was released from trust, he said this was difficult to answer; the Indian service dropped such individuals immediately and had no further contact with them. A total of 9,894 Indians received fee patents from 1906 to 1917; then as [the secretary of the interior's] mills began grinding more rapidly, some 20,000 patents were issued in the four years following.

With competency certificates and fee title to their allotments forced upon them, Indian individuals were also naturalized without their consent.[41] Allotments thus passed out of trust status, becoming both alienable and taxable. Indian land became fee land, and Indians ceased to exist as such, at least insofar as the federal government was concerned. As President Theodore Roosevelt described the effects of the policy in his December 1901 message to Congress, allotment was "a mighty pulverizing engine to break up the tribal mass, which acts directly upon the family and the individual [and because of which] some sixty thousand Indians have already become citizens of the United States."[42] The "mighty pulverizing" metaphor was apt: private ownership of dispersed parcels of land tended to undermine group self-sufficiency and interdependence, breaking up tribes and families even as it destroyed a wide variety of indigenous systems of property and inheritance (Cohen 1945, 266–268; Jones 1982, 83–86; Johansen 2000, 186; Bobroff 2001). Of those who received title, many sold their acreage at rock-bottom prices in order to survive, further dissipating an already shrunken Indian land base because neither tribes nor individual Indians could afford to purchase their compatriots' parcels (Fey and McNickle 1959, 82; Nabokov 1999, 240–243).[43] Many reservations quickly became checkerboards of Indian and non-Indian, individual and tribal, county, state, or federal ownership. As poverty and dependency grew on reservations across the country, it became obvious that the plan to get the government out of the business of managing Indians was failing (see Brookings Institution 1928; Fey and McNickle 1959).

Congress finally tried to stem the tide by indefinitely extending the twenty-five-year trust period of allotted lands, after which legal title would be transferred to the allottee, along with the attendant responsibilities of paying state and federal taxes. In other words, the land would no longer be "Indian land" and the titleholders would no longer be "Indian."[44] The imposition of federal trusteeship over privately held Indian lands (allotments) was originally intended to undermine, among other things, the status of tribes as sovereign nations by creating a new habit of land tenure dependent on the individual instead of the tribe.[45] Policy makers and Friends (including a number of prominent anthropologists) fervently believed that the Lockean ideal of private property would create the same capitalist work ethic among Indians that it had among Europeans, and would, therefore, engender an Indian cultural evolution to the next, "higher" stage of human advancement—a stage more suited to an assimilative white society (see, for example, Smith 1997, 391, and Hoxie 2001, 33). Instead, the federal trusteeship ended up perpetuating an inherently contradictory social contract whereby economic and official dependency among tribes—sovereign nations—was enforced through the brokering of Indian trust lands and assets by the Bureau of Indian Affairs.

Friends and the original architects of allotment policy placed their faith in the Indians' ability to "become civilized." The policy's first reformers, however, upon witnessing the disastrous effects of allotment policy, decided just the opposite. Where nineteenth-century Friends had been convinced (with the help of anthropologists) that Indians would eventually evolve along the same lines as whites, by the turn of the twentieth century, reformers had become equally convinced that Indians were incapable of handling their own affairs and, so, were to be provided for through the (conveniently white) exploitation of Indian lands (see Rusco 2000; Hoxie 2001).

The So-Called End of Allotment

Commissioned in the 1920s, *The Problem of Indian Administration* (Brookings Institution 1928), also known as the "Meriam Report," was just one of a number of attempts to get Congress to do something about the massive Indian land loss and concomitant human suffering caused by the enforcement of the General Allotment Act (see related discussions in Cohen 1942a/1971; Fey and McNickle 1959; see also Deloria and Lytle 1984, 43–46.).[46] Allotment was formally ended in 1934 under the Indian Reorganization Act (IRA), but, by then, the damage had been done: of the 138 million acres held across the country by Indians in 1887, more than 90 million acres had passed out of their hands. But, as Commissioner of Indian Affairs John Collier wrote in a memorandum to the House and Senate Committees on Indian Affairs in February 1934, the overall statistics were misleading: "That part of the allotted lands which has been lost is the most valuable part. Of the residual lands, taking all Indian-owned lands into account, nearly one half, or nearly 20,000,000 acres, are desert or semidesert lands. Through the allotment system, more than 80 percent of the land value belonging to all the Indians in 1887 has been taken away from them." As the chief architect of the IRA and of the reforms that brought about real, though insufficient, reform in federal Indian policy, Collier would in the same memorandum write: "The Indian Service is compelled to be a real-estate agent in behalf of the living allottees; and in behalf of the more numerous heirs of deceased allottees. As such real-estate agent, selling and renting the hundreds of thousands of parcels of land and fragmented equities of parcels, and disbursing the rentals (sometimes to more than a hundred heirs of one parcel, and again to an individual heir with an equity in a hundred parcels), the Indian Service is forced to expend millions of dollars a year" (see Cohen 1942a/1971, 216–217).

The policy changes brought about by the "Indian New Deal" and the Indian Reorganization Act were sweeping—and contested.[47] Their long-term significance continues to be the subject of academic and political concern, for a variety of reasons (see, for example, Biolsi 1992, 186). For allotted landowners, however, the upshot was simple: the IRA formally put an end to allotment but failed to contend with the dynamics of fractionated ownership that post-allotment inheritance provisions had generated. Consequently, those lands remaining in the federal trust have required increasingly intensive "management" by agency officials (see Fey and McNickle 1959).[48]

Invoking the Nations Invisible

> The fractionated heirship problem is one which is not new, one which still does not have high visibility nationally, is not seen by very many people as an emergency, and does not have any of the immediacy that problems such as hunger, lack of housing, fetal alcohol syndrome and drug use, etc. have, not to mention terrorism. The interest has never been high in tackling this problem.
> —Mariana R. Shulstad, 2001[49]

It takes some imagination to begin to comprehend, in any visceral way, the underlying, undermining significance of allotted lands. Historian Frederick Hoxie asserts that the leasing of allotments gave Indian people "few reasons to change their traditional lifeways" and, so, ironically provided opportunities to preserve elements of the very things allotment was designed to get rid of (Hoxie 2001, 158). The problem is, no matter what the divisions among Indian people, Indian country (with a small *c*)—the land itself—remains undivided and, therefore, practically and literally inaccessible to the very people whose identity is bound up with it.[50] The "undivision" of Indian land wherever allotment took its toll symbolizes by its very abstractness the invisibility of Indian land to traditional lifeways. In the end, fractionation of interest owned made land ownership tangible only in the lease checks distributed by the BIA, breaking a bond that many Indian people refer to every time they speak of "Mother Earth."

And so the same factor that works in ways, whether intended or unintended, to obstruct the sale of fractionated trust land also tends to discourage the use of trust land in ways other than those already sanctioned by the BIA, mostly in agricultural, timber, or mineral leases to non-Indian interests. Whether allotted landowners want to sell their interest in a tract of land or to let the land lie fallow, they must first obtain approval from their co-owners, one of whom may be the tribe itself.[51] Obtaining approval can be a more daunting task than it sounds if your co-owners are spread among different reservations and may not even be known to you.

On the one hand, allotted landowners may spend years contacting and negotiating with co-owners in an attempt to consolidate trust land holdings into one, continuous, and therefore accessible piece of land, sometimes to no avail. On the other hand, partitioning their share of an allotment also presents difficulties, as was the case at Fort Hall in February 2000, when a Shoshone-Bannock woman found herself blocked by her own tribal government, which, as a co-owner, refused to break up a tract of land it was leasing out. "They [the BIA] tell you," the woman recounted, "that you only own a shovelful [of land], that you shouldn't worry about it. So I pull out my calculator and multiply the acres in the allotment by my interest in it, and guess what? My 'shovelful' amounts to three acres! That's more than enough to build my house on, but do you think that the tribes are going to allow that?!" In many cases, even when the fractions represent sizable tracts of land, the economic benefits received from their inclusion with other tracts in large leases are so miniscule as to be laughable, except that these tracts remain an important resource for their owners, both culturally and (at least in their potential) economically.[52]

People sometimes ask: "Why don't Indians farm their own land?" "Why do they lease everything out to the non-Indians?" The answer lies in the colonized nature of Indian land ownership. Even for those holding title to an entire allotment or a substantial part of one, as a few elderly allottees do, the costs of farming equipment and other initial investments would usually prevent them from becoming farmers. But, you might ask, why don't they simply take out a loan like other farmers do, using their land as collateral? The answer lies in the very laws that spawned fractionation in the first place, and that prevent Indian landowners from gaining or maintaining a foothold in their own land: the federal government holds title to all Indian trust land, by definition. It is therefore inalienable, unsuitable as collateral—a guarantee of little but increasing insecurity to its Indian owners.

Fractionation Revisited

The phenomenon of fractionation emerged with the first death of an original Indian allottee. Having made no federal provision for inheritance among Indians, other than determination of legal heirs by the secretary of the interior, Congress allowed intestate Indian estates (meaning the majority of Indian estates, even now) to fall under the jurisdiction of their respective states' probate codes.[53] Because of the increasing numbers of co-owners on most allotments, the physical partitioning of inherited trust lands among heirs is a tedious bureaucratic process that few attempt.[54] Instead, inherited trust lands are usually divided virtually—that is, on paper—by allocating shares or "undivided fractional interests" in the original allotment among the allottee's surviving kin. Thus, for example, four grandchildren in line to inherit their grandmother's 160-acre allotment would on her passing each receive, not 40 acres, but rather a one-quarter undivided interest in the *entire* 160-acre parcel. Instead of one owner, there would now be four co-owners. When you multiply this outcome by several generations and many more heirs ever more distantly related to the original allottee, it quickly becomes unmanageable, exponentially so with each passing generation. In many cases, one tract of land will have hundreds, even thousands of co-owners, many of whom are strangers, if not altogether unknown, to one another.[55]

Historically, trusteeship over Indian land resides with the federal government's trustee delegate in BIA agency offices located on or near most reservations. Because of the increasing numbers of co-owners per allotment, owners of fractionated interests have had little choice but to rely on BIA services to manage their land. In turn, the BIA has generally translated into purely economic terms its mandate to manage Indian lands in the "best interest" of its Indian owners (25 *Code of Federal Regulations,* part 15, sec. 162.12). The agency acts as a broker in the leasing of Indian lands, mostly to non-Indians, though in doing so it subverts allotment's original purpose—to create self-sufficiency among American Indians (Hoxie 2001, 158). The BIA's lease brokering, when combined with what I call the "virtual land ownership" of allotment's heirs, has resulted in widespread exploitation of Indian land.

Case in point: Shoshone-Bannock elder and founder of the Fort Hall Landowners Alliance Ernestine "Ernee" Broncho Werelus returned to her home reservation at Fort Hall, Idaho, in 1993, ostensibly to retire. Since then, she and her husband, Steve, have spent the better part of their retirement fighting the passivity and corruption engendered by fractionation. As Ernee recalled in March 2001:

> My mother used to say to me, "Ernee, go up there and see what they're doing with my land." But I never had time. First I was in school, then I was having babies and Steve was off to the War. Then we moved away. Mom died in 1967, but in my head I could still hear her; she was asking me to go up there to the Agency and "find out what they're doing with my land." She said they were doing something funny. All of the elders had been saying the same thing from the time I was a little girl. I never paid any attention until we came back here to retire. That's when I finally had the time to start going through Mom's papers . . . I found out she was right! Those allotments I inherited from her? Over 30 years' time, they had gained about five dollars an acre in annual lease income. I mean, if farmland was being leased for twenty dollars an acre back in 1965, then in '95 when we started our Alliance, it was going for twenty-five dollars an acre . . . even though everything off reservation was going for a hundred and twenty-five! I'll tell you, these farmers around here . . . they've been getting some sweetheart deals.

Many of these "sweetheart deals" have wound up in litigation since the alliance was founded (see chapters 3 and 4).

The giving and taking of treaty lands under sway of the federal government was just the beginning of land loss for American Indians. The virtual land ownership of undivided fractional interests has taken people from their land as certainly as the broken treaties did. However, recent legislation—the result of decades of Indian activism—and the efforts of

Indian people and advocates all over the country pressing for reform may be turning the tide. The national news media have covered both the mismanagement of Indian trust resources, whether land, oil and gas, or mineral rights, and the mis-investment by the Bureau of Indian Affairs of monies derived from these resources (see discussion of *Cobell* litigation in "Individual Indian Money" in chapter 2). But grassroots activists and advocacy organizations on various reservations have been waging war against these and other intended and unintended consequences of federal Indian laws and policies for years. One of the primary aims of *Unearthing Indian Land* is to tell some of the stories of their long fight. Some of the stories are about legislative efforts to consolidate fractionated Indian land either in the hands of individuals or their tribal governments—a process that sometimes ends up pitting the one against the other (see chapter 3). Other stories are about lawsuits measured in the number of generations they take to resolve (see chapters 2–4). Still others are about the more mundane but perhaps most powerful aspects of decolonizing reform, ones that take place in the offices of volunteer organizations like the Fort Hall Landowners Alliance and, more and more often, in the classroom (see chapter 6).

CHAPTER 2

Appropriating the Trust

When the Indian begins to understand that he has something that is exclusively his to enjoy, he begins to understand that it is necessary for him to preserve and keep it, and it is not a great while before he learns that to keep it he must keep the peace; and so on, step by step, the individual is separated from the mass, set upon the soil, made a citizen.
—Senator Henry Dawes, 1886

A stupid despot may constrain his slaves with iron chains; but a true politician binds them even more strongly by the chain of their own ideas; despair and time eat away the bonds of iron and steel, but they are powerless against the habitual union of ideas, they can only tighten it still more; and on the soft fibres of the brain is founded the unshakable base of the soundest of Empires.
—J. M. Servan, 1767[1]

The "true politicians" of the nineteenth-century United States tried to create what the eighteenth-century French magistrate Joseph Michel Servan would have called a "habitual union" between the ideas of private property, the individual, and the social necessity of "keeping the peace." But when Senator Dawes made his statement before Congress, he could not have envisioned the kind of citizenship allotment would engender. Certainly, he did not realize the incredibility of what he proposed for Indian-American personhood. His ideal of the individual Indian citizen was exactly the opposite of what some present-day Indian landowners assert in their defense of trust land ownership, that they feel a collective identity with even so-called private land: "The land is who we *are*."

Collective identity with the land is, to varying degrees and in various ways, a place-based personhood. But there is also a felt experience of "anti-place" tied to the geographically bounded yet trans-boundary (trans-tribal) identity of the individual Indian landowner: the allottee. Individual allottees may disagree as to the appropriate responses to their particular experiences of allotment and its legacies, but they nonetheless share some fundamental understandings of what it means to be an allottee. For one thing, they must individually and collectively negotiate the cookie-cutter approaches of the BIA in its management of the federal Indian trust. No matter that the imposition of private property was supposed to separate the individual from the collective. For purposes of administration, the dominant American system yet insists upon treating the allottee—its manufactured individual—as a token of a type, the stereotyped mass that is "the Indian."[2]

What Hannah Arendt (1958, 6) described as modernism's "twofold flight from the earth into the universe and from the world into the self." appears here in another guise.[3] The anti-place of Indian land produces (or is meant to produce) an anti-person of the Indian landowner: the universal individual, the modular citizen who is everywhere and under all circumstances, supposedly, the same. In this chapter, the struggle of Indian landowners to assert their citizenship, their collective and individual personhood, within the bounds set by hegemony's own contradictory consciousness reveals a great deal about the evolving meaning of being "set upon the soil."[4]

Anchoring the Trust

> . . . how critical reactions grow from the invisible roots.
> —Jean and John Comaroff, *Of Revelation and Revolution*[5]

My introduction to Native American citizenship came in the context of Indian land grassroots advocacy, where the dialectic between the treaties and the federal-Indian trust relationship is not always evident. For one thing, as Indian law scholar, professor, and tribal court judge Frank Pommersheim (1995, 41) notes, the "treaty-based duties are not readily acknowledged by the federal government and are often erroneously subsumed under the trust relationship." Likewise, in the everyday practices of Indian landowner advocacy, the grounding of rights in the treaties is sometimes eclipsed by the government's many failures to uphold its trust responsibilities. What advocates say with insistent frequency is that the United States has used its trusteeship of tribal assets to assert its dominance over every aspect of Indian people's lives: that the "highest fiduciary standards" of the trust relationship have been violated with impunity (see discussion of *United States v. Mitchell* [1983] in chapter 3 and of *Cobell* trials in "Individual Indian Money" below). In their writings, the term "trust relationship" appears ever enclosed in quotation marks, bound and bounded by a clear sense of the absurd and the pathetic.

But the trust relationship remains a sign of something deeper, as well.[6] At the very least, it stands for the relative credibility of the treaty as a living document of relationship.[7] In dominant Western theory, the treaty is based in the Lockean ideal that governance requires the consent of the governed.[8] Of the numerous covenants drawn between indigenous and European sovereignties since at least the seventeenth century, hundreds remain in effect.[9] If advocates sometimes tend, in the words of Pierre Bourdieu (1977, 18), to "leave unsaid all that goes without saying," they do so in part because of this rich history of experience—from treaties to trust—that "finds expression [. . .] in the silences, ellipses, and lacunae of the language of familiarity."

Since its inception, the trusteeship of the United States over American Indian lands and resources has been the source of myriad legal battles in which Indian nations and individuals have sought to force the federal government to abide by its self-imposed obligations.[10] This trusteeship, or what is called the "trust relationship" between tribes and the United States, derives from federal duties outlined in treaties, held by the Constitution to be the "supreme Law of the Land" (Article VI, Clause 2; see also Wilkinson 1987,78–86; Pommersheim 1995, 41). In the context of relations with Native peoples on the part of both Britain and the United States, the treaty can be seen as a tool of colonial expansion, resting conceptually on European assumptions of the divine right of conquest, the doctrines of discovery and conquest, and Manifest Destiny (Jones 1982; Nabokov 1999, 117–144). But it has also been viewed as a "sacred pledge" and, especially in early colonial times, as a covenant and "chain of friendship," indeed, as a "constitution" reflecting a shared humanity among diverse peoples (Deloria and Lytle 1984, 8; Williams 1997, 121; Clinton 2002, 124). If, with Indian law scholar Robert Williams Jr., we think of a constitution in the British sense, "as encompassing a whole body of values, customary practices, and traditions basic to the polity, we can begin to reconstruct a much different set of *indigenous* constitutional principles generated by

American Indian visions of law and peace for the emerging multi-cultural society. [. . .] This basic foundational principle that a treaty enabled different peoples to transcend their differences and unite together is, in fact, one of the most frequently voiced themes of Encounter era Indian diplomacy" (Williams 1997, 98–99; emphasis added).

Although definitely not embraced by the colonists, the vision of "indigenous constitutional principles" has been endlessly inspiring to grassroots Indian activists—and endlessly irritating to the hegemonic powers that be.[11] The founding principles of how the "different peoples" of this expanding country were to live together would turn out to be largely those articulated in the legal opinions of Chief Justice John Marshall. Nevertheless, as the ethnographer and critical theorist Elizabeth Povinelli (1993, 13) urges, "the deployment of counter-discourses by groups neither fully within nor fully without the nation-state needs to be acknowledged." Let us do so by first locating one aspect of a counter-discourse within the legal landscape.

The Trust Doctrine

The opinions set forth by Marshall in his Court's famous trilogy of cases— *Johnson v. M'Intosh* (1823); *Cherokee Nation v. Georgia* (1831); *Worcester v. Georgia* (1832)—inspired the four sometimes slippery cornerstones of federal Indian law. Briefly, these are (1) that title to Indian land is in the federal government, though right of occupancy (beneficial or use title) inheres in the tribes; (2) that the relationship between the tribes and the federal government is exclusive, meaning that states should have no authority in Indian country; (3) that tribes are not "foreign" nations but are some kind of preexisting sovereigns, thus endowed with the inherent capacity of self-government; and (4) that the federal government is ascendant in the Indian tribes' affairs with non-Indians. Furthermore, Marshall's denomination of tribes as "domestic dependent nations" is unambiguously qualified in *Worcester v. Georgia* (1832). Although "domestic dependency" as a concept was immediately twisted to fit the internal colonizing activities of the nineteenth and twentieth centuries (the foremost of which are the imposition of the legal structure "Indian land" and its legacies), in *Worcester v. Georgia* (1832), Marshall had clearly construed "dependency" as a relationship of protection. The sovereignty of the United States held sway over the *external* affairs of tribes, which were otherwise independent and sovereign political nations. As such, their *internal* affairs were off-limits to the U.S. government.

Otherwise known as the "trust doctrine," the foregoing principles have provided the foundation for the perpetually conflicting forces of federal Indian law: for "measured separatism" on the one hand and assimilation or annihilation on the other (Wilkinson 1987, 13). They have also foreshadowed an unsettling disregard for the individual Indian person except as a "beneficiary" of federal-tribal relations. "Indian landowner" and "allottee," like "Indian land" and "Indian," are legal constructs, "determinate (real) abstractions," each conjoined to person and (anti-)place (De Genova 2002, 424). As such, they help to constitute real beings—people and places—with the capacity to take part in a "mutual structuring" (Povinelli 1993, 251). (I will pursue this aspect of my argument in the next several chapters.)

Appropriating the Trust

> When [Congress] passed the Indian Reorganization Act in 1934, Collier thought the allottees would give their land back to the tribes. But they didn't rush to.
> —Helen Sanders, 2002[12]

Given the infelicitous history of the federal Indian trust and the prevailing conceptual contradictions referred to above, why do many American Indians insist on appropriating—and maintaining—a "trust relationship" with the United States? Situated historically and pragmatically, this turns out to be a question of astonishing gravity.[13] It is like asking why Indians insist on remaining Indian.[14] In this sense, the depth of the question is but dimly illuminated in the discourses of litigation, legislation, and activism directed at the federal mismanagement of Indian trust assets that we will be exploring.

In another sense, though, the question of the trust's appropriation elicits a profound but guarded plurality of national allegiances—citizenships—based first in an awareness of a collective (multicultural) American past.[15] Although, with the Indian Citizenship Act of 1924, trust land and Indian citizenship lost their intrinsic legal connection (see Price and

Clinton 1983, 505–510), the two had been inextricably tied together under the General Allotment Act of 1887. As such, American Indian citizenship and the federal-Indian trust relationship began their coevolution under colonial assumptions of racial hierarchies, the disciplined "individual," and the "white man's burden" of European world dominance (see Foucault 1977; Clinton 2002). The trust relationship therefore retains more than just traces of the colonial order. It embodies a colonizing strategy that is self-reproducing. The question provoked by the maintenance of the trust is whether the seemingly omnipotent urge of the colonizer to govern the colonized inherent in this strategy can be transformed (see Thomas 1994, chap. 2; Bourdieu 1977 on "practical mastery" in social reproduction). The question asked implicitly and explicitly by Indian (trust) land theorists and activists alike is this: How and to what extent can institutions so steeped in the prejudices of colonialism be reformed in these ostensibly postcolonial times?[16]

In Marshall's conception, the dependency of tribes is historically grounded in a fundamental principle of inherent Indian national sovereignty under consensual protection of the United States. By making no mention of this precept, congressional and judicial fiat has tended to focus attention on the trust relationship itself, without reference to its origins.[17] But, cast loose from its anchor in the treaties, the trust floats free as a sign both of the supposedly inherent, perpetual dependency of Native peoples and, in the popular fallacy, of the federal government's largesse.[18] What emerges in practice is an apparently incoherent relationship that becomes coherent only in light of the competing discourses of power to versus power over.[19]

The paradoxical nature of federal Indian law is well known and is the subject of ongoing analysis in legal and historical scholarship (see, for example, Cohen 1942a/1971; Price and Clinton 1983; Pommersheim 1995; Smith 1997; Deloria and Wilkins 1999; Rusco 2000; Hoxie 2001; Clinton 2002; Getches, Wilkinson, and Williams 2005). What is interesting from an ethnographic perspective is the possibility that the tensions between tribal, individual, and communal interests, on the one hand, and between colonial assimilation and separation, on the other, might actually work to enhance Indian national sovereignty.[20] Indian landowner advocates end up using the very contradictions in federal Indian policy as levers to strengthen Indian national sovereignty at the level of the individual—the citizen—as well as (and sometimes in spite of) the corporate entity called the "tribe." The strife created by hegemony's inherent contradictions ends up provoking advocacy and educational efforts by Indian landowners. These efforts can, in turn, work to revitalize the assertion and protection of a community that includes not only person and group, but also earth as person (kin; see also "The Indian Land Consolidation Act" below).

Why, then, do allottees place so much emphasis on maintaining a trust relationship with an unworthy trustee? Framed historically, the question requires an engagement with the (in)appropriateness, the mutual fit or lack thereof, of the federal Indian trust to tribal sovereignty. The distinction between nationhood and peoplehood has bearing here.[21] But part and parcel with indigenous assertions of place-based identities is the ongoing appropriation of the trust to the concerns of individual and tribal landowners. As we will see, this appropriation is represented through legislation and litigation like the Indian Land Consolidation Act (ILCA) and the Individual Indian Money (IIM) mismanagement case (*Cobell*). ILCA and *Cobell* are two sides of the same, counter-hegemony coin (complete with its own contradictions) put up against the possibly irredeemable currency of the federal Indian trust.

Reaching Critical Will

> The Act of June 25, 1910, requiring that the Secretary determine the heirs of deceased allottees and issue patents in fee entailed "a vast amount of work; many allotments are now of 20 years" standing; estates are contested; and the questions of law, and particularly of fact, become extremely difficult, largely through difficulty in obtaining Indian testimony of value. As allotments have been made on 55 reservations, and upon [. . .] one of the smaller reservations [alone] there are 600 heirship cases, the work to be done under this act will become one of the greater tasks of the office.
> —"Report of the Commissioner of Indian Affairs," 1911

An understatement in 1911, that probate would constitute "one of the greater tasks of the office [of Indian affairs]" would bring hoots of derision now, almost a century and countless "heirship cases" after the United States recognized Indian inheritance rights.[22] One of the pet peeves of

Indian landowner activists and advocates is that the United States' efforts to contend with the legacies of its imposed trust have been a day late and a dollar short. But this has never been for ignorance of the problem.

Acknowledging the Problem

As one career veteran of the federal Indian probate process wrote in January 2003: "In 1913, only three years after probate authority was enacted, there were 40 thousand heirship cases waiting determination in estates collectively valued at 60 million dollars."[23] Surely it was clear then, only a generation after passage of the General Allotment Act, that there was a problem. "They knew there was a problem back when I was a baby," remarks lifelong advocate and activist Helen Sanders, "but do you think they did anything about it?"[24]

Helen Sanders was born in 1926, the same year that the famous Meriam Report was commissioned. The most comprehensive survey of Indian social and economic ills of its time, the Meriam Report (Brookings Institution 1928) offered 847 pages of detailed analysis and recommendations for governmental reform.[25] Drawn from two years of fieldwork undertaken by ten specialists working under the auspices of the Brookings Institution, the report placed the Indian "heirship problem" at the top of its list of serious issues facing the Indian Service (Brookings Institution 1928, 40).[26]

As Vine Deloria Jr. and Clifford Lytle argue, however, acknowledging the problem has never been enough to motivate systemic change. They contend that it was the work and radical reform vision of advocates like John Collier (and, I would add, Felix Cohen) that helped to transform the governing institutions themselves through the 1934 Indian Reorganization Act (IRA; Deloria and Lytle 1984, 55). Some have argued that this was a transformation whose effects have laid bare its fundamentally colonial intentions (see, for example, Biolsi 1992). Regardless of intentions, the IRA formally brought an end to the allotment of Indian land while doing nothing to counteract the debilitating legacies of fractionation and federal supervision over the lands already allotted. And even though the total failure of Congress and the Interior Department to confront these legacies of colonialism doesn't in itself prove the contention of continuing internal colonization, neither does it refute it (see Kickingbird and Ducheneaux 1973; Berkhofer 1978, 184–185; Grinde and Johansen 1995; Pommersheim 1995, 64–66; Nabokov 1999, 304–331; Rusco 2000).

Naught from the Top

> The problem is so big and involves so many aspects, that you can't get everybody to agree on something that is going to solve all of it.
> —Assistant Secretary of the Interior John Carver, 1961[27]

In 1982, BIA historian Michael Lawson wrote that, if the heirship land problem was as "amorphous" and "elusive" as the assistant secretary claimed, then "perhaps it would be best for Congress to focus on the particular needs of individual tribes rather than attempt to provide a general legislative solution" (Lawson 1984, 96).

Lawson (1984) summarizes the post-IRA history of nondecision as a backdrop for his mild criticism of congressional efforts that would soon spawn the Indian Land Consolidation Act.[28] He notes that, in 1937, several bills were proposed that would have made the Lake Traverse Reservation, in North and South Dakota, a pilot study for land reform. The first reservation allotted under the General Allotment Act, Lake Traverse was, at the time, among the most seriously fractionated reservations in the country.[29] Yet none of the bills proposed for its restoration made it past the floor. In 1938, a conference attended by Indian Affairs Commissioner John Collier and Associate Solicitor Felix Cohen produced recommendations for limiting heirship rights and land alienation. The recommendations were effectively ignored.[30]

The 1940s and 1950s were swallowed up by foreign affairs and the "Termination era" (1943–61) of federal-Indian policy making. During this time, Congress undertook major initiatives to "emancipate the Indian" by withdrawing—terminating—federal protections and assistance for some 60 tribes between 1953 and 1962; the passage of Public Law 280 in 1953; the extension of state jurisdiction over tribal matters in six states; and the approval of largely unfunded economic programs developed to encourage Indian individuals and families to relocate to urban centers. Termination-era policies were a reaction to the reform efforts of John Collier and others during the 1920s, 1930s, and 1940s, during which cultural pluralism and the Indian New Deal were vehicles of tribal revitalization (see Smith 1997).

BIA proposals to combat fractionation during these years included a variety of draconian measures, including forced sale, forced fee patenting, and long-term leasing of fractionated lands to non-Indians. But it is clear that the government "netted itself in the mix [in that] the allotted interests at issue are property rights protected by the Fifth Amendment."[31] A GAO administrative audit of the Bureau of Indian Affairs in 1956 noted dryly that "the withdrawal of Federal supervision over Indian lands [termination] is [thus] hindered by these fractionated interests" (see Gilbert and Taylor 1966, 115–116). In 1960, Congress commissioned a comprehensive study of the heirship problem through the House Committee on Interior and Insular Affairs. The following year, the committee's two-volume *Indian Heirship Land Study (see* U.S. House Committee on Interior and Insular Affairs 1961) was published. Its sampling of 9,000 heirs produced the "'rule of heirship land,' i.e., that increased fractionation equals increased Federal administrative costs and decreased heir income."[32] During the 1960s, the BIA, House, Senate, and Department of Justice all weighed in on the ever worsening problem.[33] But it would be another twenty years and a costly Supreme Court decision before the powers would settle on a general legislative strategy for dealing with fractionation (Lawson 1984, 91–94).[34]

Although Congress and the BIA were interested in surveys of "Indian attitudes," such as those gleaned by the 1961 *Indian Heirship Land Study*, federal attention to the nuances of Indian opinions has never been exemplary. Official recognition that federal agencies ought to consult with Indian tribes before carrying out activities that affect them is, at the time of this writing, only a decade old.[35] Given Indian landowner testimony regarding the lack of participation they were afforded in developing the ILCA (see below), there is little reason to believe that the foregoing federal proposals actually reflected the desires or suggestions of tribal governments or individual Indian landowners. It is especially interesting, then, that the only pieces of legislation passed to deal with fractionation prior to the ILCA were locally tailored tribal initiatives.[36]

Fixes from Beneath

Tribal initiatives have provided for the following: limitations on inheritance of fractional interests in land to tribal members or other Indians (defined variously, but usually by descent and tribally recognized status); limitations on intestate succession to tribal or Indian members of the immediate family of the decedent (spouse, children, grandchildren, siblings, parents); life estates for non-Indian spouses; escheat (transfer without compensation) to the tribe of property interests of a decedent with no Indian heirs; tribal right of first refusal in cases where property interests would otherwise devise to non-Indians, non–family members, or both.

Although some of these restrictions (especially the last two) have proven to be exceptionally unpopular with tribal members, pre–ILCA special legislation providing for some or all of them was passed for a number of reservations, including Yakima (1970), Warm Springs (1972), Nez Perce (1972), and Umatilla (1978). With similar provisions, the Standing Rock (Sioux) Heirship Act of 1980 was challenged, in *Talashie v. Lujan* (1993), for preventing a decedent's niece from inheriting fractionated property interests. The niece contended that the tribe's restriction of inheritance (as a property right) was unconstitutional, but the U.S. District Court in South Dakota disagreed. Had the disappointed heiress appealed the case, the Supreme Court might have upheld her argument, as it did in similar challenges to the ILCA, when it protected an individual's right to devise (will property). (See the discussion of *Hodel v. Irving* [1987] and *Babbitt v. Youpee* [1997] in "'Serial Experiments'" below).

One of the earliest pieces of tribal land consolidation legislation was the Rosebud Sioux Isolated Tracts Act of 1963, which allowed the Rosebud Sioux Tribe to sell, exchange, and mortgage tracts of land that were left "isolated" from other parts of the reservation after the General Allotment Act and three subsequent "surplus land" acts had severely diminished the tribal land base. The Rosebud Sioux also developed the first proactive land consolidation initiative, Tribal Land Enterprise (TLE), founded in 1943.

What Michael Lawson wrote of a land consolidation bill proposed by the Sisseton-Wahpeton Sioux Tribe in the 1980s illustrates, in part, what Indian landowner advocates think is wrong with the ILCA and, in part, what they think is wrong with the mind-set that brought the ILCA and most governmental remedies to the "Indian problem" into being. Of the Sisseton-Wahpeton bill, Lawson wrote: "[Although it] embodies a number of previously suggested remedies, [it] falls short of an ideal solution because it would arbitrarily disinherit hundreds of current and prospective heirs. Yet, over time, it should certainly work to increase the useable tribal land base and reduce the cost of Federal administration. Given the complexity of [the] heirship issue, and the failure of Congress to provide more than an extensive investigation of the problem over the last half-century, perhaps this is the best that can be hoped for" (Lawson 1984, 97).

In other words, whether emanating from tribal or federal government, the remedies to fractionation have consistently been at the expense of the unfortunate individual upon whom the "heirship problem" was foisted in the first place and for whom "the best that can be hoped" is to be arbitrarily disinherited in favor of an increased tribal land base and reduced costs of federal administration. The question of what the increased tribal land base would mean, economically or otherwise, for the individual so disinherited is not broached. Instead, as with allotment, tribal land ownership is assumed to be the same as the equally ill-defined common land ownership of pre-allotment periods (see "From Treaties to Trust" in chapter 1; the more modern tendency to conflate the incorporated with the communal tribe is discussed below). Furthermore, the cost of federal administration has usually been identified as a cost to taxpayers. Until recently, the cost to Indian individuals and tribes seldom surfaced except in the government's *internal* investigation of the problem.[37] Yet the BIA's mismanagement of Indian monies earned from the sale, lease, and development of Indian lands has been recognized by the federal government for almost two centuries, as *Misplaced Trust: The Bureau of Indian Affairs' Mismanagement of the Indian Trust Fund* (H.R. Rep. no. 499, 102d Cong., 2d sess., 1992) makes clear. "For example," reads the report (pp. 8–9), "in 1828—just 4 years after its creation—H. R. Schoolcraft described the Bureau's financial management as follows: 'The derangements in the fiscal affairs of the Indian department are in the extreme. One would think that appropriations had been handled with a pitchfork [. . .] there is a screw loose in the public machinery somewhere.'"

However, landowner advocates like Judge Sally Willett think that for Congress to lay blame on the BIA for its failures is "the equivalent of the architect blaming the contractor for design deficiencies and poor product stemming from cut rate labor and materials authorized by the former. No policy-maker or legislator took into account how Indians operate when they carved up Indian lands into parcels. Thereafter, Indians and the BIA have been subjected to constant politics, underfunding, undertraining and basically contempt from all sectors."[38] Judge Willett suggests that the "screw loose" identified 180 years ago by H. R. Schoolcraft lies in the experimental nature of allotment and its ilk (such as land cessions, removal, termination, the ILCA). These, she contends in an unpublished 2003 essay, are little more than "federal exit strategies from the 'Indian question' [that] have traditionally backfired only upon Indians." She argues that these strategies end up creating tensions between tribes and allotted landowners, whose common interest is to be treated fairly. "Sacrifice has to be mutual," she asserts, "and not all assigned to one interest [the individual allottee]. The government also has to sacrifice in creating an effective solution that, once and for all, fixes the horrendous problem that it alone conceived."[39] The solutions proposed by Indian landowners are various and not always in line with federal interests in limiting or ridding itself of its Indian problem. But the multifarious voices of Indian land ownership are no longer to be ignored, as the case studies of legislation and litigation in this and the following chapters illustrate.

The Indian Land Consolidation Act

> It is factually accurate to say that more energy has been spent trying to find ways not to shoulder the cost and burden of Indian administration, historically referred to as the "Indian question," than has been devoted to finding appropriate ways to manage or administer trust or restricted assets for the actual benefit of affected Indians.
>
> —Judge Sally Willett, 2003[40]

Congress officially recognized the "heirship problem" by enacting probate authority over allotted Indian lands on June 25, 1910 (see "Reaching Critical Will" above). Federal acknowledgment of Indian inheritance rights in real property did nothing, however, to stem the steadily fractionating ownership patterns instituted and perpetuated by allotment policies and the federal trusteeship.[41] The Indian Land Consolidation Act (ILCA) of 1983 was Congress's first concerted effort to address fractionation. Landowner advocates interpret the seventy-year delay between problem recognition and proposed solution as a chronic case of federal penny-pinching. Referring to the original and first amended versions of the ILCA, Judge Willett writes: "In the quest for a rapid fix with no cash outlay—a goal of doubtful accomplishment given the nature of the interests at stake—the government engaged in serial experiments in law in 1983 and 1984 that didn't pass judicial muster."[42] As originally enacted in 1983, the Indian

Land Consolidation Act represented an attempt to address fractionation by delegating authority to tribes to develop and adopt their own, largely unfunded, land consolidation plans and inheritance (probate) codes. With approval of the secretary of the interior, tribes with land consolidation plans and the money to implement them could begin to buy and sell trust and restricted lands at fair market value.[43] The ILCA applied especially to fractional tribal interests, which could be bought, sold, or exchanged; to fractional individual interests greater than 2 percent of any given allotment, which could be purchased by the tribe with the majority (instead of unanimous) consent of co-owners; and to fractional individual interests less than 2 percent of any given allotment, which were to automatically transfer or escheat to tribal governments if those interests earned less than $100 for the owner in the preceding year (ILCA 1983, P.L. 97-459, sec. 207). Quite apart from the irksome question of cost, various provisions of the ILCA have troubled individual landowners, tribes, and the courts alike.

Thus Indian landowners responded, somewhat belatedly, with bewilderment and outrage to the assumption that they would uniformly welcome the consolidation of their small fractional interests under tribal ownership. For their part, tribal governments rejected with some vehemence the assumption that they would be willing and able to bear the increased administrative burdens of land consolidation while also swallowing yet another assault on tribal sovereignty. Finally, the escheat or "2 percent provision," as it has come to be known, was struck down twice by the U.S. Supreme Court, first, in *Hodel v. Irving* (1987) and, again, in its revised form in *Babbitt v. Youpee* (1997). As the Court recognized in both instances, escheat traditionally applies to cases where real property has been abandoned, there is no one to inherit, or both; therefore, there is no one to compensate. The ILCA required neither that the land be abandoned nor that there be no heirs for property interests of less than 2 percent to be transferred to tribal governmental ownership, and no provision was made to compensate the owners' estates. The act was significantly amended in 2000, when (among other things) the escheat provision was removed, and again in 2004 under the new name of the American Indian Probate Reform Act (AIPRA).[44] But the ILCA and its progeny remain at the center of Indian landowner concerns as further revisions are put forth, and as national intertribal organizations try to balance or subvert the competing demands of federal, corporate (tribal), communal or collective, and individual interests. Before taking up these challenges to the act's provisions, the following section summarizes the impetus behind its passage and how the act first evolved.

"A Curious Psychological Block"

The eventual passage of the Indian Land Consolidation Act in 1983 followed a series of congressional reactions to Indian activism roused by Termination-era politics and policies. Congressional studies in the 1960s discovered that roughly half of all allotted lands were held in fractionated ownership, and at least a quarter were co-owned by more than six heirs (see *Hodel v. Irving*, 481 U.S. 704, 708–709 [1987]). There followed a series of legal debates that reflect the intractability of the problem at the administrative, bureaucratic level, if not at the level of scholarship. Gilbert and Taylor's 1966 analysis, "Indian Land Questions," suggested the existence of "a curious psychological block in the minds of federal officials. This takes the form of an over-compensative concern with the property rights of individual Indians in heirship lands conjoined with a complete aphasia concerning the practical effects on Indian welfare of the existence of such lands" (Gilbert and Taylor 1966, 116). More recently, Suzanne Schmid has taken up the question of this "curious psychological block" by framing it, as Gilbert and Taylor do, in the received wisdom of Euro-American legal authority and supposed cultural supremacy over the stereotypical "symbolic Indian" (Schmid 1989; see also Vizenor 1994; Carrillo 2002). In her legal review of the first Indian land escheat case, Schmid suggests that the "over-compensative concern" alleged by Gilbert and Taylor "stems from the fact that many of these Indian tribes originally roamed over territory now embraced within the United States" (Schmid 1989, 749n93).[45] But she argues that England's "discovery" of North America, subsequent claims to sovereignty, and recognition of only a "possessory right of the Indians over the lands that they occupied" do not give Indians a "greater property interest" (than whom she doesn't say). Instead, Schmid uncritically reasserts the apparently self-explanatory and race-based inegalitarian hierarchy imposed at "discovery": that the "Indians' aboriginal claim to lands was not fee simple" (749n93).[46] Thus the ILCA's continued uncompensated taking of Indian property interests is seen as a "natural" consequence of "discovery"—500 years after the fact.

Aside from what Jo Carrillo (2002) refers to as the "disabling certitude" entrenched in such unexamined acceptance of Euro-American jurisprudence, Indian law scholars suggest yet another block to the resolution of fractionation. This time, it lies in the Constitution itself, and in conflicting judicial and congressional interpretations of what the federal-Indian relationship should be. As suggested at the beginning of this chapter, federal courts have traditionally decided Indian property rights cases along two lines: the first grants (or takes for granted) the "plenary power" that Congress has assumed over Indian tribes by virtue of its implied guardianship over their resources (the assimilationist line); the second tends to mitigate assertions of that power based on the responsibilities inherent in the federal government's role as trustee (the separatist line; Schmid 1989, 750; cf. Wilkinson 1987, 13).[47]

The Indian Land Consolidation Act exhibits elements of both lines of interpretation and, as we will see in our discussion of challenges to its constitutionality, has twice become the nexus of legislative and judicial contention. Moreover, as with the allotment policy whose legacy it is supposed to contravene, we can identify several intentions behind the ILCA's creation—for example, to consolidate property interests in the tribes; to increase the productive use of Indian lands; to streamline the administration of those lands—all of which may be achieved with or without benefit to individual Indian landowners. This is not to say that the designers of the act didn't have the interests of individual landowners in mind, but, rather, that they assumed they knew what those interests were without having to consult anyone on the different reservations. Perhaps this was the same "aphasia" that was at work among federal officials of the 1960s.[48]

"Serial Experiments"

In July 2002, I spoke with one of those involved in the original drafting of the bill that would become the Indian Land Consolidation Act. When I asked him about it, he grimaced as if it pained him to be reminded. He said that he and his colleagues had been astonished by the vociferous rejection the act had met with among trust landowners: "We thought they'd welcome it. As long as their land wasn't going out of trust, but was going to the tribe . . . . We thought they'd be okay with that, but they weren't. They really don't trust their tribal governments, that's the problem."

The response highlights a pervasive disconnection—neither surprising, uncommon, nor necessarily of ill intent—between the world of policy makers and academics, on the one hand, and the world of those they purport to represent, on the other.[49] The distance between these worlds is illustrated by the fact that the objections from Indian landowners were neither as strenuous nor as timely as they would have been if more landowners had known at the time of its enactment that the new law's "2 percent provision" would result in the uncompensated loss of land. As landowner and advocate Ernee Werelus explains:

> It's the same old problem. Nobody down here [on the reservations] knows what's going on until it's too late. There's nobody around to explain the new laws to the people. When they go to the BIA for help, they just get shoved out the door and told not to worry because they only own a teaspoonful [of land], anyway. Say I had a 2 percent interest in a 40-acre allotment. That's almost an acre. And they call it a "spoonful of dirt"! So why do they wonder when we get paranoid every time the government comes up with a new strategy for "helping us Indians"?[50]

The same complaint is echoed elsewhere in Indian Country. For example, when the ILCA began to take effect at Pine Ridge Reservation, North Dakota, the response among tribal members is reported to have been one of confusion and mistrust: "The remoteness of many of the districts on Pine Ridge, the absence of telephones in many homes, and the fact that public transportation is almost nonexistent provides for a communication problem not only between tribal members and the federal government, but between tribal members and the tribal government as well" (Hakansson 1997, 255).

The situation is similar at Fort Hall and is one of the reasons why advocates like Ernee Werelus are invaluable to the Indian landowners' cause. Whether she travels to isolated parts of the reservation or receives visitors at her home or the FHLA office, as an elder and a native speaker she can explain the inexplicable, even if she cannot always render it reasonable (see chapters 3–5). Her criticism is the same as Lynn Trozzo's. Editor in chief of the Native-owned and -operated *Federal Indian Probate Post* (FIPP), Trozzo writes:

> My beef is this: How can policy makers write and rewrite policies for programs and peoples when they have never seen the landowners, the old

and young alike; when they have never tried to explain to an aged Indian woman whose health is fading and time is of the essence, and that even though the Agency is just five minutes from her house they are too busy to get over to see her to help her write her will? She owns 160 acres and has 10 children. Have the policy makers with all their degrees in this and that tried to sit with an elderly with a grade five education to explain heirship, fractionation and the best of all, two percent escheat?[51]

As with much dissent in Indian Country, the voices of the elderly—or at least of their advocates—were finally heard loud and clear not by the legislature but by the courts when first one, and then, ten years later, a second suit involving the constitutionality of the ILCA came before the U.S. Supreme Court.

Hodel v. Irving (1987)

The first lawsuit was filed just two months after the Indian Land Con-solidation Act was enacted, in March 1983, when Oglala Sioux tribal members Mary Irving, Patrick Pumpkin Seed, and Eileen Bissonette sued on behalf of four recently deceased tribal members whose frac-tional property interests had been escheated to the tribe under section 207 of the ILCA: the 2 percent provision. The appellants, each of whom expected to receive interests in one or another of the allotments of the deceased—in fact, 41 fractional interests were at stake, valued collectively at more than $4,500—argued that the escheat provision effected a Fifth Amendment takings violation because it compensated neither the estates of the deceased nor the expectations of the heirs.[52]

The U.S. District Court for the District of South Dakota upheld the statute under the presumption that since Congress has assumed "plenary power" over tribes, it also had the right to abolish the inheritance rights of tribal members. The Court also concluded that since the expectation to inherit is not a vested property right, the appellants' claim was not entitled to constitutional protection. The United States Court of Appeals for the Eighth Circuit struck down the lower court's decision, stating that the escheat provision was indeed a violation of the Fifth Amendment. The Supreme Court agreed unanimously, the majority reasoning that in this "extraordinary" regulation (i.e., the ILCA, sec. 207) Congress had "effec-tively abolished both descent and devise [of fractionated interests] even when the passing of the property to the heir might result in consolidation of property" (*Hodel v. Irving*, 481 U.S. 704, 716 [1987]) — supposedly a primary goal of the act.[53]

In 1984, while the *Irving* case was still pending before the Eighth Circuit Court of Appeals, Congress amended the escheat provision by widening the window of earning capacity for 2 percent fractional interests to five years instead of one — that is, the interest had to be judged capable of earning at least $100 in any one of five years following the death of its owner. There would be a "rebuttable presumption" that the interest would not be so capable if it had not earned $100 in any one of the five years preceding the owner's death. The amended provision also permitted an owner to devise his or her "otherwise escheatable interest" to a descendant who also owned a fractional interest in the same allotment, and it authorized tribes to override the provision entirely by adopting their own probate codes subject to approval of the secretary of the interior.[54] Because the *Irving* case occurred before these amendments were passed, however, the Supreme Court declined to comment on their constitutionality, though it could not long avoid the "issue skirted" (Thompson 1997, 285).

Babbitt v. Youpee (1997)

Five years after the Court issued its decision in *Hodel v. Irving* (1987), descendants of deceased Sioux tribal member William Youpee awaited the probate hearing that would carry out Youpee's final will and testament. An enrolled member of the Sioux and Assiniboine Tribes of the Fort Peck Reservation in Montana, William Youpee held several undivided interests on reservations in Montana and North Dakota. Collectively valued at more than $1,200, Youpee's interests were each willed to a single descendant. As the Court would later note, his will "perpetuated existing fractionation, but did not splinter ownership further by bequeathing any single fractional interest to multiple devisees" (*Babbitt v. Youpee*, 519 U.S. 234, 241 [1997]).[55]

Nevertheless, the administrative law judge who reviewed the *Youpee* case found that the fractional interests that Youpee had willed to his descendants fell under ILCA's amended escheat provision, and should therefore be transferred to the tribes at Fort Peck, Standing Rock, and Devils Lake Sioux Reservations. When Youpee's descendants appealed this decision to the Department of the Interior's Board of Indian Appeals, the board dismissed the appeal, stating that it did not have jurisdiction over a constitutional claim (*Babbitt v. Youpee*, 242).

At this point, Youpee's descendants took their case to U.S. District Court for the District of Montana. They named the secretary of the interior (Bruce Babbitt) as defendant and claimed a Fifth Amendment takings violation. The District Court agreed, and the United States petitioned the Ninth Circuit Court of Appeals. The Ninth Circuit affirmed the earlier court's decision, calling the escheat provision "an extraordinary and impermissible regulation of Indian lands [. . .] effect[ing] an unconstitutional taking without just compensation" (*Youpee v. Babbitt*, 67 F.3d 200 [9th Cir.; 1995]).

The *Youpee* case's arrival before the Supreme Court occasioned an audible grumble from the bench, as the justices considered "for a second time the constitutionality of an escheat-to-tribe provision of [the ILCA]," and all but one joined in a terse opinion affirming the Ninth Circuit's decision.[56] Writing for the majority, Justice Ruth Bader Ginsburg stated that "the narrow revisions Congress made to §207, without benefit of the Court's ruling in *Irving*, do not warrant a disposition different from the one announced and explained in *Irving*. The United States' arguments [. . .] are no more persuasive today than they were in *Irving*" (*Babbitt v. Youpee*, 519 U.S. 234, 235–236).

The Court's reaffirmation of its reasoning in *Hodel v. Irving* explicitly grounds the Indian allottee's property rights in the Constitution. "Testamentary freedom" is not, itself, constitutionally grounded (Guzman 2000, 626).[57] However, the Court recognized that federal law had already "significantly whittled Indian stick bundles [i.e., property rights]" through federal trusteeship.[58] Therefore, the ILCA's additional regulatory limitations on the land's disposal through the abrogation of descent and devise constituted a "potentially extraordinary economic impact" on the affected landowners. As a few commentators on the Court's decisions have noticed, the 2 percent rule was the equivalent of requiring individual allottees and their heirs—among the most disadvantaged groups in the United States (see Frantz 1999, 105–155)—to pay for the mistake of allotment. What is rather startling is that the overall assessment of the Court's rulings by the legal profession barely deemed this brazen injustice worthy of comment, instead focusing on the Court's perceived departure from its traditions, variously conceived.

An "Over-Compensative Concern"?

> The legislative, judicial, and academic reaction to fractionation and forced consolidation tells two tales with one moral: the popular view of both the extent of property rights and the nature of those who hold them is unnecessarily constricted. The Court's decision is not peculiar unless one holds a narrow view of property, just as it is not assimilationist unless one holds a narrow view of Native Americans who own it.
> —Katheleen R. Guzman, "Give or Take an Acre"

Only a handful of legal reviews managed to find more to criticize in the Indian Land Consolidation Act than in the opinions of the Supreme Court (see, for example, Thompson 1997; Schwab 1998; Guzman 2000; Welliver 2002; Shoemaker 2003).[59] In the relatively few legal analyses of the Court's Indian land escheat decisions, there seems to be a deep rift, indicative perhaps of nearly unbridgeable differences in perspective. On the one hand, there are those few scholars who feel that the Court's *Irving* and *Youpee* decisions rightly protect the constitutional rights of individual Indian landowners against the quick fix strategies of the federal government (see Guzman 2000, 599–600).[60] On the other hand, there are those who feel that the Court is undermining the economic utilitarianism of the private property tradition by protecting fractional ownership rights; and there are those who feel that the Court is wrongly upholding the colonial impulses of the United States by imposing Western private property norms over a presumed (and ill-defined) communal property orientation of tribes.[61] But regardless of their perspective, most scholars seem to take as a forgone conclusion that the corporate property interests of tribal governments are the same as the property interests of the tribe as an assemblage of co-identifying families and individuals.[62] For example, in a much longer discussion that briefly employs the ILCA cases (among many others) to illustrate the Court's tendency to reinforce the colonial roots of federal Indian law, Robert Clinton appears to ignore both the individual and the collectivity by conflating corporate (post–Indian Reorganization Act [1934]) and communal (pre–General Allotment Act [1887]) meanings of "tribe": Both *Irving* and *Youpee* "invalidated the escheat of the property interest to the Tribe, rather than merely requiring the federal government to pay compensation for the escheat. Yet, ironically, [. . .] Indian tribes have never been compensated in their governmental capacities for the expropriation of their lands for use as individual allotments. For Indian tribes whose cultures and sovereignty are entirely dependent on land ownership, the current constitutional doctrines create a no-win situation" (Clinton 2002, 203–204).[63]

Allottees likewise argue that tribal culture and sovereignty are dependent on land ownership, but they point out that Indian tribes are, after all, composed of individuals (see, for example, Assiniboine landowner Delmar "Poncho" Bigby's congressional testimony below).

Like Professor Clinton's otherwise powerful account of the colonial roots of federal "supremacy" over tribes, and with the few exceptions noted above, legal scholars have tended to use the Supreme Court's *Irving* and *Youpee* decisions as objects for other concerns. Thus they confront the cases largely as topical illustrations of what the scholars contend are the Court's tendencies in one direction or another (see, for example, Leavitt 1988, 633; Tsosie 2001, 1298). In so doing, they also tend to deal in stereotypes. For example, in his strongly utilitarian analyses, Michael Heller (1998, 1999) uses allotted Indian land, among other governmental "mistakes," to illustrate the "tragedy of the anti-commons." Heller seems to assume that fractional interests are always underutilized ("lie fallow"), creating an "anti-commons" that, he further seems to assume, cannot be "reconstituted" by facilitating land consolidation through the owners (Heller 1998, 685–687; Heller 1999, 1221–1222.[64] His assumptions thus perpetuate two common myths about fractionated ownership: (1) that fractionation automatically ends in "underuse"; and (2) that the co-owners of fractionated lands are unlikely to consolidate their interests if given the opportunity.

In fact, because BIA superintendents are empowered to broker leases of fractionated land if co-owners cannot agree as to how an allotment should be used, many fractionated allotments are included in tracts that are not "underused" but, to the contrary, are perpetually under use (see, for example, discussion of *Papse v. BIA* [2000] in chapter 4). As for Heller's second assumption — that "reconstituting [fragments] into sole ownership on any ordinary scale of use seems impossible through private bargaining" (Heller 1999, 1221) — allottees argue precisely the opposite.

They contend that fractionation can be solved by the federal government "getting out of the way" so that landowners can make their own choices regarding the use — and the nonuse — of the land. They call for, and indeed have written, legislation that simplifies and facilitates property exchanges, gift deeds, and inheritance procedures among individual landowners.[65] And they call for landowners to assert their rights of ownership by, among other things, occasionally refusing to allow their land to be leased.[66] Where Heller presumes economic tragedy in the underutilization of the anti-commons, landowners experience it, economically and otherwise, in the relentless exploitation of Indian land (see chapters 3–5 for ethnographic illustrations).[67] Since at least the 1950s, landowner advocates have litigated against absurdly low lease rates and the concomitant abuse of fractionated lands and resources by non-Indian loggers, farmers, ranchers, miners, and others. Some of these stories are recounted in subsequent chapters.

In those stories, like the one at hand, the "superficial utilitarianism" that by and large characterizes the legal and legislative approaches to fractionation "masks hidden costs and benefits" (Guzman 2000, 654). In the words of Katheleen Guzman, the one legal scholar whose review of the Court's ILCA escheat decisions reflects many of the concerns landowners have themselves expressed: "First, individuals owning potentially escheatable interests suffer a double hit but no direct gain. Preventing escheat would require that the owner incur related legal and transactional fees for keeping fastidious records; researching ownership to determine potential devisees; effecting life time transfers and hiring an attorney to effect same; appraising the property and its capacity for income; drafting a will or a will substitute; removing the property from trust or restricted status" (Guzman 2000, 654–655).[68] All of the foregoing represents not only hidden economic costs but, in many cases, insurmountable bureaucratic hurdles given the prevailing administration of Indian lands and trust resources.[69] On the other hand, the hidden benefits masked by this superficial utilitarianism are those that now have landowners calling for the return of all 2 percent escheated interests from tribes to the rightful individual owners.

In October 1998, the secretary of the interior formally reopened all estates in which property was improperly transferred to tribal ownership under the Indian Land Consolidation Act. According to landowner advocates' congressional testimony in May 2002, an estimated 13,000 escheated interests had been added to the growing probate backlog as a result of the 2 percent experiments.[70] The return of fractional interests taken during this "15-year costly diversion" remains one of the many points of contention between landowners, tribes, and the trustee.[71] In testimony before the Senate Committee on Indian Affairs, the late Delmar "Poncho" Bigby of the Assiniboine Nation of Fort Belknap Indian Reservation, Montana, explained that "many individuals blame the 'Tribes' for loss of their anticipated inheritance," even though tribes had little choice but to carry out the hastily conceived federal mandate.[72] Some compensated their members whenever they could afford to do so. Most did not know what hit them until it was too late. In the words of Sally Willett, the impact of the escheat was to divert "critical manpower resources needed for allotted land administration to a dead end purpose without ultimate benefit to the government, tribes or individuals whose cases were delayed due to the labor-intensive work required to develop the record in probates with 2 percent interests."[73]

Amazingly, an escheat provision surfaced yet again in Senator Ben Nighthorse Campbell's 1999 bill (S. 1586) to amend the ILCA. In response to the federal government's unwillingness to let escheat lie, Poncho Bigby had this to say:

What the B.I.A. fails to understand, or is totally unwilling to understand, is that to a very many of our People it makes no difference what the economic value of a tract of land may be. The real value to them is not economic, but tied to that tract of land are their culture, memories, and a sense of belonging that no money can equal. An increasing number of our members are forced to make an economic living off the reservation. To them and their descendants, this tract of land, no matter how small the interest may be, is their direct link to their ancestors and their roots. Without this link, they would be as lost as the vast majority of the dominant society. The dominant society searches for their roots to establish a personal sense of connection of who they are and where they came from, which is very sad.[74]

Echoing Bigby's impassioned statement, allottee and tribal opposition to continuing congressional interest in escheat was so strenuous that the provision was finally dropped—although it was replaced with stipulations almost as odious in the minds of many landowner advocates (see discussion of ongoing amendments below). And the problem of unreturned escheated interests continues to compound the problem of how landowners themselves might address fractionated ownership. In congressional testimony regarding ongoing amendments to the ILCA, Tohono O'odham Chair Austin Nuñez noted: "Where [escheated] title has not been corrected to reflect current ownership, real estate transactions—involving acquisition loans, sales, and exchanges—cannot be completed. Allotment owners' hands are tied until title records are corrected to reflect actual ownership. This is certainly a breach of the trust responsibility related to management of these allotments."[75] As the current and former chairmen of the intertribal grassroots Indian Land Working Group, Nuñez and Bigby here give us the less "constricted view" of "property rights and the nature of those who hold them" (Guzman 2000, 600). Human nature being the relational phenomenon that it is, Indian landowners succeed in variously confounding the expectations of their reformers by both owning land and being "owned" by it.[76]

The 2000 Amendments

The goals of the Indian Land Consolidation Act as amended in 2000 were as follows: "(1) to prevent further fractionation of trust allotments made to Indians; (2) to consolidate fractional interests and ownership of those interests into usable parcels; (3) to consolidate fractional interests in a manner that enhances tribal sovereignty; (4) to promote tribal self-sufficiency and self-determination; and (5) to reverse the effects of the allotment policy on Indian tribes" (P.L. 106-462, title 1, sec. 102, November 7, 2000, 114 *U.S. Statutes at Large* 1992).[77] The final goal was to be addressed in three ways: by restricting inheritance of trust property to Indians (narrowly defined) and tribes; through purchase of individual trust interests with the consent of a majority (as opposed to a unanimity) of the co-owners; and by providing for tribal land consolidation plans and tribal probate codes.

Although its goals seem laudable enough, allottees and tribal leaders alike objected to a number of provisions in the ILCA amendments. They were troubled by the lack of provisions to eliminate probate backlog and to return escheated 2 percent interests; by a provision imposing "joint tenancy with right of survivorship" (sec. 2206); by the lack of judicial review for regionally established "fair market values" (sec. 2214); by the narrowed definition of "Indian" (sec. 2201); by a flawed acquisition program (sec. 2212); by the lack of protection for off-reservation allotments; and by the use of adjudicators not authorized by the Administrative Procedures Act (APA). These concerns represented the most serious standing objections to a law that was, for all intents and purposes, rammed down the throats of largely unwilling landowners.[78]

Veteran advocate Helen Sanders's primary reason for wanting to stop the amended ILCA was its redefinition of "Indian." She protested: "They say only Indians can inherit trust land, and then they redefine who is an Indian. They shouldn't be legislating inheritance. That's for the tribes to do."[79] She had other problems with the law, as well—it didn't fix escheated land titles or fractionation, and it was both too complex, in its legalistic language, and too simple in its cookie-cutter approach to different reservations. But its most egregious breach of trust was that it took away the right to bequeath—that most "valuable right" recognized by the Supreme Court in the *Irving* and *Youpee* cases—both from the tribes and from the individual, and placed it in the demonstrably untrustworthy hands of the federal government.[80]

Nationally recognized Native American rights attorney John Sledd sums up the reaction in Indian Country—and shortly thereafter, in Interior, itself—when news of the 2000 amendments to the Indian Land Consolidation Act came down:

> The definition of Indian in the 2000 ILCA amendments would have forced landowners to choose between disinheriting their "non-Indian" children, and taking family land out of trust so it could be left to the children in fee, but subject to state taxation and possibly state regulation. More owners than expected chose the latter option. In parts of the country there was a trust to fee land rush (Sen. Rep. no. 108-264, p. 12). The removal of so much land from trust would have increased state tax and regulatory intrusions and seriously threatened tribal economies and sovereignty, and the threat of it caused an uproar in Indian Country. When even DOI [the Department of the Interior] began to question the feasibility of implementing the 2000 law, the fate of that law was sealed, and the stage was

set for "take 3" at Land Consolidation Act amendments. Pending further legislative efforts, DOI agreed not to issue a formal certification required by the 2000 Act before the new definition and other key provisions in that Act could take effect. H.R. Rep. no. 106-656 on S. 1721, p. 3 (Sept. 7, 2004). (Sledd 2005, 12)[81]

"Take 3": The American Indian Probate Reform Act of 2004

Between spring 2001 and fall 2004, three different bills wound their way up the Capitol steps, amid informal and vaguely defined proposals from the Department of the Interior, meetings with landowners and tribal and inter-tribal representatives, Senate hearings, and much wrangling in the ranks.[82] The American Indian Probate Reform Act of 2004 (AIPRA), P.L. 108-347, amends the Indian Land Consolidation Act and its never-certified amendments of 2000. As with earlier experimental reform efforts, Indian landowners and tribal leaders argue that the law that is emerging out of the AIPRA reflects Interior's agenda to reduce its own costs and liability more so than to live up to its fiduciary responsibilities as trustee.

The AIPRA's stated purpose is to reduce fractionation by creating a uniform federal probate code for owners of trust properties (land or money in Individual Indian Money accounts), especially those who pass away without writing a will. The act has been described as being so huge and complicated that it requires multiple careful readings even for attorneys and experienced probate judges to comprehend.[83] Landowner advocates have worked laboriously in recent years to fill the educational gap created by the fast-track reform of Indian probate; anyone interested in learning about the act and its intended and unintended effects should consult those materials (see chapter 5). In that vein, I offer two recent quotations, the first from John Sledd, discussing the push to pass the bill that would become the American Indian Probate Reform Act of 2004:

> The witness for the Indian Land Working Group [Austin Nuñez] suggested that, before taking bold action, the Senate should get some facts concerning land tenure on different reservations and how the Bill would affect it. That apparently sensible recommendation could not prevail against the combined urgency of landowners who feared [that the secretary of

the interior would certify the 2000 ILCA amendments], and DOI, which feared it would lose the chance for a major strike against fractionation and fiduciary liability exposure. Drafting continued with participants relying on anecdote and their own experience in lieu of data. (Sledd 2005, 15–16)[84]

And the second, from an unpublished essay by longtime landowner advocate and director of the Indian Land Working Group, Theresa Carmody:

> Imagine walking into your county clerk's office but instead this is the BIA Realty Office, to request information about your land. You are told that you may not be able to get a Title Status Report (TSR) for some months because the BIA is experiencing a recordation backlog. And yes, the new AIPRA provides that property in multiple ownership may be opened to forced sale depending upon whether or not any one fraction or portion of the tract of land is worth $1,500. You are then informed that now the BIA will be using an appraisal methodology that has nothing to do with valuing the land for its type and resources, but the valuations will be based on the number of co-owners.
>
> You leave in astonishment, and look for someone who is informed about these matters and who might have received some type of notice on this. You can't find anyone. Several months go by and you haven't received your TSR so you stop by the BIA Realty Office to check on it. You are told that you did not receive the information because you didn't put your request in writing—now required—and you should have received a notice about this. You are told you have to come up with your own form for this since the BIA doesn't have one and be sure to include the legal description for your land—also now required. And, oh and by the way, all the land records are now being shipped to Lenexa, Kansas, so we can centralize everything and make it easier for you to access—oh yes and we really do want you to become more self-determined about your land—what's taking you so long? (Carmody, n.d., 1–2)

Individual Indian Money: The Other Side of the Coin

In 1992, the House Committee on Government Operations published a report titled *Misplaced Trust: The Bureau of Indian Affairs' Mismanagement of the Indian Trust Fund*, which echoed the findings of various government reports and audits commissioned every few decades since 1915. For the first time, however, the House report spurred legislative action. In

1994, Congress passed the Indian Trust Fund Management Reform Act requiring a full accounting from the secretary of the interior.

It was in this context that Blackfoot Indian banker and landowner Elouise Pepion Cobell used the money she had been awarded in a MacArthur "genius" grant as seed money for what would become the largest class action lawsuit ever brought against a department of the federal government.[85] The historical, human, and monetary magnitude of the case attests to its significance in the annals of individual Indian advocacy.

According to a unanimous opinion issued by the District of Columbia Court of Appeals in 2001, the federal Indian trust was a backwater of injustice and malfeasance (*Cobell v. Norton*, 240 F.3d 1081 [D.C. Cir. 2001]). The federal trust, which includes Indian land, natural resources, and monies—earned income from Indian lands—has been undergoing a state of siege as Indian landowner activists and advocates try to wrest control of it away from the Department of the Interior (Gingold and Harper 2001). Since 1999, the government's trusteeship has been under the jurisdiction of the U.S. District Court for the District of Columbia, which has taken up the colossal and chronic mismanagement of billions of dollars of what are called "Individual Indian Monies," kept in Individual Indian Money (IIM) accounts established in concert (and complicity) with the General Allotment Act of 1887. The upheaval at Interior is occurring in the wake of this class action lawsuit against the department representing at least 500,000 Indian account holders from across the nation.[86] The crux of the problem, as the then presiding District Court judge has stated, is that "no one can say" just how many Indian account holders are entitled to just how much Indian money from the sale and leasing of Indian land (*Cobell v. Babbitt*, 91 F. Supp. 2d 1, 6 [D.D.C. 1999]).

And so, on December 21, 1999, 112 years after the General Allotment Act provided the justification that the federal government would use to open up millions of acres of Indian treaty lands in the western United States to non-Indian settlement—a justification that would obligate the government to hold the remaining tracts of land in trust for tens, now hundreds of thousands of Indian beneficiaries—the D.C. District Court ruled that the United States had consistently failed to uphold its end of the deal.

Judge Royce C. Lamberth opened his 142-page opinion with the following pronouncement: "It would be difficult to find a more historically mismanaged federal program than the Individual Indian Money (IIM) trust" (*Cobell v. Babbitt*, 4). He went on to rebuke the United States for the appalling breach of its "century-old obligation": "The United States, the trustee of the IIM trust, cannot say how much money is or should be in the trust. As the trustee admitted on the eve of trial, it cannot render an accurate accounting to the beneficiaries, contrary to a specific statutory mandate and the century-old obligation to do so. More specifically, as Secretary [of the Interior] Babbitt testified, an accounting cannot be rendered for most of the 300,000-plus beneficiaries, who are now plaintiffs in this lawsuit" (*Cobell v. Babbitt*, 4). Quoting from Chief Justice John Marshall's majority opinion in *Cherokee Nation v. Georgia (1831)*, one of the trilogy of cases that form the foundation of federal Indian law, Judge Lamberth observed: "Generations of IIM trust beneficiaries have been born and raised with the assurance that their trustee, the United States, was acting properly with their money. Just as many generations have been denied any such proof, however. 'If courts were permitted to indulge their sympathies, a case better calculated to excite them could scarcely be imagined'" (*Cobell v. Babbitt*, 4–5; legal citations omitted; see chapter 1 for discussion of *Cherokee v. Georgia*).

It is significant that the Marshall quotation is taken from one of the first judicial articulations of the trust doctrine, an opinion so twisted by the Indian-hating Jackson administration that it was used to provide "legal" justification for the eventual unilateral abrogation of Cherokee treaties, and the ensuing "Trail of Tears" removal of the Cherokee people from the state of Georgia to Oklahoma. Some fear that, here, too, the government may find its promises too burdensome to bear. It may finally twist its way out of its trusteeship even though, as Judge Lamberth wrote, "the beneficiaries of this trust did not voluntarily choose to have their lands taken from them; they did not willingly relinquish pervasive control of their money to the United States. The United States imposed this trust on the Indian people. As the government concedes, the purpose of the IIM trust was to deprive plaintiffs' ancestors of their native lands and rid the nation of their tribal identity" (*Cobell v. Babbitt*, 4–5). Now, the question is not whether the United States has succeeded in its aims, but whether the ongoing appropriation of the federal Indian trust by its Indian beneficiaries can succeed in disenthralling the federal government from its constricted and constricting view of Indian landowners and Indian land ownership.

Since the judicial opinions quoted above were issued, the most notable activities attributed in court opinions to the Departments of the Interior and Treasury have been the deliberate destruction of Indian account records, the deliberate destruction of written correspondence among officials, lying, obstruction, and various other offenses that eventually resulted in the levying of contempt of court charges against more than forty individuals.[87] In testimony, Indian landowner advocates have urged Congress to "listen to the [individual Indian] property owners because they are the ones that file suit and who win their cases in court."[88] They point to the 2 percent escheat cases (*Irving* and *Youpee*) described above, the *Mitchell* cases (see chapter 3), and ongoing *Cobell* or Individual Indian Money (IIM) litigation. And then there are the setbacks.

On July 11, 2006, after considering the latest appeal from the government in the *Cobell* lawsuit, the U.S. Court of Appeals ordered Judge Lamberth removed from the case. In part, the Court agreed with the government's concern that Judge Lamberth's "professed hostility to Interior" had clouded his ability to make impartial decisions—or, at least, to appear to be doing so (*Cobell v. Kempthorne*, no. 05-5269, at 33 [D.C. Cir. July 11, 2006]). This, combined with what it called "an unbroken string" (*Cobell v. Kempthorne*, 30) of eight appellate reversals of Lamberth's decisions "(out of more than 60 published decisions, and well over a 100 other unpublished rulings or orders, over the 10-year course of this lawsuit)" (Reply Brief, USSC 06-868, March 5, 2007, p. 2)[89] provided what many observers argue is a seriously flawed piece of judicial reasoning, with potentially grave consequences. As counsel for the "Plaintiff-Beneficiaries" notes, "It is a puzzlement" that the government expressed such concern over the "harsh language" in Judge Lamberth's opinions when the appeals court itself agreed with most of his characterizations, and even the "Trustee-Delegate" was forced to concede their accuracy (Reply Brief, p. 3). The appeals court opinion reads:

> Although [Judge Lamberth's] opinion contains harsh—even incendiary—language, much of the language represents nothing more than the views of an experienced judge who, having presided over this exceptionally contentious case for almost a decade, has become "exceedingly ill disposed towards [a] defendant" that has flagrantly and repeatedly breached its fiduciary obligations. *Liteky*, 510 U.S. at 550, 114 S.Ct. 1147. We ourselves

have referred to Interior's "malfeasance," "recalcitrance," "unconscionable delay," "intransigen[ce]," and "hopelessly inept management." *Cobell VI*, 240 F.3d at 1096, 1109; *Cobell XII*, 391 F.3d at 257; *Cobell XIII*, 392 F.3d at 463. To be sure, Interior's deplorable record deserves condemnation in the strongest terms. Words like "ignominious" and "incompeten[t]" (the District Court's) and "malfeasance" and "recalcitrance" (ours) are fair and well supported by the record. (*Cobell v. Kempthorne*, no. 05-5269, at 28–29, 30 [D.C. Cir. July 11, 2006])

Even so, on March 26, 2007, the U.S. Supreme Court declined to review the Appeals Court decision removing Lamberth. The case was reassigned to Judge James Robertson, who has pledged to move the case forward without delay.

In the midst of all this, on March 1, 2007, the Bush administration released a two-page proposal for a legislative settlement of the individual Indian trust litigation, along with more than 250 other tribal cases, as well as the government's liability in any future trust litigation. In a letter to the chairman of the Senate Committee on Indian Affairs, Byron Dorgan, Secretary of the Interior Dirk Kempthorne and Attorney General Alberto Gonzales write that "the Administration is willing to invest up to $7 billion, over a ten year period [. . .] to settle *all* existing and potential individual and tribal claims for trust accounting, cash and land mismanagement, and other related claims, along with the resolution of other related matters (e.g., trust reform, IT security, etc.)" (emphasis added).[90] This, despite Gonzales's own testimony before Congress two years previous that the government's liability in the Indian trust litigation could be upward of $200 billion.[91]

The proposal was essentially the same as one that was floated before a crowd of several hundred Indian landowners at the Sixteenth Annual Indian Land Consolidation Symposium at the Morongo Casino, Cabazon, California, in October 2006. In an unscheduled appearance the second morning of the jam-packed symposium, staffers for Senator John McCain arrived, passed around copies of the proposal, and then suggested that people in the audience "take time to digest" what they were reading. Before these words had even stopped echoing in the air, people were lining up behind the two microphones positioned at the back of the room. "Digest what?!" was the prevailing response. Like the Kempthorne-

Gonzales letter, the proposal smacked of termination, and no one needed more than a moment's glance at the "key facets of acceptable reform" in order to see that.

Assessing the significance of the Individual Indian Money litigation and proposed legislative "fixes" is beyond the scope of this study, indeed, impossible at least for now because these matters are ongoing. I touch on them here because they represent a driving and demonstrative force in individual Indian advocacy and activism—and because they clearly reveal the seemingly boundless cynicism and intransigence of the federal trustee.

CHAPTER 3

Ambivalent Allottees

> There seems to be no word in English that properly fits the situation. [. . .] if we want to categorize the special status of Indians as both dependent and independent the language fails us. Perhaps we should coin a new term, such as "ambipendence" or "ambigupendence," that could be useful generally to identify such objective situations as often exist where the subjective attitudes of people are ambivalent. Indians had to cope with "ambipendence" for centuries. [And have] evolved customary routines for living with their problems.
>
> —Francis Jennings, *The Invasion of America*

This chapter highlights the advocacy work of two "ambivalent allottees." I think of them as *ambivalent* not because they are "indecisive" or "hesitant" in the common, everyday sense of the word.[1] They are anything but that. Rather, theirs is an ambivalence of the etymologically accurate sort: they labor at times under both of "two contrary values or qualities."[2] As suggested in previous chapters, one of these is the value of capital, of land as a commodity, its Marxian use value subordinated to its exchange value. The other is the value of sentiment, of earth as community.[3]

In part, these stories are told from the allottees' perspectives and, in part, through the legal and social ramifications of their work as represented in relation to the experiences of Indian landowners—themselves and their fellow allottees. The social meanings attached to their experiences ramify, formally and informally, through the (mis)applications of federal Indian law in its articulations with the demands of a capitalist, politically racialized society. The allottees are ambivalent in the sense that they are torn between contrary desires—to meet felt needs, on the one hand, and imposed political and economic needs, on the other.

As Jennings (1975) was well aware, the problems pinned on Indians have their roots in imposed "ambipendences" like allotted Indian land.

In some ways, allotment was a grand success. In terms pertinent to its nineteenth-century supporters, its policies "legally" relieved millions of acres of treaty land from the burden of "aboriginal title"—a boon to white land speculators—and it undermined and sometimes destroyed the various communal traditions of indigenous governments and social institutions. It was an answer to the government's "Indian problem," the "native question" that has beleaguered colonial regimes around the globe for half a millennium (Mamdani 1996). In 1890, Commissioner of Indian Affairs Thomas J. Morgan would write, glowingly, that the "settled policy of the Government" was "to break up reservations, destroy tribal relations, settle Indians upon their own homesteads, incorporate them into the national life, and deal with them not as nations or tribes or bands, but as individual citizens. The American Indian is to become the Indian American" (see Cohen 1942a/1971, 23). The policy ultimately failed, but not without incalculable cost to the people whose collective identity the United States tried to destroy for the sake of its own convenience, so that it could impose the "spaces" of private property ownership on the "places" of indigenous being, and so that it could deal with "its natives" on an individual basis rather than en masse.

It seems poetic justice, then, that individual Indian landowners—both individually and collectively—have been among the most irritating thorns in the side of the U.S. federal government (see discussion of *Cobell* case under "Individual Indian Money" in chapter 2). Some of their ancestors, tribes and individuals alike, tried to forestall the imposition of private property rights on Indian treaty lands. Many actively resisted implementation of allotment, misleading commissions and avoiding the visits of census takers trying to establish the tribal rolls. By 1934, however, around 100 reservations had been allotted, either under the General Allotment (Dawes) Act of 1887 or under special legislation enacted to deal with particular reservations (McDonnell 1991, 121). In the historical record of these initiatives, government officials gave the (usually false) impression that there were options. Many tribal leaders would choose the semblance or at least the possibility of "place"—first the reservations and then allotment—rather than accepting total *displacement* for themselves and their people (for poignant examples, see McDonnell 1991; Nabokov 1999; and under "On Being Encountered" in chapter 6).

Nonetheless, it should come as no surprise that, after more than a century and several generations of imposed "private" land ownership, the heirs of allotment are now fighting to assert their rights as landowners. Although "the master's tools will not dismantle the master's house," as the black feminist-activist Audre Lorde so famously put it (Lorde 1981, 98), Indian landowner advocates are using his tools (the Constitution, treaties, federal Indian laws, the courts) to remodel it at least—by holding him to his word.

"Societies formally attach social meaning to individual experience through notions of *accountability*," observed Carol Greenhouse (1989, 1632; emphasis added) in her discussion of "temporality and the cultural legitimization of law." In the United States' social dealings with American Indian people, such "notions of accountability" were formally if unevenly attached to individual experience through treaties, citizenship, and the structures of federal Indian law. However, a notion does not an action make. Individuals must sometimes compel society to honor or repudiate certain meanings formally attached, and certain others *in*formally attached, by holding society itself—in this case, the federal government and its institutions—accountable. Here the difference between the "formally" and the "informally" attached is the distance between the best of what society has declared and the worst of what it has so far delivered. The latter—genocide, termination, institutionalized dependency—is continuously lived and remembered, creating the "customary routines" that Jennings referred to in the epigraph above. These, in turn, create the ambivalent ground of meaning for the promise, the pledge, and the hope of the former—protected tribal sovereignty, indigenous self-determination.

Tribal and Individual Allottees

But the truth has to be told. There's the tribes' version of allotment—it was bad, bad, bad. And then there's the individuals' [version]. Allotment has done a lot of good for a lot of people. The bad thing about it was in letting people sell their allotments to non-Indians. But the tribes have their own ideas. You can tell one side of the story, that's the tribes'. And you can tell the other side of the story, that's the people's. Then it'll be obvious who needs to have their butts kicked.

—Helen Sanders, 2002[4]

Telling the tribes' side of the story is not within the scope or intent of this book. Suffice it to say that the stories emanating from tribes as governing entities tend, on the whole, to have a different slant from those of tribal members. Having, over time, purchased fractionated interests from individual Indian landowners, tribal governments of allotted reservations are themselves frequently co-owners of allotted interests. As corporate entities, tribes sometimes take distinctive positions that pit them against the individual allottees to whom they are responsible and from whom (along with other tribal members) they derive their legitimacy. They do this, in part, because as sovereigns, they *can*.[5]

For example, on one reservation, an association of landowners worked in partnership with tribal officials to negotiate the renewal of a utility company's right-of-way. The negotiation team was on the verge of signing an agreement with the company—an agreement that would have significantly raised the lease income of both tribal and individual allottees—when a change in tribal leadership occurred. The new leadership decided that the renewal negotiations offered an opportunity to assert tribal sovereignty. Against the wishes of the landowners, the new leadership called for a lease payment several times in excess of the fair market value of the right-of-way. The utility company threatened to have the lands along the original easement condemned, potentially depriving the landowners and the tribe alike of much needed income. The tribe held controlling interests along the right-of-way. Had the court ruled in favor of the utility company, the case could have set a precedent because tribal lands, and therefore, it would seem, those of individual tribal members as co-owners, are supposed to be beyond the reach of condemnation.[6] Ultimately, the company was forced to negotiate because the court agreed that tribal ownership of undivided interests in allotments along the right-of-way meant that condemnation was not an option. The tribe's sovereignty thus asserted and acknowledged, tribal officials became more sensitive to the concerns of the individual landowners, and reentered negotiations with the utility company.

It is as if the United States' efforts to destroy traditional tribal governments have created a backlash or feedback effect, wherein the tribe, as a corporation, is valorized at the expense of the individual. But, generalizations about the individuation or Americanization of tribal societies aside, the contemporary fact of life, given federal-Indian legal structures, is that the tribal government and the tribal collectivity are fundamentally dissimilar beings. Allotted landowners may form "partnerships," as one advocate puts it, with their governments, but the legal and historical structures under which tribes, as corporations, and individuals, as members of an ethno-linguistic collectivity, have assumed the mantle of Indian land ownership are different. They compel and permit distinctive responses.[7] As in the vignette above, tribal government is sometimes seen as the only durable element of tribal sovereignty, outlasting the individual, and therefore deserving of special economic consideration. To this, the late Poncho Bigby, longtime tribal government employee, allottee, and landowner advocate, offered a terse dissent: "No," he said. "It's the individuals who create the economy, not the tribal governments."[8]

Fractionated Land, Fractionated Ownership

The answer to fractionation is consolidation. But landowner advocates diverge over the question of whether it is more important to consolidate land or ownership. Those emphasizing land consolidation tend to look to devices such as gift deeds, wills, and exchanges of interest among individual allottees as tools to reduce and manage fractionation among families.[9] Those emphasizing the consolidation of ownership tend to look for ways to reduce the sheer number of owners by facilitating buyouts and by endorsing regulatory provisions that transfer intestate interests to surviving co-owners or the tribe.[10]

One of the best-known and oldest programs developed to consolidate undivided fractional interests in allotted trust land is the Rosebud Sioux Tribal Land Enterprise (TLE). Established in 1943, the TLE was originally designed and implemented through the Rosebud Agency and was to be managed by an "interlocking directorate" of Indian shareholders and the Rosebud Sioux Tribal Council (Biolsi 1992, 118). Under the TLE, individual Indian landowners are allowed to exchange their fractional interests in land for "TLE certificates" (shares in the tribal corporation) of equivalent value. They may then (1) keep the certificates and receive dividends, with the tribe, from the use of the exchanged land interests; (2) convert all or some of the certificates into cash; or (3) trade the certificates back to the tribe in exchange for a TLE land "assignment" to which they may enjoy rights of use and devise as long as only one beneficiary is designated.[11]

The roots of the TLE are apparent in the reform efforts of the Indian Reorganization Act (IRA) era, as are the seeds of individual Indian discontent with those efforts. Thomas Biolsi (1992) describes a series of "Indian congresses" held in 1934 where reform-minded Interior officials met with tribal delegates from northern plains tribes, including delegates from the Rosebud and Pine Ridge Reservations. During the meetings, Indian Affairs Commissioner John Collier lobbied the delegates for their support for the Wheeler-Howard bill (later passed as the Indian Reorganization Act of 1934):

> The reformers [Collier included] believed that conveying allotments and inherited estate shares to a tribal corporation—in return for corporate shares—would allow Indian lands to be more productively used by the owners. The Indian delegates were particularly concerned about the provision in the bill giving the Secretary of the Interior the power to compel transfer of individual allotments to the chartered community. Collier explained that he expected the transfers to be voluntary once allottees realized the advantages of corporate holding, and that the provision had been included in case a single individual irrationally held out and blocked the corporate consolidation of land. (Biolsi 1992, 69–70)

Indian opposition to the provision giving the interior secretary the power to compel the transfer of individual land to the tribal corporation turned out to be strenuous enough that Collier finally recommended it be eliminated from the bill. The corporation eventually created—the Tribal Land Enterprise—by acquiring individual trust land interests from willing sellers, has certainly managed to consolidate fractionated interests and keep thousands of acres of Sioux territory from slipping out of the trust.[12] Still, some landowner advocates find the underlying message of the TLE's actions troubling.

In October 2001 at Carlton, Minnesota, Director of the Indian Land Working Group Theresa Carmody asked what the role and the interest of the individual landowner is in the Tribal Land Enterprise system. A former TLE representative told her: "Well, the tribe will be here a lot longer than the individual." A BIA official seconded this: "Some of this undivided land is a bank account. It really is. They keep it until they need it. It's a savings account. They keep it for a rainy day and then they sell [to the TLE]."

"The concept is good," Carmody commented some years later. "They're dealing with a desperate situation at Rosebud, where there's extreme poverty. But it's about education . . . letting landowners know that trading your land in for a TLE assignment is *an* alternative, not the *only* one."[13]

Rosebud tribal member Fern Bordeaux worked for the TLE for more than 23 years before taking on the development of the tribe's relatively new Sicangu Oyate Land Office. Presenting the office's new grazing ordinance to an audience of allottee advocates at the Eleventh Annual Indian Land Consolidation Symposium, Bordeaux commented: "All those years, and I never had contact with the landowners. Now, with the new land office, the landowners are involved one hundred percent. The land and tribal members are our most valuable assets."[14] Her newfound sense of association is reflected in the opening lines of the ordinance, which read:

> The "heart" of this Ordinance is the management of our lands and connecting resources through plans for conservation, protection and enhancement. The past history has been the regulation of the use of our lands by the BIA, the tribal government and the TLE for the collection of money. The debt, the unmet needs and the need to make more money available has been the deciding factor in the best interests of the people. This Ordinance places as the priority the best interests of the management of our lands and connecting resources. The best interests of the land and connecting resources will be in the best interests of the people, landowners and producers.

Other staunch advocates for the rights of Indian landowners accept tribal corporations like the TLE as one answer to the fractionation problem. Helen Sanders says, "Rosebud's TLE program is a wonderful program . . . *for Rosebud.*"[15] And Ernee Werelus notes that tribes and tribal corporations like the TLE can obtain funding for land consolidation when individuals often can't. "Where do I go to get a loan to buy out my co-owners?" she asks rhetorically. She points to the relatively recent development of a number of Indian-owned banks and revolving loan funds as a possible solution to this dilemma.[16]

Likewise, former TLE Director Ben Black Bear defends the TLE's ownership consolidation efforts in monetary terms. But he also expresses recognition of a different motivating presence: "It is the nature of tribal culture to maintain contact with the tribal homeland, no matter how small the interest. To the allottee with a minimal interest in land the issue is not economics, but maintenance of contact with the reservation homeland, extended family and the tribe."[17]

In Helen Sanders's case, the double-edged assessment of allotment she expresses in the epigraph at the beginning of this section carries special resonance. As the lead plaintiff in two precedent-setting Supreme Court decisions of the 1980s, Helen's version of allotment has a lot to do with her own business and political acumen and her liberal grit, not to mention her well-earned reputation as a rabble-rouser.[18] "I come from the reservation from hell," she quips sardonically, introducing herself at the Tenth Annual Indian Land Consolidation Symposium, to a crowd for whom she needs no introduction.[19] A founding member and chair of the decades-old Allottees Association of the Affiliated Tribes of the Quinault Reservation, twice-elected secretary of the National Congress of American Indians (NCAI), current vice chair of the Indian Land Working Group, and a frequent contributor to the archives of congressional testimony, Helen is a veteran resister of the federal Indian trust.[20]

Helen Sanders (Mitchell)

It's okay to have an allotment. It's okay to own property. Experiences from working on your land help develop people, and I would like to see us go that way.
—Helen Sanders, 2001[21]

Born in 1927 on the tiny Chehalis Indian Reservation in western Washington, Helen was initiated into the strange legacy of allotment policy when, shortly after her birth, her father applied for an allotment in her name on the heavily timbered Quinault Reservation.[22] Years later, having been elected secretary of the Chehalis Tribe, she discovered that the tribe's base census roll did not include her family. Thus, even though she had lived there her entire life and was of Chehalis descent, she was identified as Quinault. "So," she says, "I went to the Quinault Reservation and talked to the chairman. He kind of laughed and told me, 'Yeah, Helen, you're Quinault.'"[23]

Her "official" identity was to be defined by her status at Quinault as an original allottee regardless of descent and residence (two of the more common arbiters of tribal membership), and in spite of her own inherited sense of self.[24]

That said, Helen's standing as an original allottee at Quinault has given her some advantages. First, as a Quinault tribal member, she has been in a position to fight against the victimization of other non-Quinaults under intertribal forms of discrimination engendered by a flawed treaty process.[25] She explains: "As a member of the Quinault Tribe, I can vote. I can have my say over how this tribe treats the others. They [the tribal council] want to be the only ones in charge on this reservation. But the courts say they're not. We've gone round and round on this one."[26]

What is more, as an original allottee at Quinault, Helen hasn't had to labor along under the awkward weight of fractionated ownership. Perhaps this helps to explain her perseverance in helping those who do.

Helen was still in high school in 1947 when her father received a letter from the superintendent of the Western Washington Indian Agency asking him to grant the BIA power of attorney over her allotments. "The letter included a power of attorney [form] with a bogus signature on it," Helen remembers, "—mine!" Her "inklings" about BIA wrongdoing thus awakened, Helen was primed for her own coming of age as an Indian trust landowner. But she says that her real initiation came a few years later, after she had become Mrs. Helen Mitchell: "A guy came to our door one day asking about a gravel pit that was on my original allotment. I agreed to sell some of the gravel. But when we didn't hear any more about it, and never received payment, I went to the [Agency] Forestry Office at Hoquiam to see what was going on. They told me to go to the [Agency] Realty office at Everett, and when I went there, those yahoos told me to go to the Forestry Office at Hoquiam. Finally, my husband said, 'Let's just go check it out for ourselves.'" So they did.[27]

What they found out was that the Bureau of Indian Affairs had been allowing the Aloha Lumber Company to take gravel off of Helen's allotment to build logging roads on the reservation. But the BIA had been reimbursing the landowner whose property adjoined the gravel pit, instead of Helen. "It was *their* mistake, but what do you think they did?" she asks rhetorically, eyes wide, still astounded after half a century. The BIA authorized Aloha to take "the trees off of *her* [the adjoining landowner's] land, *without* her knowledge, to pay *me* back for the gravel!"

As Helen discovered, this kind of misfeasance was just a symptom of more fundamental malfeasance and nonfeasance that have come to characterize the Interior Department's criminal breach of its Indian trust (see discussion of *Cobell v. Kempthorne* under "Individual Indian Money" in chapter 2). Helen soon learned that, in the late 1940s and early 1950s, the BIA had opened up more than 90,000 acres of the Quinault Reservation allotted lands to logging. Landowners were requested to sign a power of attorney allowing the BIA to complete a sale of the timber. The trustee had divided the reservation into three 30,000-acre parcels, the Queets unit, the Taholah unit, and the Crane Creek unit, and sold logging rights to the only two companies that bid on the sale—Aloha Lumber and Rayonier. The bids, however, were hardly competitive, as retired University of Montana forestry professor Alan Graham McQuillan explains:

> The initial offering was in 1948 and only the Taholah unit was bid (one bid only, from Aloha Lumber). Queets and Crane Creek were re-offered in 1950 and this time only one bid again (on Crane Creek, from Rayonier). Queets never was reoffered again but was instead split into multiple smaller units that were sold, some as "advertised sales" of timber, but mostly as "supervised sales" of land and timber—thus moving the land out of trust—except where Helen or another allottee was the buyer. In the case of Taholah and Crane Creek, competitive bidding was not prevented; rather, few buyers were interested in such huge sales so that, in each case, only one bidder emerged. Without competition, therefore, the buyer sealed the contract at minimum or "appraised" price. The many supervised sales on the Queets unit had competitive bidding in principle but not in practice because the BIA allowed a company to buy an allotment at the south end of the unit (opposite end from Highway 101) and then negotiate an exclusive-use right-of-way to build a road to [the allotment]. When other sales came up along or near this road the company had a huge advantage [because it already had a road and right-of-way]. In this way the unit was effectively split into 5 or 6 monopolistic sub-units, each "owned" by a different company.[28]

Contracts with the companies specified the removal of countless (because uncounted) millions of board feet of timber over a thirty-year period, for what would turn out to be comparatively low sums to the landowners, against whom the agency levied 10 percent administrative fees (a point that would come back to haunt the BIA). Helen's own timber contract—signed by the agency's acting superintendent "for and in behalf of Helen Sanders"—promised a total of $7,659 for the removal of an estimated 1,259,000 board feet of western red cedar, Sitka spruce, Douglas fir, amabilis (Pacific silver) fir, western white pine, western hemlock, and other species.[29] "The appraised prices weren't that far off from average West Coast prices of the time," says Professor McQuillan. "It's just that the BIA never obtained competitive bidding, so we can't be sure what the market *would have* paid."[30] But there were bigger problems. As McQuillan explains:

> The Taholah and Crane Creek contracts had provisions for frequent revisions of price, and periodic reappraisals [of timber volume]. In the case of Quinault, revisions were nearly always late whenever market prices were going up, but right on time whenever market prices sagged because the timber companies pressed the BIA to revise the costs downward. To add insult to injury, the BIA seriously underestimated the amount of timber coming out of that forest to begin with [in 1916]. And then they undervalued that timber by subtracting fixed costs (like road building) that were, themselves, overestimated (because the costs were converted to per unit values using the underestimated volumes).[31]

They also made errors in cost estimates, like the time they measured a road as being two miles longer than it actually was, attributing a cost to the company that it hadn't actually incurred. But when an independent logger named Nelson D. Terry pointed this out to the BIA, says McQuillan, "they actually *doubled* it instead, a mistake that also took awhile to fix."

Helen Sanders takes me for a drive through lofty forests of fir, spruce, cedar, hemlock, and pine that abut and have in some places reforested the Quinault Indian Reservation. She remembers the long learning process she went through as Aloha and Rayonier pulled the reservation's most valuable trees off the forest fifty years before.[32] "Those bastards were taking sixty-foot logs and leaving everything else!" she exclaims.

FIGURE 3.1. A view of a healthy, unlogged forest on the Quinault Indian Reservation. This mainly hemlock forest was part of a 30,000-acre parcel called the Crane Creek unit, logged by its only bidder, Rayonier, Inc., between 1952 and 1986. Mismanagement of forests by the Bureau of Indian Affairs was the subject of two precedent-setting Supreme Court decisions, in 1980 and 1983. The second of these, referred to as *Mitchell II*, establishes that the federal government, as trustee, is accountable not only to tribes but also to individual Indian landowners (as beneficiaries). (Courtesy of Alan McQuillan)

According to the Taholah and Crane Creek unit timber contracts, logs were to be "scaled" (measured according to the amount of lumber that could be milled from a "scaling cylinder") at a maximum length of forty feet. The diameter inside the bark at the small end (DIBSE) of each segment of a tree gives an estimate of its milled volume in board feet. As McQuillan explains: "The rule is one-inch growth in diameter per ten feet. So, if a tree has a six-inch diameter at sixty feet from the ground, it will have a nine-inch diameter thirty feet closer to the ground." Logs over forty feet in length should have been scaled in two segments as nearly equal as possible. The scale of these segments would then be based on the DIBSE measurement of the top segment, with a one-inch "taper allow-

FIGURE 3.2. Part of the Crane Creek unit logged by Rayonier, Inc. Rayonier and the Aloha Lumber Company contracted with the Bureau of Indian Affairs to log approximately 60,000 acres of allotted lands on the Quinault Indian Reservation between 1950 and 1986. With the BIA's tacit consent, the two companies routinely left smaller but still merchantable logs on the ground. Non-cedar species simply rotted and were never paid for, while cedar logs (which don't rot) were later removed at salvage prices (see note 32). (Courtesy of Alan McQuillan)

ance" added for each ten feet in length beyond the forty- foot maximum. So a sixty-foot log should have been measured as two thirty-foot logs, one of which had a bigger diameter, and was therefore worth more. But the sixty-foot logs that Helen remembers being taken from the Quinault forest were scaled as single logs at the smaller diameter, instead of as two logs, one with a diameter at least three inches larger than the other. The logging companies were thus severely underestimating the volume (and therefore the price) of timber being removed, while reaping full value for it at the lumber mills, whose own practices ensured that each sixty-foot log would be duly valued at two thirty-foot segments, one worth more than the other. "They made a holy mess of our forest," says Helen as we

FIGURE 3.3. Harvested cedar logs from Quinault Indian Reservation. The Bureau of Indian Affairs allowed Rayonier and the Aloha Lumber Company to clear-cut 60,000 acres of allotted Indian land, high-grading the largest, most valuable trees and leaving the forest in shambles. (Courtesy of Alan McQuillan)

pass through shade and sun, shade and sun. "Then they made a killing off our wood. And the BIA just stood by and watched them do it."

By 1960, Helen had begun attending intertribal meetings of concerned landowners, first at Queets, then in Seattle, and finally in Washington, D.C. It was in Seattle that she first encountered the kind of intimidation for which the BIA has become infamous. She recounts:

> Mel Schwartz, the assistant superintendent from the Western Washington Agency was there. He started questioning me about what I was doing at the meeting. I went across the street to eat. He followed me. Sat right across from me and kept asking me why I was there. There was a five-member panel at the meeting, commissioned under the new Kennedy administration to find out what was happening on the reservations. They asked me to speak about Chehalis if the Chehalis representatives didn't show. So I said, "Okay," and when my turn came, I said that Chehalis was

just like the other communities people had already talked about, had all the same problems. Then I started talking about how the BIA Agency at Quinault, how it was selling off people's timber—and land—and should be investigated. Poor old Mel just sat there with his mouth open, he was so stunned. But the chairman from Quinault, my cousin, he hadn't said a word about it. So I did. I told them, "Don't talk to the superintendent of the agency. Talk to the people."[33]

Not long after the Seattle meeting, Helen was invited to run for secretary of the National Congress of American Indians (NCAI), the largest intertribal organization in the country. She told them that she didn't have the money to travel to their meetings. So the NCAI agreed to pay all of her travel expenses. Elected secretary, Helen began traveling back and forth to Washington, D.C. "Every time I'd go to Washington," she recalls, "I'd complain about the Quinault superintendent, how he was giving away our trees." She laughs, then reveals a bit of the rascally spirit for which this slight, stylishly gray-haired woman is infamous: "Finally got him transferred to the Dakotas!"

With a new BIA superintendent in place—one who had the interests of the Indian trust beneficiaries in mind—Helen began making her way through the bureaucratic thicket and the "airtight monopoly" that the BIA and the timber companies had held over the reservation. She describes the day she decided to ask the Small Business Administration (SBA) for a loan: "I was driving back to the Chehalis Reservation from the BIA office in Everett, when I happened to look up and see the building that used to house the SBA—it used to be the tallest building in Seattle. I turned the car around right there and headed for it. When I got there, I went inside, walked into the elevator, pushed a button, and walked out into the SBA office. I told them I needed a loan so I could start my own logging business on the reservation." Helen was told that she would have to have been turned down by three financial aid institutions in order to qualify for a loan. Her response? "No problem!"[34]

In the end, the SBA gave Helen a 90 percent guaranteed loan of $275,000. With that, she bought the undivided interests of thirty of her fellow allottees on three allotments, and hired an independent logger named Nelson D. Terry. This was the same D. Terry who fifteen years later would hire Alan McQuillan to inventory a veritable forest of felled trees left to rot by Aloha Lumber and Rayonier.[35]

Helen's determination—including her readiness to pay exorbitant road access fees levied by the big logging companies on the Queets unit—prompted one of the smaller companies, Anderson-Middleton, to lower its access fees to just 12.5 cents per 1,000 feet. Once Helen could prove better returns than what the big logging companies and the BIA were pushing, other landowners began coming forward, wanting her to log their allotments instead of letting the big companies have the profits. "There had always been only two choices at Quinault, with what to do with your land," Helen says. "You can let them log it, or you can fee patent it. I just wanted to do something different."

Meanwhile, she continued to lobby in Washington, D.C., "hammering away" at whoever would listen to her about the exploitation that continued unabated all around her. "It was common gossip among loggers that the Indians were getting beat out of their timber" (see Hanscom 1998, 10). But not only were allottees being cheated out of money and land; no reforestation efforts were in effect at all. Under the Indian Reorganization Act of 1934, federal laws mandated "sustained yield" of timber resources on Indian lands. This mandate was being utterly ignored. Finally, "some D.C. attorneys" visited Helen to discuss bringing suit against the BIA for timber mismanagement and the high administrative fees being levied against landowners. "As soon as the BIA caught wind of what was happening," Helen recalls gleefully, "they lowered the fees from 10 percent to 8 percent. So the allottees got together and agreed to take the 2 percent [that would have otherwise gone to the BIA] and use it to support a lawsuit."[36] This marked the birth of the Quinault Allottees Association. With Helen still at or beside the helm, this organization continues to educate landowners, land users, and the BIA itself about harvesting issues, land ownership and leasing information, trespass laws, development and conservation on Indian land.[37]

Mitchell I and Mitchell II

Beginning in 1971, four separate actions were brought against the United States by 1,465 individual Indian landowners, the unincorporated Quinault Allottees Association, and the Quinault Tribe (now known as the "Affiliated Tribes of the Quinault Reservation"). Eventually consolidated in the Court of Claims (now the U.S. Claims Court)—with Helen as the lead plaintiff—the case finally reached the U.S. Supreme Court only in 1979.

In what would become known as *Mitchell I*, the individual and tribal allottees sought to recover money damages for what the Court called the government's "alleged mismanagement of timber resources found on the Reservation" (*United States v. Mitchell*, 445 U.S. 535, 537 [1980]). According to the allottees and the Court of Claims, the United States had breached its fiduciary duty (its duty as trustee) under the General Allotment Act of 1887 in six areas, all of which were successfully defended in the lower courts. The allottees charged that, as trustee of Indian resources, the government had

> (1) failed to obtain fair market value for timber sold; (2) failed to manage timber on a sustained yield basis and to rehabilitate the land after logging; (3) failed to obtain payment for some merchantable timber; (4) failed to develop a proper system of roads and easements for timber operations and exacted improper charges from allottees for roads; (5) failed to pay interest on certain funds and paid insufficient interest on other funds; and (6) exacted excessive administrative charges from allottees. (*United States v. Mitchell*, 537 [1980])

In answer to these claims, the Supreme Court said exactly nothing. Instead, the question that interested the Court most was whether the General Allotment Act of 1887 "authorizes the award of money damages against the United States for alleged mismanagement of forests located on lands allotted to Indians under the Act" (*United States v. Mitchell*, 536 [1980]).[38] In a five-to-three decision written by Justice Thurgood Marshall, the Court acknowledged that the act did indeed create a fiduciary responsibility in the government, but it called this responsibility a "limited trust relationship" that imposed no management duties on the United States. In the Court's majority opinion, the government's trusteeship under the General Allotment Act was intended only to protect Indian land from alienation and state taxation; it was the allottee, the Court claimed, and not the United States who was "to manage the land" (*United States v. Mitchell*, 542–543 [1980]).[39] Unlike the dissenting opinion, which at least pointed out that "[t]he timberlands of the Quinault Reservation cannot, as a practical matter, be managed by the Indian allottees" (*United States v. Mitchell*, 549 [1980]), the majority opinion was mute on matters of fractionation and the "heirship problem" engendered not by the allottees, but by the government's trust. With this deafening silence, the Court reversed the lower court's decision and remanded the case. But it did so with a final and important footnote, the gist of which is elaborated more frankly and persuasively in the Court's dissenting opinion. The footnote reads: "The Court of Claims did not consider the respondent's assertion that other statutes [. . .] render the United States liable in money damages for the mismanagement alleged in this case. Nor did the court address the respondent's contention that the alleged mismanagement is cognizable under the Tucker Act because it involves money improperly exacted or retained. The court may, of course, consider these contentions on remand" (*United States v. Mitchell*, 545 [1980]).[40]

The ellipsis in the quotation above hides a reference to the first footnote in the decision, wherein the justices listed several relevant statutes that (according to the decision itself) "require the Secretary of the Interior to manage these forests, sell the timber, and pay the proceeds of such sales, less administrative expenses to the allottees" (United States v. Mitchell, 537 [1980]). Thus, between its footnote and its dissent, the judiciary ended up sending a clear message — a "notion of accountability" — to the allottees as to how they might hold the executive responsible for its alleged failures.

As *Mitchell I* wound its way back through the Court of Claims to re-present the contentions suggested by the Supreme Court (and asserted all along by the allottees), Congress was in the process of passing the Indian Land Consolidation Act (ILCA), its first attempt to confront the systemic problems spawned by the General Allotment Act of 1887 and its progeny, the federal Indian trust. By the time *Mitchell II* emerged from the Court of Claims to ply its way to the Supreme Court on March 1, 1983, the ILCA had already — two months after its passage — begun to reap a harvest of claims against the unconstitutionality of its escheat provision, the rule that allowed small fractional interests in land to be taken from individual landowners and given to their tribes (see discussion of *Hodel v. Irving* [1987] under "'Serial Experiments'" in chapter 2).[41] Although the Supreme Court would not confront its first ILCA case for another four years, with *Mitchell II*, it would at least begin to officially recognize the significance of the heirship problem — and of the individual Indian landowner — to the United States' self-imposed trusteeship.[42]

In *Mitchell II* (1983), the Court agreed with the Quinault Reservation allottees that, under timber management regulations promulgated over the years by the Interior Department as directed by Congress, the United

States must compensate allottees and tribes for "violations of its fiduciary responsibilities in the management of Indian property" (*United States v. Mitchell*, 463 U.S. 206, 228 [1983]).[43] In a six-to-three decision, and in language that would become foundational to future Indian trust litigation, Justice Thurgood Marshall (writing for the Court) reflected on the Court's decision in *Mitchell I*, resolving that

> [i]n contrast to the bare trust created by the General Allotment Act, the statutes and regulations now before us [. . .] establish a fiduciary relationship and define the contours of the United States' fiduciary responsibilities. Moreover, a fiduciary relationship necessarily arises when the government assumes such elaborate control over forests and property belonging to Indians. All of the necessary elements of a common-law trust are present: a trustee (the United States), a beneficiary (the Indian allottees), and a trust corpus (Indian timber, lands, and funds) (*United States v. Mitchell*, 224–225 [1983]).[44]

Against a dissent written by Justice William Powell that accused the majority of simply asserting (rather than demonstrating) the fiduciary obligations of the United States as well as its consent to be sued for damages, the Court's majority opinion stands as a short course in the history of the federal Indian trust. It recounts (among other things) how episodes of federal mismanagement of Indian timber resources eventually led to the promulgation of a comprehensive body of regulations governing Interior's "literally daily supervision" over "[v]irtually every stage of the process" of timber harvesting on Indian lands (*United States v. Mitchell*, 222 [1983]). Given the lack of control Indian trust beneficiaries have been allowed over their own resources, the Court argued that the trust relationship between the United States and "an Indian or Indian tribe" should be seen as including "as a fundamental incident the right of an injured beneficiary to sue the trustee for damages resulting from a breach of trust" (*United States v. Mitchell*, 226 [1983]).

As Helen Sanders muses over whether to pursue the Quinault Tribe itself into the courts for what she asserts is *its* mismanagement of the reservation's timber resources (in the years since *Mitchell II* [1983]), she notes that the Supreme Court ultimately recognized that "the [U.S.] government has two trusts—one to the tribes and one to individual Indians."[45] And although, as critics of the *Mitchell II* decision point out, the Court continued to refer only to "alleged" mismanagement and "alleged" breaches of trust, its remand of the Quinault case to the Court of Claims for determination of mismanagement claims and possible determination of damages eventually resulted in a settlement (out of court) of $26,000,000 to the allottees and the Quinault Tribe (for lands held in tribal ownership).[46]

Ambivalent Judgment

> You don't pay twenty-six million dollars out if you think you're right.
> —Helen Sanders, 2002[47]

Although the decisions in *Mitchell I* (1980) and, especially, *Mitchell II* (1983) stand as important precedents in the establishment of Indian landowner rights, there remains a telling oversight in the Court's arguments. There is no explicit recognition of the causal connections between what I call the "virtual ownership" of Indian land and the federal policies from which it has arisen. Helen Sanders points to a similar oversight in her testimony opposing one of the many bills proposing amendments to the Indian Land Consolidation Act. In reference to two of the bill's findings on "fractional allotment ownership," she states: "There is no understanding by the bill's authors that the so-called 'inordinate' administrative costs [of fractioned lands] are the product of failed BIA policy and not fractional ownership itself."[48] In that case, the costs of administering fractionated Indian lands are implicitly levied—symbolically if not actually—against the Indian landowner, not against the social and cultural institutions that led to the creation of Indian land and fractionation in the first place. Likewise, in the Burger Court's argument in support of the Quinault allottees' right to compensation from the federal government, Justice Marshall writes: "To begin with, the Indian allottees are in no position to monitor federal management of their lands on a consistent basis. Many are poorly educated, most are absentee owners, and many do not even know the exact physical location of their allotments. Indeed, it was the very recognition of the inability of the Indians to oversee their interests that led to federal management in the first place" (*United States v. Mitchell*, 227 [1983]).

In a case marked not by any "inability of the Indians" but by the alleged mismanagement of the federal trustee, for which the United States paid

$26,000,000 in damages, the implicit burden of blame is nevertheless laid at the door of the Indian allottees. There is no acknowledgment that the relatively powerless position of Indian allottees is an effect, not a cause, of more than a century of mismanagement by the federal trustee, and there is utter silence regarding the history of Euro-American racism and greed that led to Congress's self-serving "recognition of the inability of the Indians [. . .] in the first place." And even though *Mitchell II* was a victory for Indian landowners, its price was all too predictable. Indian subjection is represented as if it existed wholly apart from the supposedly blameless and, in *Mitchell II*, apparently martyred federal Indian trust.

Ernestine "Ernee" Broncho Werelus

> The land is still trying to take care of us.
> —Original allottee Walter Nevada, 2001[49]

> I told the elders that I'd do my best to get this thing going so they'll see some benefit from it before they die.
> —Ernee Werelus, 2000[50]

Ernee Werelus likes to say that she celebrates two birthdays every year, once in September and again in October. For years, she thought that she had been born sometime in September of 1929. Then one day she retrieved her birth certificate from the Bureau of Indian Affairs, where her birth date had been recorded as October 1. She asked her mother about the date, and recalls her mother's response: "'Well, it was sometime around then. The leaves were turning.'" But it had to be in September, Ernee continues, "because that's when the Blackfoot fair is. Mom's water broke at the fair when my brother bumped into her tummy. It might have been a couple of weeks before anyone got around to telling the BIA. They probably just wrote me down for whatever day they got the news that I'd been born."

Ernee was born in a "moon house"—a sweat lodge–type structure—out behind her parents' house. Her father delivered her. She and her mother remained in the moon house for several weeks following her birth, her father bringing food to her mother during the customary isolation period. Her mother was Bannock, her father Shoshone. Her parents spoke to one another each in their respective native tongues, understanding the other's language but responding in their own.[51] Ernee grew up listening to and speaking both languages, her trilingual fluency a rarity in these post–boarding school days.

Her father passed away when Ernee was but a young teenager. That autumn, her mother sent Ernee and four of her younger siblings to the Indian boarding school at Stewart, Nevada. Ernee describes a year spent "feeding chickens and rabbits and mopping floors." When the five children returned to Idaho for the summer, she told her mother, "I'm not goin' back." She explains, "Mom didn't like it, but I told her I didn't learn a thing that whole year! So I moved in with my sister and, that fall, I put myself in school at Blackfoot, in the public school. I even held myself back a year 'cause I knew I hadn't learned a damn thing at that boarding school."

After graduating from high school, Ernee enrolled in a three-year nursing program at Saint Anthony Hospital in Pocatello, where she lived in a dormitory until her money ran out, a year and a half into the program. "I needed to finish my training, so I ended up joining the Navy," she says. "They told me that there was a medical program in the works. That never happened, but they sent me to a dispensary in Great Lakes, Illinois. That's where I met Steve."

At 23, Ernestine Broncho married Steve Werelus, a non-Indian orphan of Polish descent from western New York. Steve's soft-spoken ways and (to this day) manifest adoration for Ernestine earned him acceptance into the Broncho family at Fort Hall. Once married, the couple moved to Pocatello and began attending college. During those and later years, Ernee's mother would occasionally plead with her daughter to go to the BIA and ask about the family's allotments. "The checks just keep getting smaller," she would tell the young Ernestine. "Go find out what they're doing." But it would be many years before Ernee would have the time and energy to heed her mother's pleas.

When the Korean War broke out, Steve was called to active duty in the Medical Services of the Navy, and then the Marines. The now pregnant and dangerously anemic Ernestine moved home to the reservation, where her mother and extended family could take care of her. Four years later, Steve finished a degree in pharmacy at Idaho State University (then Idaho State College), and the couple moved away to begin life together anew. They would spend the next twenty years working for the Indian Health

Service, Steve as a pharmacist and chief administrator, Ernee as a dental therapist, educator, and administrator. They moved from reservation to reservation in Oklahoma, the Dakotas, and western Washington until, in 1991, they finally decided to retire and move home to Fort Hall. They built a house adjacent to the Broncho allotment where a moon house once stood.

Although Ernee is not an original allottee, her parents were.[52] Her family had successful cattle and horse operations during her childhood, cutting native grasses for hay and grazing their animals (collectively with other tribal members) on tribal land assignments in the mountains and the lush bottomlands along the Snake River. But, with the advent of sprinkler watering systems in the 1950s and 1960s, the BIA redoubled its efforts to develop allotted Indian lands.[53] Non-Indian farmers, who (unlike Indians) had the social and economic wherewithal to obtain bank loans, were encouraged to lease and clear the Indian lands of sagebrush. Ernee and others at Fort Hall remember the 1960s as "the decade they plowed up the desert." Thousands of acres of sagebrush grassland were put into potatoes, sugar beets, and grains. With the urging of the BIA, Indian ranching soon gave way to non-Indian farming.

Ernee recalls conversations with her mother during those years with a look of humor mixed with a tinge of sadness: "Mom always told me that since I had Steve to take care of me she wasn't going to give me any land when she died. But I guess she wasn't so tough after all!" Ernee's mother died in 1967, leaving her strong-willed daughter several large, undivided interests in her allotments. But it wasn't until the fall of 1995 that Ernee would finally have the time and energy to begin looking into what the BIA had been doing with her mother's—now her own, her siblings', and her cousins'—inheritance. She says, "All those years, I'd get mail from the Bureau and I'd just throw it up on top of the fridge. Who knew what it was for! The forms were all so hard to read, they didn't make any sense."

With retirement and their return to Fort Hall, however, Ernee and Steve were faced with the files of paperwork from the BIA that Ernee's mother had kept. It wasn't hard to detect the patterns of bureaucratic malfeasance. Studying records on the allotments she had inherited from her mother, Ernee discovered that in the 28 years since her mother's death—from 1967 to 1995—the annual rent had risen all of five dollars. Ernee recalls:

I thought to myself, I can't be the only one. This must be happening to other people, too. I remembered the old people coming to visit my mom and dad when I was young. They were always saying things like, "We think the government's stealing our land. We think the Bureau's taking our lease money." But I guess there was nothing any of them could do about it. If they did go to the Bureau, they'd just get told that they shouldn't worry, that the Bureau was taking care of things for them. Hah! They were taking care of things all right! That's why Mom kept asking me to go up there. I can still hear her saying, "Ernee, go look into my land."

Then, one day, a farmer came to the door of the Wereluses' new house. As Ernee remembers it, the farmer introduced himself and told Ernee that he leased some of her land. He wanted to renew the lease. She told him that she would need to look into it and would get back to him. She thought that it would probably require an up-to-date appraisal, and a renegotiation of the terms—neither of which had occurred through the Fort Hall BIA for over 25 years. Frustrated, the farmer informed Ernee that he didn't have to deal with her at all. As he backed away from the Wereluses' front door, he exclaimed: "You don't own the land, anyway. The Bureau does!"[54]

With two voices—the farmer's and her mother's—echoing in her head, Ernee paid a visit to the tribal business center and reserved the Council chambers for the following week. Then she made up fliers and put an ad in the reservation newspaper asking her fellow allottees if they, too, had questions about what the BIA was doing with their land. Her notice invited them to come to the Council chambers to talk about what could be done. She posted fliers everywhere she could think to post them, and then went home to pore over the federal statutes and regulations governing trust land. As for what kind of response she thought she'd get from other tribal members, she recalls:

> I had no idea what to expect. I'd been gone for more than 30 years! But when I pulled up to the business center for our meeting that next week, the people were already there, waiting. That's a big room, the Council chambers, you know. It must seat, what, three hundred people? Well, we packed the place! There was standing room only. They were lined up against the walls. All ages—elders who knew my parents, kids whose parents I used to know when they were kids. And not just that night. We packed the place every Tuesday evening for the next three months. It

seemed like *everybody* had a story to tell! They even started coming to the house, day and night. Calling all the time. It was too much! So at our last meeting, I asked them, "What are we going to do about this?"

At the public meetings, everyone had agreed that the central grievance was the low rental rates they were receiving for their interests in allotted land—a symptom of racism and bureaucratic malfeasance (as described below) but also of the disempowering effects of fractional land ownership. In 1996, the average lease rate per acre of allotted agricultural land at Fort Hall was $60, compared to an average of $240 per acre of comparable land off the reservation. This was barely an improvement over the fixed-rate policies of earlier years; indeed, income disparities between on and off the reservation had actually become more pronounced. As reported in independent economic development studies of the 1950s, 1960s, and 1970s, allottees at Fort Hall (including the tribal government) were being bilked out of millions of dollars per year in lease income while their non-Indian lessees were profiting handsomely.[55]

In 1958, Joseph Hearst, dean of liberal arts at Idaho State University in Pocatello wrote of Fort Hall's economic prospects: "We have 522,036 acres of land, yet our total estimated income was little more than one dollar an acre. The total for last year, estimated by the Agency, was $588,765, of which $157,314 was tribal, and $431,451 was individual. The point to be made here is that there is great difference between the possession of resources and the means and ability to use them."

In 1968, the Kennedy subcommittee staff, together with Senators Robert Kennedy and Frank Church, would report: "The non-Indian farmer-businessman is in firm control of Fort Hall's rich land. Though the Fort Hall Indians own the land, their average yearly income is only one-third that of their non-Indian neighbors. Non-Indians increasingly dominate its use and, therefore, the profits it yields."[56]

In 1973, the national, private research firm Economics Research Associates stated in their study of the Fort Hall Indian Reservation: "What is clear is that lease rates on the order of 2.3 percent of the gross have no parallel elsewhere in American agriculture, and their presence on the Fort Hall Reservation requires a great deal of justification. It would seem that the lessees (and the BIA, as historical administrators of existing leases) properly share the burden of proof that such rates are equitable, and are the result of competitive market forces, rather than the result of insufficiently aggressive stewardship coupled with the normal pressures of special interests" (Economics Research Associates 1973, 2).

In 1974, a General Accounting Office (GAO) report commissioned by Congress at the request of the Fort Hall Business Council documented that at Fort Hall: "The average net income per acre for irrigated reservation cropland leased to non-Indians was about $60 less [$75.41 for non-Indian land and $15.36 for Indian land] than the average net income per acre for similar non-reservation land" (GAO 1974, 11).[57] The GAO report is interesting in that it tries to "explain away" such disparities in income by blaming certain "tangible and intangible factors" (for example, reputedly higher water and irrigation costs, higher winds, sandy soils, heirship problems, and, ironically, the "absence of risk to the Indian landowners") that "impact on reservation land" but not on the lands adjacent to the reservation (11–15).

In response to the GAO's assessment of a catch-22 situation at Fort Hall, another report, privately prepared by a Boise consultancy firm in 1976, refutes each factor in turn and bluntly concludes: "Since the GAO report was released, it has been criticized by virtually every knowledgeable person who has studied it. What is clear is that the GAO [has] far from even a cursory understanding of irrigated agriculture in the West; and that the GAO investigation—although requested by a legitimate tribal government in order to resolve long-standing disparities—was biased in favor of the BIA and a non-Indian constituency which are the major causes of the disparities" (Peterson & Associates 1976, 13).[58]

By the time Ernee and Steve Werelus retired and returned to Fort Hall, all of the well-meaning reports and studies had led to little in the way of ameliorating the "intolerable anachronism" represented by the reservation's land-leasing situation (Peterson & Associates 1976, 16). And the group of Indian landowners who responded to Ernee's appeal didn't need to be told that something was "unconscionably amiss" in the management of their land (see Hanscom 1998, 10). They were well acquainted with the inequities. But their sense of accountability had atrophied for lack of exercise—with hardly an instance that anyone could point to and say, "They cheated us, we caught them, they were punished, and we were repaid." So when Ernee asked, "What are we going to do about this?" only a small group, fewer than a dozen landowners, stepped forward to help answer the question. Most of these people were elders, like the ex–tribal chairman Frank Papse Sr., who (at greater than 80 years of age, and using machinery almost as old) still farms his own land, and has already lived through the tiresome ebb and flow of many formal reform efforts.[59]

By late in the fall of 1995, these volunteers had founded the Shoshone-Bannock Landowners Association, and the Werelus house became a favorite impromptu meeting place for concerned landowners with a renewed sense of empowerment. In August 1996, the group was formally recognized by tribal resolution as an organization dedicated to helping individual allottees—otherwise unrepresented within the tribes' governmental structure—with regard to lease disparities and the conservation of their land resources.[60] With the help of Idaho Legal Aid attorney Howard Belodoff, the group developed its bylaws and constitution, changed its name to the "Fort Hall Landowners Alliance" and, in November of 1997 received its 501(c)(3) nonprofit charter from the State of Idaho.

Fort Hall Landowners Alliance

Although one of its long-term goals was to incorporate under the tribes' governmental structure as a service department, economics and reservation politics have forced the Fort Hall Landowners Alliance, Inc. (FHLA), to operate as a volunteer organization, with Ernee and Steve Werelus as its principal, if not only, personnel. The tribes have, however, donated space and overhead for the FHLA office in the reservation's Human Resources and Development Center. This support is renegotiated every year and, every year, Ernee expresses the hope, tongue partly in cheek, that "maybe this year they'll kick us out so I can quit this nonsense and get back to my gardening!"

The frustrations of grassroots advocacy aside, the history of how the alliance became an "office" shows something of its inimitable presence at Fort Hall. In 1997, FHLA board members requested office space in the Tribal Business Center so that the Wereluses could reclaim the privacy of their home. Council members and tribal administrators responded to this request by setting aside a room the size of a large closet—roughly 8-feet square—for Alliance business. It was from that tiny space that the office operated during its first year as a formal organization.

In 1998, the director of the tribes' Education, Employment, and Training (EET) program sent a memo to the chairman of the Business Council, updating him on EET's recent change of space utilization, with the following justification:

> Over the past ten months there has been a steady flow of public traffic to the Landowners office making the service being given to the tribal members obvious to even this casual observer. There are people coming and going all the time. This seems to be a valuable service that is utilized by a large number of tribal members. Because of this observation, I have agreed to allow the Landowners to move into the larger space. This will provide a more reasonable setting for the services being offered at no cost to tribal members.[61]

The council recognized this expression of the people's will by consenting to the Alliance's continuing use of this significantly larger space.

As of this writing, the Alliance has an official membership of around 400 individuals (some 10 percent of total tribal membership on and off the reservation), many of whom represent extended families. More than 90 of these individuals have entrusted either Ernee or Steve with powers of attorney for various lease negotiations. Many others—from Fort Hall as well as other reservations—seek out the Wereluses' advice and legal representation without formal membership in the Alliance. The FHLA serves nonresident Shoshone-Bannocks who own interests in land on the Fort Hall Reservation, as well as serving Indians who own interests in land on other reservations.[62] It has also served the tribal government, whose interests are included in many of the leases the alliance helps to negotiate (for a discussion of the range of the FHLA's activities, see chapters 4 and 5).

Walter Nevada

> The Reservation is home. It is a place where the land lives and stalks people; a place where the land looks after people and makes them live right; a place where the earth provides solace and nurture [but] paradoxically, it is also a place where the land has been wounded; a place where the sacred hoop has been broken; a place stained with violence and suffering. And this painful truth also stalks the people.
> —Frank Pommersheim, *Braid of Feathers*

Of the core group of a dozen or so landowners who helped to found the Fort Hall Landowners Alliance, one allottee in particular embodied what motivates Ernee and other landowner advocates—Walter Nevada. A centenarian at the time of my original research, who passed on in June 2007, Walter was one of the Shoshone-Bannock elders who would visit the Alliance office frequently to ask questions about his land. While there, he would check up on the status of various negotiations and lawsuits brought by the Alliance against non-Indian farmers, utility companies, and the Bureau of Indian Affairs. A lot of people come to the Alliance office to get help with their allotments and leases, with the government mail they receive and can't interpret, with worries over who is inheriting what. Walter would also come just to visit with Ernee, his 75-year-old "daughter, Indian way" (by affection).

Walter could speak English, but didn't unless he had to, preferring his native Shoshone. Sometimes he would come into the office and sit down without saying much, listening to whatever conversation was already underway among the visitors already present. Ernee would turn her attention to him as quickly as she could without offending the others, trying to provide the verbal white space—the silences—that might encourage Walter to say what was on his mind. When he started talking, Ernee would listen, rapt, quietly shushing those who walked into the office, and beckoning them to sit and listen, as well. Sometimes, after he had asked and received answers to his land-related questions, and with a bit of prodding from Ernee, he might start to tell stories. With long, thin hands and feathered voice, using old words whose meanings were sometimes lost on his fellow elders, he would fashion bygone people and animals and places out of the stale indoor air. If more visitors came in while Walter was talking, they would settle onto whatever chairs or desktops were available, and focus their attention on him, answering his threads of story with an occasional nasal *haa'* just to let him know they were listening.

Until his passing in 2007, Walter was one of Fort Hall's few living original allottees. "Original allottee" is a redundancy. Technically, only those who were apportioned land under the General Allotment Act of 1887 are allottees. Those who have inherited land from an allottee are heirs or landowners, not allottees, even though what they have inherited is still considered an allotment—usually just an undivided interest in an allotment—and they are referred to as "allottees" as often as not.

As an original allottee, Walter probably did all right even by non-Indian standards, though you wouldn't have been able to tell it were you to meet him. Until he was injured in a car accident on the reservation in September 2005, he drove an old blue sedan between his house and the tribal business complex where the Nutrition Program serves a daily meal to tribal elders. He would wear a pair of clean faded jeans, leather lace-up boots, and a long-sleeved cotton plaid shirt over a white T-shirt. His wispy white hair would be covered by a cap bearing the logo of a feed store or a tractor brand across its front.

Being an original allottee, he still had use rights to the land he was allotted as a child. And being a widower more than once, he had inherited half-interests in the allotments of his late wives. Like his fellow landowners, most of his land was leased out to non-Indian corporate farmers, who would use it to raise one or more of the region's cash crops: barley, wheat, potatoes, sugar beets, or alfalfa.

Once a year, the farmers send their lease payments to the local or "agency" BIA, and the BIA agency sends that money and the record of payment on to the Interior's Office of Trust Funds Management (OTFM) in Albuquerque, New Mexico. With the assistance of the U.S. Treasury Department, OTFM deposits these checks into one, single Individual Indian Money (IIM) account.[63] Then, from time to time, OTFM cuts checks to the individual landowners or allottees like Walter. The checks are sent en masse back to the agency BIA on each reservation. The agency then distributes the checks either by mail or in person during mass "distribution days." The BIA advertises distribution times and places on message boards and in the local newspaper. On that day, all landowners who are expecting lease payments descend on the distribution center to pick up their checks.[64] The checks seldom represent just one payment from one lessee, but multiple payments from multiple lessees for various tracts of land leased. None of that information is included with the check, though. Except for the words "grazing" or "pasture," the checks bear no record of what the lease amounts are for. Between payment and receipt, the lessees disappear.[65]

Unlike many of his compatriots, Walter always had a pretty good idea of what lease payments his checks comprised. He knew the farmers, and he kept track of who owed him what. He wasn't afraid to go knocking at the BIA's door when payments were delinquent, or when irregularities appeared, although he complained that the explanations they gave him often didn't make sense. Whether this was a hearing problem or a language barrier, Ernee wasn't sure. She wondered whether it was just that the BIA officials—whether Indian or not—didn't know how to act and speak in "Indian friendly" terms. Regardless, Walter began coming to Ernee with his questions. Ernee would pull a chair up next to him so that she could shout her answers into his ear. She would give him her full attention for as much time as he required. In fact, with most of the people who came to see her, she would try not to act "too busy," even though she was. But this was especially true with Walter and the other elders, and even some of the younger people who would come in. She says, "If you turn them away once or ignore them, they will never come back."

Unlike the tribal members who rely on Ernee and Steve to provide answers that are unforthcoming elsewhere, tribal and BIA officials were less than supportive of the Fort Hall Landowners Alliance. Some of them perceived in Ernee and Steve the threat of outsiders "who think they know everything," "who come around here and just cause trouble, throwing their weight around with their stupid book of [federal] regulations."[66] During the Alliance's first years, the Tribal Council only grudgingly put up with its activities, agreeing to continue to provide free office space and phone service for the Alliance's activities only because a growing crowd of Indian landowners (upward of 1 percent of the reservation's population) demanded it. BIA officials tended to be less accommodating, posting threatening warnings in the agency building against tribal members who were too "demanding."

Ernee and Steve continue to help make things happen for landowners, whether by urging, requesting, negotiating, or suing. But Indian land ownership presents challenges that also require something other than persuasion and coercion. Like Walter. The one thing he really had trouble swallowing, even with Ernee's patient explanations, was fractionation. He couldn't understand how land that had once belonged to himself and his family could suddenly belong, now, to himself and a lot of other people who were somehow related to him, though some of them he had never even met. He would ask, incredulous, "How did all these people get on my land?" Then, when he received a check for the lease of his land, he would shake his head and mutter to Ernee the Shoshone equivalent of "We don't take care of her, but she's still trying to take care of us."[67]

The Power of "Property"

> The land yearns
> for us.
> The people yearn
> for the land.
> Loss and separation
> are hard to bear.
> —Simon Ortiz, *Woven Stone*

The juggling of imposed and implaced versions of property finds some expression in Walter's case, somewhere between the "my" of ownership and the "we" of kinship. But the sense of tension over contrary notions of property often simply gets subordinated to the struggle, as Elizabeth Povinelli (1993) suggests, for property itself. That is, allottees must struggle to control the *actual* land itself before they are ever afforded the opportunity to vie for control of how it is variously represented, as, for example, "mother earth," or "property."

A complaint I often heard from elders at Fort Hall was that, because farming and development have taken priority, people have to travel much farther for useful plants that were readily available close by in earlier times.[68] The economic practice in question—whether it is farming at Fort Hall or logging at Quinault—treats land purely as a commodity, a source of productive output whose essential significance is to increase the exchange value of the farmer's or logger's labor. This is not to lambaste all lessee farmers or loggers, some of whom carry a guiding environmental ethic (which may or may not also be a "sentimental value") even onto the lands they only lease (for a discussion of the allottee-lessee relationship, see chapter 5). But these are the exceptions to a rule that is the essential truth of capitalist production anywhere: the business of agribusiness (whether farming or logging) is not to produce potatoes and grain or lumber, but to make money.[69]

So what are the "epistemological relations," as Elizabeth Povinelli (1993) puts it, between the economic practice of capitalist production and the cultural identity of the individual Indian landowner? The cultural identity of the individual Indian landowner is said to imbue earth with the significance of family, a sentimental value that ought to constrain the uses to which property is put. However, the landowner's *social* identity—as heir, lessor, and beneficiary of the federal Indian trust—leaves little or no room for the exercise of practices other than those associated with the property's commodification through lease payments funneled from the farmer through the BIA. Likewise, the landowner's social action, as land-owner, has to do (often of economic necessity) with lease negotiations and lawsuits—if, for example, the farmer doesn't pay or the BIA doesn't collect. In either case, the epistemological relations formally encoded in property reflect the presence of only one value system (that of capital) even when allottee sentiment and rhetoric tell us that, in reality, there are two.[70]

In sum, then, the allottees of the foregoing narratives seem to be engaged in struggles to gain economic control over versions of property—signs of ownership—that are distinctly Euro-American: private property, allotment, the undivided interest. Whether objectified in the economic yields of farming or of logging, mining, or grazing, the struggle for power is one that remains ensconced in the domain of capitalist production. And the sentimental value being asserted has less to do with the qualita-tive aspects of property as earth or even trust land than it has to do with the quantitative aspect of property as an economic unit: less to do with community than commodity.

Or does it? Is the drive to protect the rights of the individual Indian land-owner rooted only in a distinctively non-Indian conception of property?[71] Or is it a facet of a larger campaign for a distinctive kind of indigenous sovereignty? Or is it perhaps something else altogether?

Speaking Power's Truth to Power

> If, in the context of the modern nation-state, aboriginal people wish to claim some form of control over their lands, and they wish those claims to be seen as legitimate by others, they must speak "in a language that power understands." And that language is, and has long been, the language of property.
> —Paul Nadasdy, 2002[72]

Treaties and, to a greater extent, allotment delivered earth and place into the colonizer's world of endlessly replicable, bounded spaces (see Ruppel 2004; see also Casey 1997; Arendt 1958). With this in mind, the "allottee" might be thought of as simply the inverse of Gerald Vizenor's "simulated Indian" (1994).[73] As such, the colonizer's dream of the assimilated native is the Christianized, detribalized, private landowner: the "simulated white" of allotment (see, for example, Thomas J. Morgan's remarks at the beginning of this chapter). Under this interpretation, the allottee's "performance of territoriality" would be nothing more than a recolonization of the already colonized: a reflection and an echo of the dominating nation-state's design (cf. Malkki 1992; Carrillo 2002; Perry 2002; Povinelli 2002).[74]

But what of the white-haired Ernestine Werelus standing up to a tribal councilman who wouldn't yield the floor during the tribes' annual meeting of the general council (the people)? Her hand shooting up, Ernee gets to her feet. "This is not a council meeting!" she shouts, telling the councilman to take his seat. "This is the people's time to talk." (see Hanscom 1998, 1). The people did talk that year, three years into the shake-up initiated by Ernee's question to her fellow landowners—"What are we going to do about this?" And they voted. They voted to fire the chairman of the tribal business council. And they voted to get rid of three local BIA staff members (see Hanscom 1998, 1).

But the difficulties encountered in the performance of territoriality—in the process of "redefining" notions of accountability—are reflected in the fact that change is sometimes infinitely slow. Although tribal chairmen come and go, the three BIA staff members remained. They stood accused of allowing trespass on trust lands, illegal assignment and subleasing practices, late and noncollection of lease payments, preferential treatment of non-Indian lessees, and numerous other violations. The Fort Hall Landowners Alliance and (later) the tribes have sued the Fort Hall Agency BIA for all of the foregoing violations, at one time or another, presenting the ample evidence at hand to the federal courts (see chapter 4). But since the BIA protects its own—and isolates, threatens, and (if need be) punishes the whistleblower—some of those so protected continue to use the trust to their own ends.[75] As long as they do, allotted landowners have no choice but to continue to call the trustee to account in language that the trustee understands. This, for now, *is* their practice of place, their performance of territoriality.

But to consider all such performance as evidence of domination would be to trivialize those moments when performance is also a personal, and powerful, negotiation of conflicting demands about what it means to be *in place*. For, in the performance of Indian land ownership, the struggle for the power to control epistemological relations begins not by reflecting, but by redefining. Thus landowner advocates challenge the notions of unaccountability that are *in*formally attached to the individual's experience: for instance, that Indian land is "cheap land" or that it is "really" owned by the BIA or that Indian landowners mustn't have their "routines" upset.[76] From there, the struggle proceeds apace to the ongoing redefinition of notions that are formally attached, as well. In Peircean terms, the federal Indian trust—whose immediate object is the BIA's performance of its fiduciary duty, with its notions of accountability formally attached—has a dynamic object that begs to differ. As Indian lands and assets get illegally exploited beneath a veneer of federal guardianship, the so-called echo and reflection of domination answers back. But it is no echo, and it is no reflection. It is the voices and images of Ernee Werelus and Helen Sanders and others who are unhesitatingly ambivalent in their appropriation and re-envisioning of the relations of power, and the meanings of "property."[77]

CHAPTER 4

Continuance

> Indian success, in my opinion, is measured by survival. I recognize that my standard for success appears to be a low one. It is not if you take Indian survival in context of what all has been thrown at us in serial and concentrated doses: extermination, disease, removal, cessions, reservations and reductions, allotting, surplusing and opening reservations to entry, forced fees, repeated funding failure, termination, relocation and, the ever-present, inconsequentiality.
> —Judge Sally Willett, 2003[1]

In the winter of 2002, Ernee Werelus was invited to speak about Indian land ownership at a "Land Retention Summit" in Epes, Alabama. Hosted by the Rural Training Center of the Federation of Southern Cooperatives, the summit was the first of several to bring together "land retentionists" and activists from different American minority communities.[2] But Ernee was too occupied with her endless efforts at Fort Hall to attend. She was collecting affidavits from allottees to support one of the Fort Hall Landowners Alliance's lawsuits against the BIA. She was advocating for landowners at bid openings for their lease renewals. She was showing an elder how to make a will, or a youngster how to read a map. So she suggested that I go to Alabama in her stead. "I'm too tired," she said, "and, besides, you can talk about what we do as well as I can." Of course this wasn't true. No one can match Ernee's affable but irreverently frank presence. In her advocacy for fellow Indian landowners, she is infuriated, frustrated, and funny. In one of her updates for the reservation newspaper, she wrote about a meeting with the BIA: "The realty staff did provide a packet of information to be used in the leasing process which included a [. . .] form titled 'Fort Hall Agency Leasing Process,' another titled 'Tenure and Management,' another titled 'Instructions To Potential Lessees Of Indian On The Fort Hall Indian Reservation.' I'm sure that this last form omitted the word 'Land' after Indian, or do they intend to lease us out now?"[3] I could *tell* her story. But she *is* the story. She is the one who dares, and in so doing (though she doesn't believe it), she inspires.

But I went, painfully aware of the distances between Ernee's lifelong experience and my short-lived fieldwork, between her historical interpretations of felt memories and my mere consciousness of history. So it was with relief that I arrived in Alabama to find that another endearing rebel from Fort Hall, LaNada War Jack, was attending the summit with her ex-husband, Gus.[4] Gus was there to talk about his tribe's history and program of land acquisition. LaNada passed around copies of a passage from Felix Cohen's writings on the mythology of American "conquest," and together we tried to relate stories of earth and Indian land to the land tenure struggles of other minorities. Aside from the distance some Indian people say they feel from the term "minority"—which lumps them in with others for whom "difference" may have nationalistic overtones but no constitutional basis—the gap between Indian and other stories of land retention was substantial.[5] In its space was captured, on the one hand, the emancipation of American slaves with its vetoed promise of "40 acres and a mule" and, on the other, the allotment of American Indian lands with its kept but encumbered promises of 20, 80, or 160 (arid) acres and sometimes plows and mules or horses and cattle (however decrepit; see "The General Allotment Act" in chapter 1). Also there, explicitly, in that space, were black and Hispanic claims to land stolen from Indians by whites, much of it now enclosed in national parks and public spaces. Implicit were the different assumptions rooted in western versus eastern experiences of land and history in the United States.[6] And running almost uncommented upon through all of this like a herd of ghostly buffalo were the provisions of the federal-Indian contract, which, however contradictory, firmly define the federal Indian trust.

Late one evening, after Gus and LaNada had described some of the obstacles they have faced in their respective careers as (sometime) tribal officials, activists, and educators ("troublemakers," says LaNada with a cackle, "like Ernee"), I asked them how, against the odds, the deep historical differences, and the widespread ignorance of who they are and how they got here, they remained optimistic. How did they keep going on? Both of them smiled, amused, and Gus shrugged a little. "It's just something to do. Keeps me busy," he said, as if his advocacy were nothing more than incidental to the long vision and patience of survivance.

"And then later on in the ancient and deep story / of all our nights," writes the poet Simon Ortiz (1992, 108) in "The Significance of a Veteran's Day," "we contemplated,"

> not the completion of our age,
> but the continuance of the universe,
> the traveling, not the progress,
> but the humility of our being here.
> Caught now, in the midst of wars
> against foreign disease, missionaries,
> canned food, Dick & Jane textbooks, IBM cards,
> Western philosophies, General Electric,
> I am talking about how we have been able to survive insignificance.

The land tenure of individual Indians barely registers in the American scheme of things. Indeed, being "in the midst of," it seems insignificant. When Indian landowner, Colville Business Council member, and activist Deb Louie sees the words "Who Owns America?" printed in green on a canvas book bag at a conference by the same name, he shouts with a rambunctious, infectious laugh, "We do!"[7] The Confederated Tribes of the Colville Reservation, where Deb Louie is from, is one of the slowly expanding cohort of tribes to take the day-to-day management of reservation lands out of the hands of the BIA.[8] But the question itself—Who owns America?—is dressed in well-meaning but academic and largely speculative attire.[9] And its answer is ordinarily expressed in quantitative terms.[10] Indian lands, including Alaskan Native lands, reservations, Indian communities, and *rancherias*, currently make up 55.7 million acres, over 2 percent of the total landmass of the United States. Some 11 million acres, or nearly one-fifth of Indian lands, are trust parcels owned by individual Indian allottees.[11] And of those 11 million acres of land, most is fractionated—held in undivided interest by ever larger numbers of heirs—its "value" buried ever deeper beneath layer upon layer of history.[12]

These statistics indicate, but they do not involve. They tend, in fact, to generate a "social space of insignificance" similar to the "spaces of non-existence" described by theorists of migrant "illegality." In his review of that literature, Nicholas De Genova (2002, 427) writes: "The social space of 'illegality' is an erasure of legal personhood—a space of forced invisibility, exclusion, subjugation, and repression that 'materializes around [the undocumented] wherever they go' [Coutin 2000, 30] in the form of real effects ranging from hunger to unemployment (or more typically, severe exploitation) to violence and death—that is nonetheless always already confounded by their substantive social personhood."

Among allottees, by comparison, erasure is accomplished in the social space of the *legal*, of unwieldy and poorly understood (because badly structured) forms of private (trust) land ownership and the vexed inheritance of undivided interests. And whereas the allottees' "legal personhood" is at least nominally protected under the guise of trust land ownership itself—which, as a rule, can be realized only by a member of a federally recognized Indian tribe—the protection has been a spurious one: "like the fox guarding the henhouse," says Ernee Werelus.

The social space of the "legal," like that of the migrant "illegal," is the space of the supposedly demonstrable: the "delimitation of reality to that which can be documented" (De Genova 2002, 427). It is allotment itself, whereby tribal rolls were first established; it is Indian identity measured in drops or fractions of lineal blood; it is the legislated taking of quantitatively "minute" fractional interests in land, a taking that (for some) was interpreted as the immeasurable, because qualitatively perceived, loss of heritage (on allottee reactions to this taking, see "The Indian Land Consolidation Act" in chapter 2).

In short, the social space of the legal replaces the personhood of place with a social space of insignificance—a percentage—that, for now, must at the very least be survived. I say "at the very least" because the statistical near insignificance of Indian land is contested by what Simon Ortiz (1992, 32) calls "continuance" itself: not just the *per*sistence of the place-centered "indigenous reality" but the *in*sistence that this is the reality and the ground of what I am calling "neighborhood," the face-to-face encounters and practices of *neighboring*. Chapter 5 will characterize that continuance in terms that relate to the activism and advocacy of Indian landowners, in litigation, negotiation, and education.

Litigation

The lawsuits brought by the Fort Hall Landowners Alliance and discussed below typify those brought by Indian landowner advocacy organizations generally. The testimony of individual Indian landowners before the courts tends to dominate discussion of who Indian landowners *are*. This is, in part, because conflicting legal forces really do dominate an engaged Indian land ownership, and the legal documents that emanate from that engagement narrate the struggle to define and claim rights. It is also because the identity of individual Indian landowners confirms and, at least in part, conforms to the stories of that struggle. Where it does not, we encounter the social silences of insignificance, and the repercussions of relevance.

Proof of Suffering

In 1996, the Fort Hall Agency BIA got caught red-handed. During negotiations with Idaho Power Company (IPC) over the renewal of its easement across the reservation, landowners with allotments along the company's right-of-way went to the BIA offices and requested the names and addresses of their fellow allottees—their co-owners—so that they could meet and come to some agreement over the new lease rate they wished to receive. The landowners knew that the BIA had already given their names and addresses, and the names and addresses of their co-owners, to IPC.[13] But, when they asked to be given the same information, the bureau realty employees and the superintendent refused. The landowners were told that the names and addresses of their co-owners were protected under the Privacy Act (5 *U.S. Code*, sec. 552a [b] [1]–[12]).[14]

Represented by Idaho Legal Aid Services, the Fort Hall Landowners Alliance and the affected landowners challenged this denial of disclosure under the Freedom of Information Act (FOIA). They said that the BIA had failed to uphold the government's trust responsibility either by violating the privacy of Indian landowners or by refusing to give them the information they required to manage their land.[15] Why, they asked, if landowner information was protected under the Privacy Act, was it freely given to the power company but withheld from the very people whose ownership interests were at stake?

At the same time the FHLA case was making its way through the federal courts, legislators were putting the finishing touches on new amendments to the Indian Land Consolidation Act. Partly because of this case, one of these amendments explicitly mandated that landowner information be readily available to co-owners and prospective lessees alike, thus facilitating landowners' management of their own land (see P.L. 106-462, 114 U.S. *Statutes at Large*, 1991, sec. 217[e]). But in a twist typical of the United States' trusteeship over Indian assets, the government tried to use the new law against the Indian landowners themselves. U.S. Attorney Nicholas Woychick argued that the government would not contest the landowners' Privacy Act claims. Any alleged violation of the landowners' privacy was thus made moot, not only by the government's concession, but also by the new ILCA amendments that made landowner information available to interested third parties (such as the power company). Any unfair treatment of the landowners in the past, he contended, was "unintentional."[16]

In response, the landowners and the FHLA's Legal Aid lawyer Howard Belodoff argued that the government's concession and the ILCA amendments were inadequate remedies for the decades of exploitation suffered by landowners because of the BIA's alleged breach of trust.[17] They insisted that the Fort Hall Agency's Realty Office had consistently served the interests of the lessees over those of the lessor-landowners, and that the BIA had exhibited a pattern of knowingly, intentionally, and willfully violating the privacy of its Indian charges.[18] The BIA's recklessness had prevented landowners from receiving "fair and adequate compensation for their land" and had caused needless suffering among the landowners.[19]

Now they want "proof of suffering," Ernee wrote me in December 2001.[20] She quoted the government attorney, who stated: "You have contended that the disclosure of the plaintiffs' confidential information without notice or their knowledge or consent was an invasion of privacy and caused the plaintiffs to suffer embarrassment, anger, frustration, humiliation, loss of self-esteem, harassment, stigmatization, mental and emotional distress, and trauma." The government wanted proof, documentation. The government's attorney asked the plaintiffs' legal representatives (FHLA and Idaho Legal Aid) to please "[i]dentify all documents in your possession, custody or control relating to said 'embarrassment, anger, frustration, humiliation, harassment, stigmatization.'" The Boise-based Legal Aid lawyer, Howard

"Howie" Belodoff had passed all of this on to Ernee, who had consulted with the affected plaintiff-landowners:

> Howie is still working on the "privacy" case, and he has asked me to put together some kind of wording, for [two of the plaintiffs] about how their names being released has affected them. The government lawyer Woychick filed a brief asking the plaintiffs questions about the ill effects they encountered by the actions of the BIA. We could say, since the government put them on reservations and promised to take care of their resources and look out for their best interests, and now they find out that the BIA had not protected their interests, it makes them feel exploited. They attend tribal traditional religious meetings to help them with their anger, humiliation and mental, emotional distress.
>
> [A plaintiff's] wife said that [he] has developed some cysts on his chest area because of worries. He is now having dialysis four times a week, and he has problems with low self-esteem.
>
> [Another plaintiff] on the other hand is fighting depression and is treating himself with prayers and traditional healing medicines.
>
> I'm not sure how one answers questions like "Identify all documents in your possession, custody or control relating to said 'embarrassment, anger, frustration, humiliation, harassment, stigmatization.'"
>
> Could one say, that all the trust Indian people had is broken. Tribal religions are complexes of attitudes, beliefs, and practices fine-tuned to harmonize with the lands on which the people live, therefore what the government has done to us serves great pain to our minds and souls.
>
> I am really struggling with this. [. . .] Trouble is, I don't know how, if one suffers internally or even mentally when done wrong, how do you prove it. You know, Indians don't visit therapists or even psychiatrists when depressed.

Eight months after Ernee wrote these lines, in August 2002, the FHLA's Privacy Act case was certified as a class-action lawsuit, a heartening fact that nonetheless seems to have had little to do with the landowners' suffering, except inasmuch as it could perhaps be demonstrated through the loss of lease monies. The landowners' legal complaint was amended to include "all owners of trust land on the Fort Hall Indian Reservation who had their names, addresses, and land ownership information disclosed by Defendants in violation of federal regulations and the Privacy Act."[21]

As such, the case went far beyond the BIA's transgressions in service of Idaho Power Company—although those offenses alone extend back more than fifty years.[22] The court agreed that the landowners have suffered "adverse effects" because of the BIA's disregard.[23] But the government disputed whether its disclosures of the landowners' information were "willful and intentional," a challenge accepted by the judge as an element of the case to be decided at trial.[24]

Proving that the government's lopsided disclosures of personal information were intentional would turn out to be as problematic as establishing that the landowners suffered anything but monetary losses as a result of those disclosures. The nuances of their complaints as Ernee described them appear to have gotten lost in the legal shuffle. Instead, their strongly felt grievances were flattened out to fit the language of the law and the legal structure in question (that is, the Privacy Act).

The "said 'embarrassment, anger, frustration, humiliation, harassment, stigmatization'" inhabit a social space of insignificance for which there is little or no legal accommodation. The Privacy Act violation acknowledges the possibility that the landowners were prevented from getting fair market value for their land—a claim whose value can be appraised in dollar terms. But the attendant aches and uncertainties of repeated violations—the cumulative complications of institutionalized economic exploitation—can be neither measured nor necessarily attributed to any breach in particular because, precisely as Ernee suggested, they are not documented. They are merely embodied and declared.

They are, in the words of critical legal scholar Patricia Williams (1991, 110), "injuries made invisible by the bounds of legal discourse." Injuries like these are part of a larger complex of suffering for which Anglo-American jurisprudence, with its "clear taxonomies that purport to make life simpler in the face of life's complication," literally has no space, or place (Williams 1991, 8).[25] Without causal proof, suffering is suspect and therefore attributable to "extrinsic" factors beyond the supposedly "objective" ken and control of the courts.[26]

In cases like these, harm suffered by the landowners due to the wrongs committed by the government is, at best, assessed in dollars. And so it was, on December 3, 2007, when the Idaho Federal District Court awarded $2.3 million to the trust landowners identified in the class. Some non-Indians will grumble and say of this resolution that "Indians are only ever interested in money." For their part, some of the plaintiffs, after cashing their checks, said, as others have in similar cases: "We've been bought off."[27]

And to the extent that the myth of the "conquest" still carries weight, perhaps the cynics are right.[28] In conquest mythology, indigenous Americans "lost" while Anglo-Americans "won" and, so, the Indians have to play by "our" rules, "our" rules being the ones that excuse the violence of domination by cloaking it in the convenient innocence of the "unintentional" or the "inevitable," if they acknowledge it at all (Carrillo 2002, 42; see also Povinelli 2002; Chomsky 1993). A boundary is thus created "beyond which lies the 'extrinsic' and beyond which ignorance is reasonably suffered" (Williams 1991, 114). Williams goes on to describe the ignorance of domination parading as authority because it *can* in terms that immediately evoke the violations of Indian land ownership and fractionation: "It is not only the individual and isolating fact of that ignorance; it is the violence of claiming in a way that denies theories of group rights and empowerment, of creating property that fragments collectivity and dehumanizes" (114).

"You don't own the land, the BIA does!" cries an irate Anglo farmer defied for the first time by an equally irate Indian allottee. Meanwhile, a BIA employee warns a bewildered landowner, "You'd better sign that consent form or you won't get any lease money at all."[29]

The rules by which this game is played assume a polarity of quantitative (objective) and qualitative (subjective) ways of knowing, and then privilege the former over the latter. A violation of the Privacy Act is translated into a monetary loss, thus privileging the loss of rights to private property over the loss of privacy: the recorded loss of income over the felt but unverifiable loss of self. It is then doubly ironic that the cases brought by individual Indian landowners against the federal trustee are often about the trustee's inability to keep quantitative accounts of the tangible, whether money, land, resources, or even people.[30] None of these has the government been able to document, much less keep track of, and yet the beneficiaries of its trusteeship are expected, indeed required, to document the *in*tangible.

The critics may be right. An award of damages without rectifying systemic inequities and without an end to the violence of claiming, denying, fragmenting, and dehumanizing may be nothing more than a payoff.

Then again, this time, the system itself *has* been changed, if only infinitesimally and perhaps accidentally, by the actions of the landowners themselves.[31] Their right to access information about the identities and whereabouts of those with whom their economic lives are tied has, for better or worse, been codified.

For the historically empowered, it is somewhat shocking that such a right should need to be codified. But perhaps it is part and parcel with empowerment that such a right should be taken for granted, as simply "proper"—an expectation appropriate to a person's sense of self (which is always) in relation to society. Indeed, when I have described the FHLA's Privacy Act case to anyone even casually familiar with the entitlements and conditions of private property ownership off the reservation, the response is something like "Well, why shouldn't they be able to access their ownership information? After all, anyone can walk into a county courthouse and find out who owns what if they have a good reason for wanting to know." Here again, Williams's impassioned critique of "the alchemy of race and rights" is instructive: "For the historically disempowered, the conferring of rights is symbolic of all the denied aspects of their humanity: rights imply a respect that places one in the referential range of self and others, that elevates one's status from human body to social being. The attainment of rights signifies the respectful behavior, the collective responsibility, properly owed by a society to one of its own" (Williams 1991, 153). The attainment of rights generates *significance* in the social space of the legal. And significance, like its negation, creates its own conditions of survival.

On Surviving in Significance

In 1995, the Fort Hall Agency superintendent approved an illegal lease to McNabb Farms Partnership, a large local corporation later implicated in an illegal sharecropping arrangement with the BIA (see discussion of Conservation Reserve Program subsidies under "Staying Power" in chapter 5). The five-year agricultural lease included two allotments for which the landowners' consent to lease had not been given. The landowners (one of whom was FHLA Chairman Frank Papse Sr.) had refused to accept an offer of $16 per acre based upon a BIA appraisal, and had requested $25 per acre instead. This higher rate was consistent with surrounding off-reservation leases. When McNabb failed to return Papse's telephone calls, and the landowners heard nothing more from the BIA, they assumed that their allotments would lie fallow until a willing lessee came along.

Two years later, Frank Papse decided to pay a visit to the allotments, which are located some distance from where the allottees live. A lifelong farmer himself, Papse discovered "grain up to my knees."[32] The allotment had obviously been planted and was being farmed. When Papse contacted the BIA, he found that the superintendent had gone ahead and approved the lease at $16 per acre, ignoring the landowners' written and verbal objections. Soon thereafter, the landowners each received back payments for the previous two years' unauthorized "rent" at a rate of $16 per acre. They refused to cash the checks and contacted the FHLA, seeking to bring trespass charges against the farmer under the American Indian Agricultural Resources Management Act of 1993 (AIARMA; 25 *U.S. Code*, sec. 3701; 107 *U.S. Statutes at Large* 2011).

Represented by Ernee and Steve Werelus and Idaho Legal Aid Services (ILAS) attorney Howard Belodoff, the landowners appealed their case to the BIA's Portland Area Office, where the area director agreed that the superintendent had no authority to lease the allotments without the landowners' consent, and that the farmer was therefore in trespass. However, the director told the landowners they could not receive trespass damages above the $16 per acre already paid by the farmer as "rent." The AIARMA did indeed provide for severe civil penalties in cases of trespass on Indian lands—giving double the crop value plus damages and interest to victims of Indian land trespass. But because Secretary of the Interior Bruce Babbitt had failed to issue regulations implementing the AIARMA, the director advised them, its civil penalty provisions could not be put into effect. In other words, because the interior secretary had neglected his federal trust responsibility, the landowners had no legal recourse against either the trespassing farmer or the malfeasant trustee delegate at Fort Hall.

The American Indian Agricultural Resources Management Act

Enacted in 1993, the AIARMA is supposed to provide for greater tribal and individual control over all aspects of land management, particularly over trespass violations on Indian-owned land. Under a congressional mandate, final regulations implementing severe trespass penalties under the AIARMA were supposed to be issued within one year of its enactment, while regulations implementing its other provisions were to be promulgated within two years. However, instead of doing what the act required, the Interior Department simply proposed some confusing and not very far-reaching changes to the existing *Code of Federal Regulations* (*CFR*), Title 25 ("Indians"). These proposed changes were published in June 1996, and a public comment period was provided.

During the comment period, Indian advocacy organizations demanded that the AIARMA regulations be dealt with separately and immediately rather than being buried in and confused with other proposed changes to the existing *CFR*. Under the Administrative Procedures Act (APA), the Interior Department should have taken these comments into consideration and responded in a timely fashion. Instead, Secretary Babbitt's department did nothing. The proposed changes to the *CFR* as well as the AIARMA languished for several more years before litigation (the FHLA trespass case included) and the fast-track frenzy of the end of the Clinton administration finally forced Secretary Babbitt to respond to the rising protests of Indian people around the country.

Papse v. BIA

By the end of 1999, the landowners and their representatives at the Fort Hall Landowners Alliance and Idaho Legal Aid Services had exhausted all administrative remedies offered by the Bureau of Indian Affairs and the Department of the Interior. They finally filed suit in U.S. District Court (*Papse v. BIA* [D.C. Idaho 1999]). Under the Administrative Procedures Act, they challenged not only the amount of trespass damages and the interior secretary's failure to issue AIARMA regulations in a timely manner. They also challenged the appeal procedures used by the Portland area director, who had based his decision on evidence not disclosed to the landowners, a violation of federal regulations and a breach of his trust responsibilities.

According to ILAS attorney Belodoff, "What disturbed [Idaho Chief District] Judge [B. Lynn] Winmill more than anything was the fact that the Area Director had been allowed to make a decision based on evidence that the landowners were prevented from contesting, or even seeing." That evidence, finally extracted from the BIA during discovery before the Interior Board of Indian Appeals, showed that the BIA had based its appraisal on the commonly used "comparative income" approach, which yielded a lease figure of almost $30 per farm acre. However, the BIA then discounted that rate by 60 percent under the assumption that the land would be allowed to lie fallow every other year. The fact that the land was actually being cultivated *every* year apparently did not enter into the equation. "But they proved our point," exclaimed Belodoff, "that the land, by their own calculations, was actually worth more than the farmer was paying, and more even than the landowners were asking."[33]

In September 2000, Idaho Chief District Judge Winmill granted the landowners partial summary judgment under the AIARMA and ordered the BIA "with all deliberate speed and without further delay [to] issue final regulations [as required under the AIARMA] no later than December 31st, 2000" (D.C. Idaho, Order, September 21, 2000 [CV99–589-E-BLW], p. 2.) Upon receiving the court's decision, the government offered to settle the case and pay damages of $10,000, a payment not requested in the landowners' complaint, but accepted nonetheless. Though the money that the landowners received did not—could not—compensate them for trespass damages, it did finally reimburse them at a fair-market rate for the McNabb's illegal use of their land. Belodoff was reimbursed for his travel between Boise and Pocatello, Idaho, and for the cost of filing the case. Ernee and Steve Werelus received no compensation except the hard-earned knowledge that their work had made a difference, whether by increasing the income of some Indian landowners, or by compelling federal agencies to abide by their own policies, or by helping to create law. Seven years after its congressionally mandated deadline, the Department of the Interior finally issued regulations implementing the AIARMA as part of the revised *Code of Federal Regulations* Title 25, published in winter 2001.

Fast-Track Reform

But that's not the end of the story. The sword of significance—in this case, a federal court order to a federal agency mandating "deliberate speed"—cuts both ways. On July 14, 2000, two months prior to Chief Judge Winmill's order, the Department of the Interior had published a set of proposed changes to *CFR* Title 25, including changes ostensibly implementing the AIARMA.[34] The new regulations were to revise four major sections of the *CFR*, some of which were remnants of Termination-era rule making (see "Acknowledging the Problem" in chapter 2): part 15, "Probate of Indian Estates"; part 115, "Trust Funds for Tribes and Individual Indians"; part 162, "Leases and Permits on Indian Lands"; and part 166, "Grazing Permits on Indian Lands." When the proposed regulations were published, interested tribes, tribal members, and advocacy organizations were given 90 days to assess the proposed changes—changes that affected the BIA's management of over 54 million acres of tribal and individually owned Indian lands in 2000, the administration of trust monies derived from the use of those lands, and nearly every aspect of economic development, agriculture, and housing within Indian Country—and to provide comments to Interior.[35] The BIA's self-imposed timetable allowed another 90 days—from mid-October 2000 to mid-January 2001, a holiday period in an election year—during which its task was to review, summarize, and respond to the comments provided by the public, redraft the regulations according to the agreed-upon changes, present the regulations in redrafted form for review by the Department of the Interior, the special trustee, and the Office of Management and Budget, and redraft them again for final publication in the *Federal Register*.

Responding to widespread concern in Indian Country, Secretary of the Interior Babbitt and Assistant Secretary Kevin Gover insisted that the revisions be expedited to keep pace with the trust reform processes mandated by Congress and the *Cobell* (Individual Indian Money) Court. Thus the fast-track reform was already well under way when Chief Judge Winmill issued his "deliberate speed" order from the Idaho District Court on September 21, 2000. Intertribal organizations and landowner advocates had been fighting the precipitous pace of these revisions for months already, even as they scrambled to amass and organize their critiques and counter-proposals in an effort to present a more or less unified voice and to leave a record of their opposition should Interior refuse to yield. Among their more urgent objections was that the new regulations actually regressed from the "self-determination" ideals of the post-Termination decades to the earlier paradigm of "wardship," wherein the "best interest of the Indian" was to be paternalistically decided by the secretary of the interior.

And among their critiques was a recognition of historical and political context. In October 2000, at the Tenth Annual Conference of the Inter-Tribal Monitoring Association, Chairman Greg Bourland commented with characteristic rhetorical flourish: "Mr. Babbitt, you had eight years to do something for Indian Country, and now you want to leave a legacy in ten months?"[36] At the same conference, General Counsel John Dossett of the National Congress of American Indians (NCAI) commented in frustration that the BIA central office was "already implementing regulations that have not been finalized. So how serious are [Interior officials and Congress] about listening to tribal comments?"[37] In a letter signed by eighteen senators and dated the day after Chief Judge Winmill's order was issued, the chairman and vice chairman of the Senate Committee on Indian Affairs, Senators Ben Nighthorse Campbell and Daniel K. Inouye, had written to Secretary Babbitt urging restraint upon the administration in light of the concerns voiced by many tribes and tribal members.[38] But to no avail.

Interior went ahead and published the final regulations on January 20, 2001, over the urgent and repeated objections of tribes, intertribal organizations, and landowner advocates. The department hadn't needed the prodding it received from Chief Judge Winmill's order. But the irony was still hard to escape: the significance of the landowners' win at Fort Hall was co-opted and twisted by its timing, which could only strengthen Interior's "single-minded determination to meet a self-imposed deadline."[39] The hegemonic discourse ran true to form, responding with a flurry of confusing revisions to calls for substantive reform by the courts in Indian trust lawsuits such as the *Cobell* and Fort Hall trespassing cases. It seemed that, even *in* significance—in the formal achievement of recognition and rights—the counter-discourse could prevail, if at all, only in continuance.

Negotiation

This chapter and the next divide the continuance of Indian landowners into three basic units of analysis: litigation, negotiation, and education. Although the three units affect each other and overlap, it is possible to roughly characterize the main thrust of each. Litigation represents Indian land advocacy as it is bound up in the highly formalized conventions (regulations, laws) of the federal Indian trust, and (as proposed in chapter 5) education represents Indian land advocacy as it creates new possibilities for the future of Indian land ownership, whereas negotiation represents Indian land advocacy as it asserts itself through the surprising and sometimes shocking presence of Indian land ownership conveyed through humor, anger, and the stubborn expectations of civility.

"On the Whip End of Someone Else's Crazy"

> The task is [to envision] a larger definition of privacy and property: so that privacy is turned from exclusion based on self-regard into regard for another's fragile, mysterious autonomy; and so that property regains its ancient connotation of being a reflection of the universal self. The task is to expand private property rights into a conception of civil rights, into the right to expect civility from others.
> — Patricia Williams, *The Alchemy of Race and Rights*

> I like to turn the "fractionation" mess back on the intellectual authors. "Fractionation" is a symptom. [. . .] It is the natural consequence of congressional policies that do not take into account any practical aspects of Indian existence, ever, but think they do. Indians are living with what [historian] Angie Debo calls "the tangled effects of good and evil" or, as I say to friends, "on the whip end of someone else's crazy."
> — Judge Sally Willett, 2001[40]

A buxom woman with long, thick, strawberry-blonde hair and merry blue eyes stands before a ready audience of Indian landowners and agency personnel at the Tenth Annual Indian Land Consolidation Symposium. "You better be careful who you run with," she warns her audience in a Southern drawl, "or your kids will end up looking like me." Indians from various tribes and as diversely hued as the speaker is "white," laugh in jovial agreement. So begins another of Judge Sally Willett's lectures on the (needlessly arcane, she argues) complexities of Indian probate reform.[41]

A member of the Cherokee Tribe and a career civil servant from a landowning family, Judge Willett—everyone calls her "Sally"—has worked as an administrative law judge for twenty-seven years, seventeen of which were spent at the Department of the Interior deciding Indian probate cases among the more than sixty tribes in the American desert Southwest. Besides her full-time employment, she volunteers as a "probate/fractionation tech" for the Indian Land Working Group, and does volunteer training on allotted land, fractionation, and Indian estate planning for tribes, individuals, and federal agencies. With ICC Indian Enterprises, she conducts a yearly Indian probate class for BIA and tribal realty personnel from all over the country.[42] And she is a prolific essayist on matters of Indian law, policy, and history as they bear on contemporary life, sovereignty, and jurisdiction in Indian Country. A sampling of titles from her published and unpublished essays hints at the Molly Ivins–esque style and acerbic wit with which she delivers her lines: "Consult, Not Insult—A Study in Drive-By Consultation"; "Saving Indians from Saviors"; "The Full Court Press: Termination by Adjudication"; "'Fee' Fi Fo Fum"; "The Idiot's Idiot."[43]

Judge Willett's Indian probate expertise was gained during nearly two decades spent "explain[ing] Indian inheritance laws to community members" from some of the most "traditional" (i.e., kinship/place-oriented) tribes in the country. So, in her writings and public appearances, she reserves her prickliest criticism for those who draft Indian "reform" legislation without understanding (or caring about) its practical consequences for Indian people. She argues that, like allotment, forced-fee patenting, termination, relocation, and the 2 percent escheat provision, federal reform in Indian affairs continues to be an experimental process driven by cultural and technical ignorance, chronic underfunding, and the "Aim, fire, ready" politics of assimilation. "BIA has to administer exactly what politicians and ardent Indian fighters give [it]," she writes: "cheap, improvident systems that blow up on Indians."[44]

So she urges an audience of laypersons and professionals to do what Indian reformers are infamous for *not* doing. "Analyze the proposition," she says. "Don't just accept the conclusion."[45] In context, she's talking about S. 1586, the Senate bill that would become the Indian Land Consolidation Act Amendments of 2000 (see "The 2000 Amendments" in chapter 2). But the comments are also apropos to her stance as a volunteer advocate, a legal professional, and an Indian landowner. "When I get a draft of a new bill," she tells her audience, "I ballpark it out. I sit down and play out its consequences over a generation . . . or five. You have to do the same."

Joint Tenancy with Right of Survivorship (JTWROS)

For instance, landowner advocates tried to predict the on-the-ground effects of this provision of the Indian Land Consolidation Act—commonly known as the "new 207," or the JTWROS provision of the ILCA—on Indian families (sec. 207[c] of the Indian Land Consolidation Act Amendments of 2000).[46] For a while, JTWROS replaced the 2 percent escheat (the "original 207") as the key mechanism in the ILCA amendments for reducing the fractionation of small ownership interests. Under the proposed provision, an undivided interest of more than 5 percent that would have passed by intestate succession to more than one person in the same parcel (that is, fractionated) would have been inherited by those persons as "tenants in common." However, an interest of *less* than 5 percent that passed by intestate succession to more than one person in the same parcel would have been inherited by those persons as "joint tenants with right of survivorship." The difference is, whereas "tenants in common" can pass their interests to their heirs, "joint tenants" cannot. The interest of a deceased joint tenant belongs to the surviving co-tenants, or the tenant's survivors.[47]

Congressional, departmental, and tribal government supporters of the provision thought it worthwhile because, besides reducing the further fractionation of small interests, it would have (theoretically) reduced the government's administrative workload by creating an automatic transfer of rights to surviving co-tenants. There would (theoretically) be no need to probate intestate ownership interests until the death of the last survivor, in whom all interests would eventually be consolidated. And the provision would have (theoretically) presented an "incentive"; if landowners wanted to avoid becoming joint tenants, it was assumed that they would simply write a will.

Indian landowners (only half-jokingly) suggested that this was another of the United States' ways of "getting us to kill each other off," since the "survivor" inherits everything. On a more mundane but similarly unsettling note, Helen Sanders commented: "The Department of the Interior cannot find 61,673 account holders now. How would they track families with multiple marriages with children from each marriage to know who was the last one standing?"[48] As others argued, whereas JTWROS might be an acceptable instrument for estate planning, it is most definitely not appropriate for *intestate* cases, and especially not cases of *Indian* intestacy.[49] It is for the tight-knit family unit whose members agree that the last living member should inherit the land. Indian landowner advocates contrasted this model with the "normal" case of intestacy involving fractionated trust allotments, "where 30, 50, and 60 heirs from 3 marriages are thrown into a JTWROS where no one in the family knows everyone else; most don't know the other family components; and they are looking to Interior to tell them who the heirs are."[50] In such a case, JTWROS would actually have increased the government's workload, requiring staff to perform extensive reconstructions of family history and death dates under a system that is already buried under a mountain of probate backlog.[51]

Regarding the "incentive" argument, as the late Assiniboine elder Poncho Bigby once said, "Nobody writes a will unless they're ready to die."[52] Ernee Werelus nods in agreement, saying, "A lot of people feel like it's a bad omen to write a will, like they're tempting fate or something." Sally Willett points out other unexamined effects of experimental fixes like JTWROS on divergent cultural norms, such as traditions of matrilineal inheritance.

And, throughout, there is that curious but (given historical precedents) predictable lack of regard for the autonomy of individual Indians. By targeting "small" intestate interests across the board, the JTWROS provision would have experimented with supposedly irrelevant Indian land interests that, when measured, are actually of quantitatively significant, as well as qualitatively meaningful, size. If partitioned, a 5 percent interest in a 160-acre allotment would be 8 acres—or, "a potential homesite"—the same argument landowners have marshaled, twice before, against the unconstitutional 2 percent escheat provision. In the Indian Land Working Group's first formal newsletter, published spring 2003, Judge Willett writes:

> Until reformers and policymakers accept and act upon the proposition that allotted landowners dually view their allotted interests: as heritage and property—often the former primarily—they will continue to underestimate the level of active resistance reform proposals will encounter. The most inflaming, seen dominantly in past Department of Justice and DOI memoranda pertaining to the 2 percent rule, are those that embody a value judgment that the landowners' interests are *de minimis* and/or nonproductive. That fact is asserted as justification for summary extinguishment of the individual's rights with resultant transfer to a third party.[53]

"Always challenge the assumption," says Sally, echoing one of her fellow speakers, an Osage legal consultant named David Harrison, in his cautionary advice to landowners to "be careful of unsaid things."[54] "And remember," she continues, "valid comments to your congressmen are 'I don't understand this' and 'I don't want you to do this to me.'"[55]

She delivers this second "valid comment" as if she were punching the air with every word. Like her counterparts at Quinault and Fort Hall and the Indian Land Working Group and elsewhere, she vehemently rejects the continued paternalism that allows reformers to impose serial "new dawns" in Indian Country without ever realizing that the sun they are re-creating has careened across this sky before.[56] As she would write the following year, under the pall of 9/11, Interior's fast-track promulgation of new regulations, and Congress's stubborn enactment of the new ILCA amendments (all of which have tended to give people termination déjà vu all over again): "Indians have had it with being the laboratory rats for every new savior that comes down the pike with some screwball idea. Helen Sanders said [at the 2001 Indian Land Conference] she is fed up with 'little white boys [in Washington, D.C.] who don't even know who Indians are.'"[57]

This kind of "incendiary rhetoric," as one consultant called it in July 2002, may not contribute to solving the problems created by the historical and contemporary agents of "Indian reform." But, if the rapid development of grassroots landowner organizations throughout Indian Country means anything, such rhetoric is an important index of a smoldering exasperation among those who deal daily with the human and institutional vehicles of Indian land trespass, land and landowner exploitation, probate backlogs, and the pervasive malaise of fractionation as a way of life.

Intertribal organizations like the National Congress of American Indians have traditionally represented only tribal governments (although they have begun to reach out to allottee organizations),[58] and tribal governments are assumed to represent only their constituencies. Federal agency personnel consult, if at all, with tribal governments and intertribal organizations like the NCAI. On some reservations, tribal land use departments deal only with tribally owned lands, and yet carry out decisions that affect all trust lands (because tribal and individual interests are mixed in many allotments). In situations like these, individual Indian landowners truly are on the "whip end of someone else's crazy." Their marginalization as "troublemakers" or "militants" is predictable, but no less irksome.[59]

Troublemakers

After Sally's talk, the conference attendees disperse for lunch. Ernee Were-lus and I head for the hotel restaurant to save a table. Soon, we are joined by Sally, Helen Sanders, and the force of organization and leadership behind ILWG, Theresa Carmody. Troublemakers all. Sally is still churn-ing from her talk, and Helen is in the process of getting whipped up for hers, following lunch. Helen ponders what to order. Thinking out loud, she decides to have her usual—steak and potatoes—to which Ernee replies candidly, without looking up from her menu: "No, Helen, we don't have time to chew that."

Theresa, Sally, and I burst out laughing. Ernee and Helen—the white-haired among us—exchange looks of surprise and then join in the hilarity, repeating the statement to each other through hoots of laughter. Theresa suggests creating conference T-shirts with the words "We don't have time to chew that!" printed in bold across the back, a motto befitting both the vital humor and the sense of practical absurdity that attend Indian land ownership and advocacy work. She persists with the idea, deciding that the T-shirts should sport a whole list of similar "You had to be there" gems beneath Ernee's statement, like Helen's grumpy assessment the previous day of a fellow conference attendee: "Yeah, she was kinda human." The one-liner jokes of Standing Rock Sioux funnyman and conference modera-tor Del LeCompte also crop up one by one during the course of lunchtime conversation: "If we're not at the table, we're on the menu." "The world's messed up, but I'm okay." "Dear Son, I'm writing this letter real slow 'cause I know you can't read too fast." And perhaps the most ironic of them all, considering the spirited motivation for this gathering: "An Indian father says to his little boy as they stand on a hilltop, surveying the reservation lands, 'Son, someday none of this will be yours.'"[60]

The Definitions of "Indian"

Like humor itself, continuance has a way of puncturing the smooth sur-faces of hegemony with its sheer presence: with the infinite and infinitesi-mally interconnected facts of "being here." Institutional and sociocultural structures that historically have had no space for the stubborn facts of indi-vidual Indian land ownership—much less Indian landowners—consider

FIGURE 4.1. "Troublemakers." Left to right: Theresa Carmody, director of the Indian Land Working Group; Helen (Mitchell) Sanders, of *Mitchell v. United States* fame and chair of the Allottees Association and Affiliated Tribes of the Quinault Reservation; Ernee Werelus, director of the Fort Hall Landowners Alliance; Steve Werelus, Ernee's husband and partner in the alliance's and her endeavors; Judge Sally Willett, landowner advocate and administrative law judge; and Marcella Giles, Muscogee/Creek land rights attorney and director of the Oklahoma Indian Land and Mineral Owners of Associated Nations. (Courtesy of Sally Willett)

the civil rights and civil liberties of individual Indians to be little more than inconveniences. As one tribal attorney stated in July 2002 in a moment of frustration over allottees' demands that tribal governments (and not just the federal government) remain accountable to their constituencies: "*Mitchell II* should be overturned!"[61]

But landowner advocates insist that being pro-landowner is not the same as being anti-tribe. It is, rather, about gaining tribal as well as federal recognition that the imposition of allotment had some unintended consequences, the foremost of which are changes in Indian land ownership itself. It is rooted in the historical promises of tribal sovereignty, emerging through the arid rocky soils of political, economic, and environmental exploitation and social neglect, and sprouting in the gusty political winds of contemporary promises: of tribal self-government and self-determination, of indigenous cultural autonomy—and of individual rights.

Expanding the definition of private property among individual Indian landowners, then, involves their developing traditions and protections of the *personal* autonomy necessary for making choices about how they relate to the land or earth within certain established limitations. Specifically, most landowner advocates agree with tribes that individually owned trust land must remain in trust. For better or for worse, it must remain "Indian land" in order to preserve a land base over which tribal governments can assert what jurisdiction and sovereignty they have managed to retain. Within this conceptual and physical constraint, say advocates, Indian landowners should be able to lease, buy, and sell without the approval of the interior secretary, and they should be able to gift-deed and will trust land to their children and grandchildren, regardless of whether those offspring are enrolled "tribal members" or are considered "eligible to enroll" (as per the amended ILCA definition of "Indian").[62] The lineal bloodline (not blood quantum) heir of Indian trust land, as far as landowner advocates are concerned, should be "affirmed to be Indian for purposes of inheritance, land management and administration."[63]

Since federally recognized tribes have the power to determine whether the lineal descendant and heir is also a tribal member, some tribes, like the Oglala Lakota, passed new enrollment codes in advance of the ILCA's narrowed definition of "Indian." The Oglala code provides that anyone who is a lineal descendant of an enrolled member of the tribe qualifies for enrollment and, therefore, could inherit trust property even under the proposed ILCA amendments. Without these kinds of changes at the tribal level, argue landowner advocates, the amended ILCA definition would have excluded thousands of people who may have documentable "Indian blood" (in terms of lineal descent), but not "enough blood" (in terms of blood quantum) from any one tribe to qualify for membership in those tribes that have blood quantum requirements.[64] Ironically, legislation meant to restrict fractionation (and reduce federal expenditure) could have actually increased it by prompting tribes to relax "minimum blood quantum" membership criteria lest thousands of tribeless yet genetically, ethnically, and culturally "real" Indians be automatically disinherited.[65] On the other hand, BIA probate personnel reported that thousands of unenrolled Indian landowners and enrolled landowners with unenrolled descendants across the country applied for fee patents on their trust interests as soon as news of the ILCA amendments hit the wires. They did so out of the fear that, once certified, the amendments would make it impossible for them to will their trust interests to their descendants, now redefined as "non-Indians."[66]

The possibility that newly created "non-Indians" (that is, unenrolled Indians) might inherit trust land, and, that trust land within the bounds of reservations might go out of trust because of the fear of disinheritance introduces one problem in particular that federal reformers seem loath to deal with—jurisdiction. Recent Supreme Court decisions have already weakened tribal sovereignty by rejecting various kinds of tribal jurisdiction over non-Indians within a reservation.[67] When reformers informally proposed creating a "passive trust" provision that would enable unenrolled landowners and those whom they called "non-Indian," that is, unenrolled, descendants of enrolled tribal members to hold or inherit Indian land without its passing out of the trust, landowner advocates railed that it was yet another piece of "experimental legislation." What might the presence of a new class of "non-Indians"—not to mention a new type of "trust"—do to further weaken tribal sovereignty? Landowner advocates pointed out that Interior would have had to introduce an entirely new system for tracking its newly defined "non-Indians." Why not, they asked, simply return to the earlier, simpler ILCA definition that allowed inheritance by lineal descendants? Other ILCA amendments had already restricted descent to first- and second-degree blood relationship. There was no need, advocates argued, for redefining who was an Indian.

Sometimes the arguments work. The passive trust provision disappeared with the drafting of S. 1721, the bill that would eventually be signed into law as the American Indian Probate Reform Act of 2004 (AIPRA), amending ILCA. Under AIPRA, landowners can, by will, pass trust land in trust to any lineal descendants regardless of how far removed they are from enrollment eligibility.[68]

At Fort Hall, where the Shoshone-Bannock Tribes resisted the pressure to impose blood quantum restrictions under the Indian Reorganization Act of 1934, the tribal membership has more than once voted down proposed amendments to the Shoshone-Bannock Tribes' constitution and by-laws. Two such amendments would have established a one-quarter blood quantum eligibility requirement, on the one hand, and given the Fort Hall Business Council final authority in determining enrollment, on the other. The membership has so far firmly rejected both options in favor of retaining the tribes' 1936 "descendancy" requirement. Not long after one such amendment was defeated, Ernee Werelus felt compelled to send a letter to Senator Ben Nighthorse Campbell with regard to S. 550 (the Senate bill that would become the American Indian Probate Reform Act of 2003) and the new definition of who is an Indian. "Ancestry is a spirit of presence," she wrote,

> of a kinship felt when one is truly an Indian, not measured by DNA or determined by a government entity. A fourth or quarter blood quantum is the formula used to determine when the "turning white" is [. . .] accepted as part of Euro-American society. [O]ur survival as Shoshone-Bannock Tribal members is at its critical crossroads when we have non-Indians defining our existence and with only a stroke of a pen or tap of a computer key to wash away our children, our babies. All I ask from the government is not to certify the [ILCA] 2000 amendments until tribal members and representatives and tribes are invited to the table with the work groups formed by different Indian Organizations.[69]

For their part, landowner advocates seem to want to decouple tribal membership from Indianness—or, to clarify that neither tribal member-ship nor federal regulation is the arbiter of who is Indian. This is not about opening up limited Indian resources to non-Indians. It is about empower-ment and choice. It is, for instance, about enabling today's Indian parents and grandparents to will or gift-deed their trust land interests to their children and grandchildren without the economic and perhaps greater personal loss (of identity) that would follow the loss of trust status.

CHAPTER 5

One More Arrow

In 1916, the Office of Indian Affairs (as the Bureau of Indian Affairs was called at this time) instituted a special ceremony to mark and publicize the passage of individual Indian landowners from "incompetent" tribal members to "competent" American citizens through the (often forced) fee patenting of trust allotments. Fort Hall was one of the places where this practice was ritualized. The ceremonies on various reservations were reported in newspapers and magazines of the time, as historian Frederick Hoxie describes:

> The proceedings always began with an order to the entire reservation to assemble before a large ceremonial tipi near the agency headquarters. The crowd would look on while their "competent" brethren were summoned individually from inside the lodge. The candidates for land titles were dressed in traditional costume and armed with a bow and arrow. After ordering a candidate to shoot his arrow into the distance, the presiding officer, usually the agent, would announce, "You have shot your last arrow." The arrowless archer would then return to the tipi and reemerge a few minutes later in "civilized" dress. He would be placed before a plow. "Take the handle of this plow," the government's man would say, "this act means that you have chosen to live the life of the white man—and the white man lives by work." The ceremony would close with the new landowner receiving a purse (at which point the presiding officer would announce, "This purse will always say to you that the money you gain from your labor must be wisely kept") and an American flag. (Hoxie 2001, 180; see also Madsen 1980/2000; McDonnell 1991)

Those who agreed (or were forced) to accept fee title to their lands were summarily dropped from Interior's supervision and faced the flood of "tax collectors, auto dealers, and equipment salesmen" on their own (Hoxie 2001, 183; see also Debo 1985). Those who were deemed "incompetent" or refused fee patenting took up, once again, the mantle of ambivalent federal regulation and passed it on to their descendants. But, as Hoxie observes, "both groups—the competent who received titles to their lands and the incompetent who remained under federal supervision—lost control of their resources" (183).

Beyond lost resources, the "last arrow ceremony" also marked a division that, to this day, reminds Native people of their loyalties. Those whose ancestors "shot the arrow," though they may have since regained tribal membership and ownership in trust land, are sometimes looked upon as traitors. Their families chose the white way, regarding land as if it could be exchanged for mere money. In a sense, of course, whether their ancestors shot the arrow or not, "the purse" was imposed. What really remained for those who stayed was the vitality of place-bound kinship, which is what some allottees strive not only to express but also to pass on.

Education

This kind of vitality begins to emerge when a balance is achieved between tradition, with its endless elaborations of custom and convention on the one hand, and presence, with its frankness, its grounding, and its now comic, now derisive jabs at the other. What emerges is never "pure" possibility but, rather, an openness toward change borne forward by the weight and momentum of the established system. What emerges is Ernee and Steve Werelus's attempts to change the system at various levels. What emerges is Sally Willett's tongue-partly-in-cheek attempt to make legal inheritance procedures more "Indian friendly." What emerges is the potency of those who remained, and the empowerment of those who have found one another.

Staying Power

> There are alternatives that would be much better than having our lands farmed, grazed and poisoned the way they are now. Is it worth one or two dollars per acre to have livestock in certain areas causing erosion, damage and polluting our streams and doing away with our traditional herbs and medicines? This is what one of our elders, a landowner, complained of. Remember when we could picnic and fish in the mountains. The amount we are getting from leasing doesn't seem worth the price of killing our mother earth.
> —Ernee Werelus, 1997[1]

Although much of the Wereluses' time is spent negotiating higher lease rates for landowners, helping heirs with probate proceedings, or amassing evidence for court cases, their work through the Fort Hall Landowners Alliance has also helped to introduce alternatives, as Ernee once wrote, to "killing our mother earth." For instance, the Fort Hall Reservation constitutes its own Conservation District, one of only fourteen such reservations when my original research took place. The number has since risen to twenty-six.

The USDA's Conservation Reserve Program (CRP) provides per county subsidies to landowners who want to replant native vegetation to help restore habitat. Because of its newfound status as a Conservation District, Fort Hall is an area distinct from the four counties it comprises, and is therefore eligible for CRP funding above and beyond that provided for those four counties. However, this formal recognition came only after months of political and administrative wrangling spurred by a visit from Dick Rush, the director of Idaho's Farm Service Agency (FSA). Rush's visit, in turn, was prompted by a letter from Fort Hall Landowners Alliance Coordinator Ernestine Werelus and Chairman Frank Papse Sr. in October 1997, a letter written after interested Indian landowners had repeatedly applied for and been refused CRP funding. "One of the main reasons we are here," said Rush at an informational meeting convened at Fort Hall a month after his receipt of the letter, "is I received a letter from Ernestine and Frank, Fort Hall Landowners Alliance." The alliance had made "a specific request, this is probably why we are here, there is a lot of other things going on but I am here to respond to this."[2]

Ernee and Frank's letter describes the competitive nature of the CRP bidding process off the reservation, the lack of information available to tribal members, and past inequities resulting in a major federal investigation of an illegal sharecropping arrangement between a CRP–subsidized non-Indian farmer and the BIA (see "On Surviving in Significance" in chapter 4). Pointing to well-known examples of local pollution and overgrazing, the letter concludes: "The Bureau of Indian Affairs had and has a trust responsibility to preserve and protect our lands but they have failed us. We look for assistance from the U.S.D.A. and all of its agencies to assist and guide us in promoting the health of our lands and environment. All of the surrounding cities and communities are affected by the water we all drink, the air we all breathe and the land that serves us all."[3]

On the one hand, Rush's prompt response to the letter from the FHLA was motivated in large part by concerns stemming from litigation against the USDA brought by black landowners in the Southeast.[4] On the other hand, it was the letter from the FHLA that focused attention not only on the government's past offenses and neglect but on the real possibilities of change. Likewise, it was the persistence of a few landowners who, by repeatedly approaching and working with state Farm Service Agency officials, brought to light the problem as well as its solution.

The problem was that neither the Fort Hall Business Council nor many tribal members were aware of the potential economic and environmental benefits of the Conservation Reserve Program. Without the designation of the Fort Hall Conservation District, reservation lands had remained largely ineligible for the program simply because early bids from off the reservation routinely exceeded the per county limit.[5] Fort Hall now has its own state FSA extension agent, and more than 40,000 acres of trust land (at the time of this writing) are in CRP, creating economic benefit for the tribes, tribal members, and non-Indian lessees alike; and initiating the process of rebuilding soils and habitats degraded by more than a century of overexploitation.

During my conversations with Ernee, it became clear that, in fact, many of the frustrations of Indian land ownership stem from lack of knowledge, either on the part of landowners themselves, the tribes, the BIA and other governmental agencies or on the part of the surrounding non-Indian population. A shallow sense of history leaves Indians and non-Indians alike with the impression that fractionated ownership is a "normal" state of affairs on reservations. A shallow sense of institutionalized inequity and racism leaves those in positions of authority—even some of the well-meaning ones—to conclude that the problems of Indian land mismanagement are beyond solution.[6] And, most important, a shallow understanding of the fundamentals of owning trust land—including applying for federal funding, reading maps and appraisals, figuring ownership interest and income, negotiating a lease, refusing a lease, writing a will, and so on—leaves landowners, themselves, with the sense that the problems of trust land ownership are insurmountable, or can be tackled only by experts.

To help combat the sense of helplessness and apathy, landowner organizations like the Fort Hall Landowners Alliance have begun producing educational materials targeting landowners, the youth, and tribal leaders. During the course of my research, for instance, the alliance received two small grants from nonprofit and educational institutions to develop such resources. And because I was interested and available, several months of my fieldwork were taken up with the development of these projects.

In the first instance, we created *Trust Land: Landowner Organization Handbook* (FHLA 2001), which details the history of the FHLA while providing basic how-to information (regarding, for example, details of incorporating, finding funding, developing a database) for landowners on other reservations seeking to start their own advocacy organizations. In the second instance, we worked with teachers at the reservation high school to develop a semester-long series of "Indian Land Units" that present Indian land in its historical, legal, political, and sociocultural contexts. We also worked with elders and students together to produce an accompanying documentary film on fractionation, *Nations Undivided: A History and Healing of Allotted Indian Land.*

The handbook is currently being marketed (to cover costs of printing and mailing) at Indian land conferences. And Ernee brings it along whenever she is invited to give workshops to landowners on other reservations. Still, most people seem more likely to ask her to come speak or to call her on the telephone with their questions rather than to look up answers in a book.

Likewise, the educational units and video, which belong to the Sho-Ban Junior/Senior High School, may at some point be distributed beyond that venue to the surrounding non-Indian schools. For now, only the Sho-Ban School social studies teacher and a few others have used them in classes. The state school board has shown interest in them, but the tribes have no plans to distribute them to other schools in the region. On the other hand, the video has been well received by audiences both on and off the reservation, as it was when Ernee showed it to the elders involved in its production, including the then-centenarian Walter Nevada. After the showing, Walter—who doubted during production that anything would ever come of "all this talking"—approached Ernee: "We should make another film," he told her. "I have more stories."

Similar things have been happening on other reservations, especially where there is financial and institutional support for such endeavors. For example, since the 1980s, the Fort Belknap Tribes have worked with Montana State University's Extension specialist Marsha Goetting to produce and distribute fact sheets—"Planning for the Passing of Fort Belknap Land to Future Generations"—and to develop a series of coordinated landowner workshops. The USDA Risk Management Agency has provided substantial funding to develop a second set of fact sheets in the wake of the American Indian Probate Reform Act of 2004. These are now available online (at http://www.montana.edu/indianland) so that tribes and landowner organizations can access and adjust them to their particular situations.

Sinte Gleska University on the Rosebud Reservation in South Dakota, where there has been a long history of concern for land consolidation strategies, runs a landowner education program called the "Land Curriculum Project," funded by the Tribal Land Enterprise (TLE; for more on the TLE, see under "Fractionated Land, Fractionated Ownership" in chapter 3). The Confederated Tribes of the Umatilla Reservation in Oregon have worked with the Intertribal GIS Council to develop a Geographic Information System (GIS) that coordinates land ownership information, cultural and market appraisal data, and other land use statistics for the tribes and tribal members. There are many other examples, including the land-related courses offered through tribal colleges, although not all of these engage issues of fractionation and consolidation.[7] Educators and advocates contend, however, that even with growing grassroots influence, fractionation and its associated ills will continue to spread as long as Congress and the federal agencies act only when they are compelled, and impose reforms based on culturally and legally inappropriate assumptions. Meanwhile, with or without the support of public institutions and governments, acting as educators, allottees continue to try to open up new avenues to help landowners help themselves.

In her "Plain Language Indian Will," Judge Sally Willett presents allottees with a version of the present that bends the rules without breaking them and that, embracing the past, throws it forward into an uncertain but compelling future, full of potential. In the sample will, which she distributes freely along with her essays, historical timelines, probate diagrams, and inheritance flowcharts at conferences and training workshops around the country, a fictional "Willie aka William Veree Wildman" has written:

This is my will. I am an allottee. I am old. I am not crazy. I know what I am doing. I throw out all prior wills and codicils.

1. This is an Indian will so I don't have an executor.
2. I owned property all over the place. But I sold it when I was young and not too bright. Now I just own Arizona property at Pavilion Acre on the Salt River Reservation. I got it from my first wife, Priscilla Palm Springs. She died. We didn't make any kids. I don't like 'em.
3. I have a new wife: Missy Hot Stuff. She's nineteen. She's not Indian. That's why I'm making this will.
4. I give Pavilion Acre to my first wife's two brothers: Jim Bob and Bob Bob.
5. I ain't got nothing else I don't see why I have to fill out some fancy "residue" clause.
6. That's all.

See me and my witnesses signatures below. Signed by his left thumb print: William Veree Wildman.

In the same fashion, Willie's fictional friends, "Wanda Will Witness" and "Wilma Will Witness" sign a sample "Witness statement," which reads: "We saw William Veree Wildman sign this paper. He was okay when he did it. We didn't see anybody force him to do it. It looked all right to us." Then Willie puts his fictional thumbprint to an "Affidavit to Accompany Indian Will," which reads: "I Willie aka William Veree Wildman made my will today. It's attached. I say again that I am not crazy and know what I am doing. I want my property to go like it says in the will." A second "Witness statement" signed by Wanda and Wilma assures any judge that: " We, the witnesses, know we have to say this again in case BIA can't find us when William Veree Wildman kicks the bucket. We say again that Willie was okay when he made his will. Cranky but okay. See the copy attached. He did it on his own and he wanted his property to go just like it says in the will." And, finally, the notary's authority seals Willie's will with a simple: "Those people up there swore all this before me today (date) _____ Notary Public."[8]

People chuckle when they read this, recognizing a "cranky" uncle or father-in-law who so far refuses to write a will. Then they tuck it away in notebooks jammed with materials that they take back to their reservations and homes.

Power in Numbers

> Every generation is the seventh generation.
> —Poncho Bigby, 2000[9]

By appealing to the institutions of power—local, regional, and national BIA offices, the tribal council, and the courts—"troublemakers" like Ernee and Steve Werelus and their allies at Fort Hall have succeeded in raising lease rates on some allotments by 25 to 100 percent. Their organization is famous among landowner advocates for the "19 leases" illustration that Ernee pulled together one year to convince the Fort Hall Business Council that landowners could successfully negotiate their own land transactions, either personally or through the FHLA by power of attorney. Frustrated, Ernee randomly pulled the contracts for nineteen leases from her files. In a table, she listed the lessees for each allotment, the old lease rate negotiated by the BIA, the new rate negotiated by the landowners, and the resultant changes in income under the new five-year lease contracts. Once added together, the difference in just these 19 leases—the Fort Hall Bureau manages the renewals of over 700 such leases per year—amounted to an increase of more than $4,660,000 in individual and tribal revenues over five years.

Most of the leases listed in the table were renewed in 2002. Unfortunately, a recent update shows that some of the increases didn't stick. A variety of factors have conspired to reduce the overall income, including the BIA's reappraisals (downward) of certain properties, the leasing of "unitized" allotments minus those allotments where landowners were demanding higher lease rates, and a reduction in the number of lessees bidding on properties. Ernee and others continue to spend most of their time in ongoing struggles against the private interests of the few large farming corporations that, with the help of the BIA, have historically controlled almost all agricultural lands on the reservation. As discussed in previous chapters, the Fort Hall Landowners Alliance has had to directly challenge the Fort Hall Agency BIA over its neglect of its fiduciary duties. But the challenges are not only in the courts. They are the face-to-face challenges where Ernee goes to the BIA and asks them why they don't advertise lease renewals as per code. No lease renewals had been advertised at Fort Hall for 25 years prior to the FHLA's advocacy efforts. It isn't just the fault of the farmers, a few of whom "have voluntarily raised their rental rates since we started," Ernee once explained to a local newspaper reporter. "We've found that when others who want to farm on the reservation come in offering more money for a lease, their offers have been rejected by the BIA, which tells them the land is already under lease, even though the lease has expired and a new one hasn't yet been agreed to by the landowners" (see Hone 1998, 1).

Many say there is a cartel, formed by farmers who are members of the Mormon Church, and facilitated by some of the Mormon employees of the Agency BIA. The allegation is grave, yet, in these parts, unsurprising. Until it can be either proved or disproved, the FHLA chips away at a seemingly unlimited array of obstacles to an engaged Indian land ownership.

> And the land — assaulted, stolen, leased, bulldozed, and flooded — continued as a source of group cohesion and an inspiration for continued activism.
> — Frederick Hoxie, *A Final Promise*

The single most important development emanating from the critical mass of individual landowners is the Indian Land Working Group (ILWG), spearheaded by one of its founders, Theresa Carmody, and steered by a committee of 40 tribal and landowner association representatives. Predating *Cobell* litigation by several years, the Indian Land Working Group grew out of a land consolidation conference convened in 1991 by the Confederated Tribes of the Umatilla Indian Reservation. The conference was supported by three nonprofit organizations: the Northwest Area Foundation, the Northwest Renewable Resources Center, and the First Nations Development Institute. The purpose of this first conference was to bring tribal representatives together with individual Indian landowners to facilitate the exchange of ideas about the use, management, and control of Indian land. Nearly a hundred tribes were represented at the first conference. Since then, the ILWG has organized its annual Indian Land Consolidation Symposium in cooperation with a different tribal host every year, and the number of tribal representatives and individual landowners in attendance has continued to climb.

The annual Indian Land Consolidation symposia are major, four- or five-day gatherings where every topic of conceivable importance to Indian landowners and interested tribes is dealt with exhaustively in workshops and by panels. Representatives from tribes, intertribal organizations, landowner associations, the BIA and related agencies, legal aid organizations, and nonprofit land consolidation groups speak on the latest threats and possible enhancements to Indian land tenure. Past symposia topics include proposed legislation updates, litigation updates, regulatory revision updates, international movements and court opinions, estate planning, developing a land ownership database, petitioning to reopen probate cases, organizing a landowner association, landowner initiatives, fee to trust transactions and regulations, filing for return of 2 percent interests, developing land consolidation plans, developing tribal inheritance or probate codes, the EPA and the environmental review process, and USDA Indian programs. The list goes on.

With "the seventh generation in mind," symposium presentations are meant to engage "programs and processes which protect cultural, economic, and political growth," writes Austin Nuñez, chairman of the Indian Land Working Group and of the San Xavier District of the Tohono O'odham Nation. The "restoration" of Indian land and tenure must include "curriculum development, claims research, land consolidation plans, preservation of sacred sites, codes to preserve native use and ownership, and co-management initiatives."[10]

To encourage these kinds of "programs and processes," the working group early on developed a series of educational videos and manuals on Indian land ownership. Video topics include: estate planning and probate (video and manual), land exchange and consolidation (video and manual), land acquisition and financing (video), land data (video), and Indian land leasing (video). A separate *Indian Land Consolidation Manual* (Carmody 1998) covers the history of allotment policy and fractionation; attempts to solve the problem (from the Indian Land Consolidation Act of 1983 onward); tribal and landowner association models for reform; consolidation strategies (including inheritance codes, appraisals, land acquisition and exchanges, financing, will writing, and joint tenancy); "recent developments" (such as the formation of the ILWG itself, a [then-recent] GAO study entitled *Profile of Land Ownership at 12 Reservations* [1992], and the *Oversight Hearing on Fractionated Ownership of Indian Lands before the Select Committee on Indian Affairs*); strategies for supporting land consolidation (including revolving loan funds, grants, will writing, congressional field hearings, the ILWG's draft legislation addressing fractionation); and contact and publication information for interested tribes and landowners. Since enactment of the American Indian Probate Reform Act of 2004, the Indian Land Working Group has also produced the *Estate Planning and Probate Manual* with accompanying DVD and resource CD. The DVD includes interviews with allottees and tribal representatives talking about fractionation and its possible solutions, the probate process, and the importance of tribal probate codes. The CD includes copies of the relevant laws (Indian Land Consolidation Act of 1983 and American Indian Probate Reform Act of 2004), and information on will writing and the relevant forms, as well as forms used to gift-deed allotted land interests.

For almost two decades, the working group has been bringing the collective concerns of individual Indian landowners to national attention by proposing land reform legislation and by adding its voice to those of other landowners and advocates testifying before Congress. It has also continued to produce educational materials, most recently creating the plain-language *Estate Planning and Probate Manual* (Carmody 2006), which explains—and, just as important, critiques—the complicated provisions of the American Indian Probate Reform Act of 2004, while offering a variety of proactive steps that landowners can take to "take ownership" of their land.[11]

In 2002, the Indian Land Working Group helped to launch the Indian Land Tenure Foundation (ILTF), an organization generously funded by the Ford Foundation and dedicated to bringing all lands within reservation boundaries "and other areas of high significance where tribes retain aboriginal interest" under Indian ownership and management (Carmody 2001, 20).

The Indian Land Tenure Foundation's strategies include increasing the economic assets of Indian landowners, using Indian land "to help Indian people discover their culture," and reforming "legal mechanisms governing sovereignty of Indian land to recapture physical, cultural, and economic assets of Indian people" (Carmody 2001, A2–A4). Through grants and training opportunities, the foundation encourages landowners to work with the support of their tribal governments, where possible. Where this is not possible, the organization provides support geared toward the production of educational materials, especially videos and Indian land curricula. Taking its cue from the expressed priorities of

Indian landowners throughout Indian Country, the ILTF's first priority
is a long-range strategy of educating every Indian landowner (whether
tribal or individual) and the public about issues of land tenure "so that
knowledge becomes power when decisions to create positive futures are
made" (Carmody 2001, A1). Guided by a "new tribalism," the Indian Land
Tenure Foundation appears to represent a growing ambivalence among
America's undivided nations, where the "individual ownership concept,
created by the [General Allotment Act of 1887], is alive and even desired,"
on the one hand, but where also having "a strong Indian community for
the future" is "a universally held feeling," on the other. "Indians want
a strong and increasing land base for tribes as well as opportunities for
individual ownership" (Carmody 2001, 15). Undoubtedly, the strongest
resistance to this "new tribalism" will come, as it did to the old tribalism,
from America's indivisible nation of strangers.

Powers of Interpretation

> I've never quite understood how Americans conceive of themselves as
> American especially when they relate to those whom they have "mar-
> ginalized," including, and maybe especially, themselves.
> —Simon Ortiz, March 2002[12]

In the fall of 2002, I was teaching at Idaho State University while gearing up
to write the dissertation that is the basis for this book. One of my courses was
"Issues in Indigenous Resource Management," a small seminar attended
by four graduate students (two in biology and two in anthropology) and
two undergraduates (both anthropology majors).

From the outset, as the students and I read case studies and discussed
issues of relevance—deforestation and environmental degradation, intel-
lectual property rights and global capitalism, cultural patrimony and cultural survival—I sensed (and probably projected) a growing frustration.
The case studies that offered hope of a different future, when reflected in
the fractured glass of postmodernity, postcolonialism, and globalization,
seemed naive. Our own thinking about the apparently insurmountable
problems of exploitation in "the fourth world" seemed to give the lie
to the accepted belief that education, itself, could empower. Before the
end of the first month, we were ending each week's classes in such a

gloomy funk that I decided to propose an entirely different approach to our subject. Several of the students had already expressed interest in hearing what indigenous people, themselves, might have to say about "indigenous resources." Reading about our subject—even in studies authored by indigenous people—was not enough. We needed to deal with it face-to-face. So it was that we talked ourselves into organizing a public forum on "indigenous resources" as a class project.

In the ensuing weeks, we invited various Shoshone-Bannock tribal members as guest speakers to come and tell us of their own engagements with "indigenous resources," which we broadly defined as those assets available to indigenous people. Our classroom guests—who were also prevailed upon to participate in the public forum, if they could—spoke to issues of tribal governance, archaeology and ceded territories, nuclear waste management, Indian-white relations, indigenous languages and education, federal Indian law, and, of course, Indian land ownership and advocacy. In preparation for the forum itself, we twice visited Fort Hall to meet and brainstorm with groups of invited speakers. As the date of the forum drew near, we contacted area television and radio stations, newspapers, and colleges. We reserved ISU's ballroom in case large crowds decided to attend. We used our meager class funds and donations of time and money from the Student Anthropological Society and a fellow anthropology instructor, Sharon Plager, to provide meal tickets for the invited speakers, and gallons of free coffee and tea for the public. We even baked cookies.

When the day came, on November 22, 2002, all but two of the twenty-one speakers who had agreed to participate showed up. Several stayed through the day, sometimes listening to the other speakers, sometimes mingling with the bystanders standing by at the back of the ballroom. We started at eight o'clock in the morning with tribal elders giving opening prayers and introductory comments on community and traditions.

One of the early panelists set the stage for the rest of the day. A tribal elder known for his caustic orations against whites began to speak about the importance of the treaty and the tribes' historical associations with the federal government. In long braids and cowboy hat, he recited stories of nineteenth-century politicians who came, pen and treaty in hand, to ask for Indian acquiescence to white passage or settlement. Then, without explanation, he began speaking in Bannock. He spoke for several minutes, gazing about at his audience as his words flowed around the room.

Bannock is not widely spoken at Fort Hall, so few could be expected to follow what he was saying. Most looked about or whispered among themselves. Some smiled. Others shifted in their seats. Finally, he stopped. "Now," he said, "how many of you understood what I just said?" A few Indians, most of them elderly, raised their hands, some tentatively. "Okay," he continued, "so put yourselves in the shoes of our ancestors. Every time these white politicians came and wanted us to sign something, they'd give a speech. Sometimes they'd have a translator. Sometimes not. Sometimes we couldn't understand the translator. But every time they came and said this was the last time, if we'd just sign something. And every time, we'd lose more land. That's what all those words they said amounted to." He paused and looked about, a slight smile forming in the shadow of the brim of his hat. His voice lowered as if he were imparting a long-kept secret, he concluded: "Now it's different. We speak the language. We've learned a thing or two about politicians. And we understand our treaty rights in ways our ancestors couldn't. In ways most of you can't understand."

Throughout the course of the day, four panels in succession focused on Shoshone-Bannock history and sovereignty, treaty rights and governance, natural resources, and cultural resources. After each panel, there was time for questions from the largely silent audience, and panel discussions. We wound up the day at five o'clock in the afternoon, exhausted. One of my students had calculated that around five hundred people must have come and gone through the course of the day.

Our sense of accomplishment and completion was tempered by a nagging suspicion that those who came and went hadn't really connected with what was being offered by the speakers. And to those of us who had stayed for the whole day, speakers included, it was clear that we had tried to cover too much ground. The panelists had touched on everything from indigenous education to tribal sovereignty to groundwater pollution to reservation economics to the repatriation of human remains, and more. Even with ample preparation and "face" time with some of the speakers, as my students had enjoyed, it was more than anyone not already familiar with the issues could absorb, much less intelligently discuss or "think with" (as the late anthropologist Clifford Geertz used to say). But, for me, the import of that realization—the regret over having, in a sense, squandered an educational and "neighboring" opportunity—didn't sink in until I received an e-mail from a well-educated white acquaintance who had attended all of the panels. "Good forum," he began, "too bad more tribal members weren't there."

Why, I wondered, did he think that more tribal members (other than the speakers) ought to have been there (though many others, such as members of ISU's five Native student clubs did, in fact, attend)? All but two of the speakers were tribal members invited primarily to help educate my students and me and, in the process, any who wished in the community at large. The intended audience did not exclude tribal members, but many of them would have already possessed at least some firsthand if not book-learned and professional knowledge of what was being presented. That is why they were asked to speak. The intended audience, in fact, was the *non*-Indian majority, with little or no awareness of the day-to-day realities of "indigenous resource management." And it was the non-Indians who might have made a better showing.

The e-mail message continued, "I had a question that I was just dying to ask, but was afraid they would take it the wrong way: We have always heard about how Native Americans are so close to the land, interconnected with their environment, etc., YET, when you travel around the country and cross a Reservation, there is usually a lot of trash, junk cars, weeds, etc. What's up with that? Know anyone with an answer to that one?" Dubious of what would be the "*right* way to take it," I decided not to reply, and instead posed the question to my students the following week. They responded with some of the answers considered below. But I have neglected until now to attempt an answer either for myself or for the questioner.

My students' responses to the question went rather nimbly to the superficial and self-referential nature of the questioner's implied critique. "Sounds to me like he's already got the answer he's looking for," said one. "That's so stereotypical!" said another, comparing the "surface" littering of the landscape in all parts of the country (not just on reservations) with the more damaging but less conspicuous effects of industrial agriculture, as mostly non-Indian farmers deplete aquifers and pollute soils and rivers with pesticides and herbicides.

But it isn't just that "trash, junk cars, weeds, etc." are more likely to be symbols of the questioner's aesthetic or environmentalist sensibilities than signs of a Native eco-cultural disconnection. It's that the questioner's "concern" is with his own interpretations of signs—the symbolic or in-harmony-with-the-environment Indian "we have always heard about" versus the clear evidence "we" see as we drive across reservations, evidence that marks a divergence from "our" preconceptions of what the Native environment ought to look like (free of trash, junk cars, weeds, etc.). Our "concern," as Martin Heidegger calls it, is with our own "interpretive tendencies" instead of with the beings we are drawn to but are afraid of encountering.[13]

CHAPTER 6

Encounters

At least one genre of contemporary writing emanating from the (mostly non-Indian) intermontane West has engaged the notion of place as an emblem of personhood in the western United States. Indeed, a peculiarly Western sense of place has tended to dominate the works of writers from Wallace Stegner to Edward Abbey to Terry Tempest Williams and those who have followed in their literary footsteps. But something in that literature has always rung hollow to me. In this chapter, I try to capture a sense of the *mis*placed in the region instituted (as Heidegger would say) by Pocatello, Fort Hall, and the Lemhi Valley and of the face-to-face encounters I have experienced there—and, in so doing, to situate the struggles of Indian landowners within the larger, yet still local, complex of Indian–non-Indian relations, on and off the reservation, past and present.

Border Towns

> But the past, by definition, is not a series of measurable statistics. It is also the shame, the silence. It is what is willfully forgotten. [. . .] They would survive. They would prosper. They would even triumph, though they would never forget. But the darker sound, the unarchived, unrecorded, senseless noise of the past, remains.
> —Eavan Boland, 2000

It was Native American Awareness Week at Idaho State University, April 2001. The student union building bustled with attendees from the university community, the city of Pocatello, and the reservation, come to campus to partake of powwows, fry bread, and a full slate of public discussions and talks aimed at bringing the region's non-Indians and Indians—together. My Sho-Ban companions and I, armed with steaming cups of weak coffee ("strong water") from the university food service, made our way to the conference rooms upstairs where most of the week's events were taking place.

We followed a small, loosely organized crowd that moved down a broad, carpeted hallway to the Salmon River Suite, where a sign welcomed attendees to a panel on community relations. Inside the conference room, rows of padded chairs faced a podium that stood between two long, linen-swathed tables, bedecked with evenly spaced water glasses and microphones, one per seat.

The room was already peopled, but randomly, with that unstudied and typically Western attention to space, to spaces between—to "personal space." Margins for safety, a luxury afforded those who live in sparsely populated places. Every other chair or so was filled, except where friends allowed their margins to be crowded or shrunk, or whatever happens to margins when they push up against one another. Of the 50-odd persons present, perhaps a dozen were Native Americans, mostly Shoshone-Bannock tribal members from the Fort Hall Indian Reservation that borders the city of Pocatello and its suburbs to the north, west, and northeast.

As we in the audience found our seats, the panelists also began to take their places at the front of the room. Among the invited speakers on this panel were the mayors of Pocatello and its northern suburb, Chubbuck; a representative of the Pocatello Chamber of Commerce; various heads of city, county, and tribal departments; and a former Shoshone-Bannock tribal councilman from Fort Hall. The composition of the panel was two-thirds non-Indian, one-third Indian. Besides the panelists, there was a local non-Indian news broadcaster who expressed uncertainty about his role on the panel except as an apologist for the media; and a local non-Indian businessman whose role was to moderate, which he did with the unflappable air of someone who is convinced that he is always right and also wise, although a self-conscious smirk betrayed his uneasiness. He welcomed the audience with rules of order for the forum, and then asked the panelists to introduce themselves in turn, starting at his far right.

The audience listened silently as the speakers gave their names and occupations and briefly summarized the subject to which they'd each been invited to speak. Then hands began to go up all over the room. The moderator, reluctant but obliged to follow the overwhelming will of the audience, called on one person after another. For the better part of the next three hours, audience members directed questions and often angry comments to a white-haired gentleman in khakis and a monogrammed cotton sweater who had introduced himself as a former "Chief" of a group called the "Pocatello Chiefs."

The "Chiefs," as they are known locally, have traditionally represented the City of Pocatello on civic occasions such as ribbon-cutting ceremonies and parades. They serve as a kind of booster club for the Chamber of Commerce. At public celebrations and parades, their members customarily don headdresses made of colorfully dyed chicken feathers as a way, they say, of recognizing "the true settlers of this valley." During "naming ceremonies" meant to honor nominees of the organization, the group's members bestow monikers that are supposed to reflect the occupations and expertise of those being named. The white-haired panelist who introduced himself as a former "Chief" said that he himself had been dubbed "Chief Teach-'em-Good-uh-Well." As a onetime "Chief of Chiefs," this panelist had fended off public criticism of the group's traditions in the past, and he was prepared to do so again.

In a newspaper article published the day after the debate that arose from his presentation, Chamber of Commerce general manager Sam Nettinga would lament with annoyance that "every Chief of Chiefs for the past five or six years has had to deal with this [protest]."[1] Swimming in the chagrin of the audience that day, I thought that the "Chiefs"—an organization with pre–Depression Era origins—might finally bow to public pressure and look for a new, more insightful way of celebrating Pocatello's multicultural past. But it was not to be.

Instead, their champion began by declaring that the group's dress and naming practices were performed "in a positive way to show respect to this community [and] its history in relation to Native Americans of this area . . . in a positive light." Furthermore, it seemed to him "perfectly logical and reasonable . . . that really [the headdresses should be] a representation of the history of Pocatello and certainly its Native American, or Indian. . . ."

Here, the former "Chief of Chiefs" abruptly interrupted himself to ask for help from the Native members of the audience regarding which term they would have him use "because of the fact that I'm told," he stumbled, "different things at different times." Insisting on this thought, he opened wide the window of opportunity to the restive audience with an assertion of his own postion and a question to them: "It doesn't matter to me, but do you have a preference?" Nervous rustles of laughter and sighs emerged from the audience. Finally, a Shoshone-Bannock tribal member stood to explain that the speaker might, in fact, be "missing the point," concluding obligingly that, regardless of the term he chose, Indians, or Natives, or Sho-Bans, "are humans!"

After applause and some further nervous debate over terms, the moderator finally informed us that there was a "lack of consensus" on the matter, and suggested that we "move on."

Undeterred, the speaker resumed his defense of the Chiefs and their outmoded practices: "The headdress seems like a natural recognition symbol as it relates to the name 'Pocatello Chiefs.' At any rate, the headdresses that we wear are made out of chicken or turkey feathers. They are attractive. In that sense, we use them in a different way. [They] are nothing other than having some resemblance like the ones that are used for tribal customs." As these words fell across our ears, one of my companions leaned over and whispered how familiar the speaker's reasoning seemed, especially in the wake of the state legislature's recent refusal, in the face of public protest, to change ninety-one offensive place-names in Idaho. In that case, as the defense had submitted: no one actually *intended* these place-names (like "Squaw Butte" and "Chink's Peak") to be hurtful or insensitive. In fact, as the argument went, and historical usage notwithstanding, words like "chief" and "brave" as commonly used by non-Indians, however offensive to Indians, were actually meant to *honor* them. So it was with a distasteful mixture of incredulity and lack of surprise that the transparency of the speaker's words hit me.

Now, with hindsight and the benefit of a video recording of the forum, I find myself wondering whether this man was aware of what he was saying, whether he had intended to be so forthright. There was more truth in his statements than perhaps even he realized. After all, he did say that the Pocatello Chiefs wanted to show the history of Pocatello "in a positive light." In other words, someone might logically argue that the Chiefs' practices had about as much to do with any accurate interpretation of Pocatello's past as chicken feathers have to do with actual headdresses. As far as this speaker was concerned, the costumes and names used by the Pocatello Chiefs were truly not intended to mock or dishonor the valley's "true settlers" because, after all, the Chiefs portray a fantasy—not history, and certainly not the day-to-day realities of this border town.

That same someone might ask how many people in the general population—non-Indian and even Indian—grasp the degree to which our misconceptions of one another are underlaid by a basic and continually, officially reproduced ignorance of how we all "got here." Of how we own and don't own our land. Of who paid what kind of price. Of what debts continue to build.

"In a Positive Light"

So what of "positive light"? Perhaps it is a characteristic of border towns—whether on the margins of Indian reservations or of other nations—that they function out at the edge of consciousness, where the light is either fading or just beginning to dawn, but is seldom bright like day. By definition, borders and margins are places where division and fusion coexist, where the individual or collective self has no choice but to butt up against—to acknowledge or not, or at times to actively disregard—its other. Border dwellers are not all necessarily defined by this characteristic, but the city of Pocatello's official self-image certainly reflects only select bands of the broad spectrum of available light.

The details of Pocatello's historic—and ongoing—appropriation of Indian lands and symbols usually remain hidden in the shadows beyond "positive light." For instance, among the brass and stone interpretive plaques found about campus at Idaho State University, there is sparse reference to the lives and communities displaced by the valley's "second" (as opposed to "true") settlers, the Euro-American throngs that began flowing into and through the area by the mid-1800s.[2] Instead there are commemorations like the following, prominently sponsored by the Daughters of the Utah Pioneers and the Church of Latter Day Saints (Mormons) followed by a list of names of local civic organizations and businesses. Erected in 1963 alongside several yards of replicated narrow- and standard-gauge railroad track at the west edge of campus, and emblazoned with beehive and ox-harness, the plaque reads:

UTAH AND NORTHERN RAILROAD—This monument marks the route of the first Idaho railroad. The Utah and Northern narrow gauge was started as a Mormon co-op at Ogden, Utah, in 1871. It reached Franklin, Idaho in 1874. The Union Pacific interests extended the line to Garrison,

Montana between 1878 [ten years after the establishment of the Fort Hall Indian Reservation] and 1884, a total distance of 466 miles. The route through Pocatello was changed in 1883, and the gauge was standardized on July 24, 1887 [the year Congress passed the Dawes Act]. The Utah and Northern brought new life to the entire area.[3]

The "old life" that remains on reservations and off, reposed in oral histories—and to a lesser extent in history books—somehow seldom ends up in bronze. Seldom is it publicly observed that Pocatello, at its illegitimate birth (even if not at its official founding) was in the middle of Shoshone and Bannock Indian territory, treaty lands rescued by the Shoshone and Bannock forefathers in negotiations with federal officials in the 1860s. Hardly a "border town," the city of Pocatello began its life literally as a wide spot in the path of white "progress" through already designated Indian treaty lands. Whether the expansion of the original "Pocatello Station" into an actual town was a result of thoughtless impulse or cynical planning is unclear.

Nevertheless, as written history tells it, the original north-south Utah and Northern Railroad line memorialized in the bronze plaque described above was pushed through the Fort Hall Indian Reservation without regard to the tribe's official existence, and without thought to giving just compensation to the land's original inhabitants.[4] It was not until a junction with the Oregon Short Line Railway from the west was contemplated in 1882 that any consideration was given to actually seeking a right-of-way from the tribes. By that time, so many non-Indian people were living around Pocatello Station that railroad company attorneys simply requested an unusually wide right-of-way there: a fact, however, that did not go unnoticed for its oddness by federal officials reviewing the request.[5] Despite years of wrangling with mostly protesting Shoshone and Bannock leaders, the railroad companies' request for an extra-wide easement was finally granted. In the minds of non-Indian officials, the de facto existence of a town at Pocatello Station precluded the cession of an easement sufficient for the mere maintenance of a railroad, a limitation that had been promised time and again to the Shoshone and Bannock people. But promises could easily be disregarded when, as the editor of the *Pocatello Tribune* blithely observed in his paper's 1895 Christmas edition, "the crowding of a pushing and enterprising population into the narrow limits of the railroad right-of-way at once resulted in agitation for more room" (see

Madsen 1980/2000, 118). The alternative of removing the non-citizens of this non–town site was considered unthinkable, given their "enterprising" if volatile nature.[6]

And so, their people outnumbered and embattled, the Shoshone and Bannock leaders were forced to relent—then, and several more times after—until by 1900, when Congress ratified the Pocatello Cession Agreement, the reservation had been reduced to less than one-third its original 1.8 million acres. Now, a straight east-west running strip called "Reservation Road" describes one of the southern boundaries of the Fort Hall Indian Reservation, several miles north of the original railroad junction at Pocatello.[7] Further land loss occurred with allotment, the bulk of which did not occur at Fort Hall until after 1911 owing to the intervening need to build irrigation canals to make farming feasible. The diminished reservation has been augmented some over the years through tribal land acquisition initiatives, so that Fort Hall now encompasses nearly 550,000 acres of land, 96 percent of which is held in trust by the United States for Indian individuals and the tribes. The present appropriation of Indian land by non-Indians is accomplished, at Fort Hall as at all other allotted reservations, through the leasing of fractionated Indian heirship lands to non-Indian corporate interests (whether for agriculture—as is the primary case at Fort Hall—or for timber, minerals, oil, gas, or utility easements). But that story has been pursued in previous chapters. Here I want only to share a place-specific sense of context in general historical and contemporary terms.

Left Out

> Don't ever learn to clean fish, then you'll never have to.
> —Tante Louise

Only in the legal realm is ignorance no excuse. Elsewhere it seems to serve quite well as a defense against the unknown and the hard to handle. In the case of Pocatello and its relationship with its neighbor, the Fort Hall Indian Reservation, the advice of my mother's sage "Tante" (Norwegian for "aunt") comes unbidden to mind, but her words in this instance serve more to explain the blissful, abysmal lack of awareness that seems to permeate this place than to advise those who live in it.

In a recently installed tribute to the past, a "History Walk" at ISU commences with the university's founding in 1901. Certainly, there is legitimacy in commemorating ISU's centennial year. What seems misleading, however, is the almost total silence (except perhaps in university museum displays) regarding the old life of this place. Nor is there any attempt to recognize the particular kind of consciousness that blanketed the beginnings of white settlement, even though period newspapers displayed it proudly. For instance, in 1894, just seven years before the founding of the college that would become Idaho State University, the *Idaho Herald* quoted from another local paper a sentiment that found common play in Idaho's newspapers of the period: "The silly twaddle about this land belonging to the noble red man and that we have no right to rob him of what was given him by the creator, and a great deal more of like nonsense, should cease [so] that [in] the place where painted savages held weird revelries would spring up colleges and sanctuaries of peace" (see Madsen 1980/2000, 118).[8]

Here there is no attempt to disguise or lighten the intent. This 1894 comment is far more transparent than the claim by the former "Chief of Chiefs." Explicit in the one and implicit in the other is the right to rob and to replace. Yesteryear's "sanctuaries of peace" become today's harbors of "positive light."

Perhaps it is unfair to take to task a well-meaning leader of a civic organization like the Pocatello Chiefs or a not so well-meaning newspaper editor from a previous century for naïveté or brute ignorance. Or, for that matter, a town for its officially "positive" and self-congratulatory attitude about itself. The problem is, in a border town like Pocatello where historical context is ignored if not negated in the interest of at least surface amity, it does not take much to provoke the hostility that lurks beneath. In a newspaper article published the day after the Pocatello Chiefs were held up for public scrutiny at ISU's "Community Relations" forum, Chamber of Commerce general manager Sam Nettinga huffed: "We're getting tired of getting hit in the nose all the time. If [the Indians] want to get left out of the culture, then we'll see if we can accommodate that."[9]

Leaving aside questions about exactly what "culture" the Indians are being so generously "left out of" and by whom, the easy martyrdom squeaking through Nettinga's comment is revealing. Like the headdresses and names bled of their vital and complex symbolic import, what passes through the "invisible iron curtain," as one tribal member calls it, between Pocatello and Fort Hall is only what's deemed suitable for public consumption. Everything and everyone else gets "left out."

What of the more traditional and indigenous wisdom of honoring and offering thanks to a prey animal before it offers itself to be taken—and partaken of? As is common among subsistence-oriented indigenous societies throughout the world, the predator-prey relationship is a partnership that involves intimate and mutual knowing, by which both are sustained. And through which both are honored in their entirety (see, for example, Berkes 1999; Grim 2001). Where in modern Euro-American experience is this kind of mutual and profound reverence between self and Other to be found? Do we "accommodate" difference only by discounting, discarding, or devouring it?

Margins of Safety

Debate over the Pocatello Chiefs exhausted and unresolved, ISU's "Community Relations" forum wound itself to a fitting end. Seated at the right hand of the still smirking moderator, the gray-haired mayor of Chubbuck (the suburb that lies between Pocatello and Fort Hall) brought out an old book that had belonged to his mother. From between the pages of the book, he extracted a yellowed newspaper clipping from which he read a translation of a speech given by a Bannock Chief during the 1920s, at the dedication of the American Falls Dam west of Pocatello. The building of the dam meant the eventual flooding of approximately 26,000 acres (or about half) of the Fort Hall bottoms—the lush areas along the Snake River where archaeologists have uncovered evidence of several thousand years of seasonal human occupation.[10] The chief's speech and his gestures, described as at once "impressive and expressive," detailed how the dam and the flooding would bring hardship upon his people, how they would suffer immense loss not only in terms of fish, land, and pasturage, now that they were expected to be farmers and ranchers, but also in spiritual terms as the reservoir flooded their cemeteries and seasonal homesites.

The elderly mayor finished reading the translation of the chief's words and began to fold up the old piece of newspaper. He had only recently discovered it, he said with some emotion in his voice, while going through his late mother's belongings. He had "looked at that [reservoir] how many hundreds of times" and had never thought about what its creation had meant for the Indians, about "how much they've sacrificed and given up just to help out their white neighbors in need!"

Seated at the left hand of the moderator, the former tribal councilman smiled in weary recognition, then shook his head and said, "To justify it they give a little dialogue to say how great it was to sacrifice. But somehow it always ends up being land. Beware the man with the beads." I thought of the words this same man had spoken not an hour earlier, also apparently unheeded by the mayor, when he had described the frustrations he had experienced in trying to deal with the City of Pocatello, and his perception of what "community relations" between Pocatello and Fort Hall really means:

> You know, every time we come together in a forum like this, here, we have to sit back and try to give some kind of a history, background . . . why we are the way we are. I was invited to a City Council meeting a while back [where I] tried to pick up on what I could contribute. I wasn't too sure, so I sat back and listened. They have their own issues . . . and nothing to do with the Tribe, per se . . . "Community relations," the way I perceive it is . . . "let's get to know these Indians a little better over there because they happen to be sitting on a bunch of land that . . . we would like to grow into." Because Pocatello is basically stifled. It cannot grow any more north because of the Reservation.

It was like two flocks of birds had just flown through the room, coming from opposite directions, flying past one another, awkward but unwaveringly accurate in their determination *not* to touch or be touched. They dodged each other without even brushing wingtips, margins of safety intact.

Both Pocatello and Fort Hall are imbued with a sense of the safety, the borderline consciousness, of the margins. To get a handle on their neighborhood, their identity as a region made up of distinct yet interdependent places, you have to take hold of not just Pocatello and Fort Hall, but also the profound historical juncture they emerge from, remain enmeshed in, and yet are largely unaware of.

In this sense, they share one place—a space permeated with the spirits of the past. Gibson Jack, Pocatello, Tyhee, all participants at different times in the relentless "negotiation" that finally yielded Fort Hall *and* Pocatello. All place-names now—a drainage, a creek, a town, a school. And more than place-names, too. The names each refer to someone's great, great, great grandfather, uncle, *Chief.* Their bearers wore headdresses earned one golden eagle (not turkey or chicken) feather at a time, and names of merit. They bore news to their people, and tried their best to leave something for their grandchildren.

So where in all the commotion that is present-day Pocatello are we reminded of what was *lost*? Not just the land, whose loss tribal members are reminded of daily. But the sense of sacrifice that was not by choice, not for "our friends the whites," but for the lesser of two evils: some semblance of place rather than no place at all.

In the spring of 2002, I was living in Pocatello, working with Ernee Werelus and the Fort Hall Landowners Alliance, teaching at ISU, and exploring, through my writing, the margins as place. The preceding pages represent my first, more objective attempts to do so. The following pages represent a more personal approach, one involving both poetry and storytelling, and inspired by the poet Simon Ortiz.

The White Problem

> The prairies and rivers did not say anything.
> The mountains and hills did not say anything.
> Everything was astounded and quieted in dismay.
> — Simon Ortiz, "Past Poems"

Except for a remnant of a life
displaced some generations back but
near as the knowing we allow ourselves

A child's bracelet fashioned out of old wire
laying on a rock in the sun
in the mountains of Montana or
maybe it was Idaho
It doesn't matter

A child's bracelet
fashioned out of old wire
undisturbed by the decades, unsettling
the silence[11]

A hundred-plus miles northeast of Pocatello and Fort Hall, across the broad quiet desert that makes up the basaltic bottom of Idaho, three parallel valleys rise up between the Beaverhead, Lemhi, Lost River, and White Knob ranges. The easternmost of these valleys climbs along the Birch Creek drainage to Gilmore Summit, at greater than 7,000 feet, between the Beaverheads to the east and the Lemhis to the west, before descending less than a thousand feet along the Lemhi River into the Lemhi Valley proper. As you travel north, up Birch Creek and then down the Lemhi Valley, past Nicholia and Gilmore—mining towns gone bust—the first extant settlement you come across is Leadore, originally established by the Gilmore and Pittsburgh (G&P) Railroad as a loading station for shipments of ore and cattle to Montana.[12] The population at Leadore ("lead ore" not "le adore") hovers around a hundred in a good decade.[13] But its establishment meant ruin for its nearby predecessor, Junction, of which nothing remains but memories (Benedict 1996, 255; see also Benedict 2006).

Among those memories is the fearful one provoked by the flight of Chief Joseph's band of Nez Perce toward Canada during the summer of 1877. Two years after President Grant's Executive Order of February 12, 1875, establishing the marginally sufficient Lemhi Valley Indian Reservation for the "mixed tribes of Shoshone, Bannock, and Sheepeater Indians" (see Madsen 1979/1990, 200), white Lemhi Valley residents prepared to defend themselves against attack, certain that the valley's few hundred resident Indians would unite with the "warring" Nez Perce.[14] The whites built fortifications and they organized protective, vigilante-like military associations. Meanwhile, under the leadership of the Shoshone Chief Tendoy, most of the valley's Indian residents tried to dispel their neighbors' growing panic. Tendoy went so far as to commit young Indian "warriors" to assist the whites in their defensive preparations. As historian and long-time Lemhi Valley resident Hope Benedict writes: "Despite indications to the contrary and protestations of neutrality from the Lemhis, the whites of Lemhi County feared the worst, making plans to build stockades in both Salmon City and Junction. In this and subsequent skirmishes, the whites of Lemhi County found their greatest allies to be Tendoy and the Lemhis" (Benedict 1996, 135–136; see also Benedict 2006).

Nevertheless, within three decades—by the time Junction had given way to the slow but steady advance of the G&P—white pressure and, worse, federal stinginess had succeeded in driving the Lemhis out of the valley. According to Benedict (1996, 150), the whites who wanted the Indians to leave were actually in the minority. Some actually pled their case, albeit in self-serving ways. For example, in 1874, a local businessman and retired Army colonel named George L. Shoup wrote a letter on behalf of Chief Tendoy to John Hailey, Idaho's territorial delegate to Congress.[15] According to Benedict, the colonel argued that the Lemhis' presence created "a barrier between the white settlers and 'other Indians who were not good.'" With this as his rationale, Colonel Shoup requested that "Tendoy and the approximately 450 Lemhis be granted a reserve within the bounds of their homeland" (150). In later efforts, he even argued that the Lemhis were to be consulted and their consent obtained before being removed to Fort Hall (Madsen 1979/1990, 123).

How Shoup's sense of expediency and later efforts ought to be viewed in light of his earlier frontier exploits is a touchy subject. Just ten years earlier, he had participated in the infamous Sand Creek "battle" in Colorado, during which some 900 volunteer soldiers attacked a winter encampment of around 750 Cheyenne who had agreed to surrender their weapons in exchange for protection of the U.S. military. Sleeping beneath white ("surrender") and American flags, most of those who were killed were women and children (by the soldiers' own accounts), and all of those slaughtered were then hideously mutilated. Colonel Shoup appears among the "Bloody Third" — Colonel John M. Chivington's Third Colorado Volunteer Cavalry Regiment — as it marched triumphantly through the streets of Denver.[16]

Although Congress and the War Department agreed at the time that Sand Creek was indeed a massacre, not a battle, no charges were ever brought against the volunteer perpetrators of this crime. Given the general acceptance of the day that "extermination" was a valid solution to the United States' "Indian problem," it comes as little surprise that the Lemhis were eventually forced — even over the objections of influential and "Indian fighter" whites like Colonel Shoup — to leave their valley. In a densely packed historical analysis of the community and "sense of place" created by Lemhi County settlers after 1866, Benedict indicates how thin the line was between white acceptance of the Lemhis' presence in the valley and white willingness to see them go. Quoting from letters and memoirs gathered from valley residents descended from those who witnessed the Lemhis' departure to Fort Hall (where descendants of the Lemhis still reside, some still reluctantly), Benedict observes: "They trailed out through the valley with their families and pack horses, dragging their wickiup poles. They were weeping as they went. The ranchers along the way could hear their crying for some distance before they passed their homes. The ranchers were near tears and some did cry. Despite their sorrow, the white community of Lemhi County did not consider the Lemhis integral members. Tendoy's people had been helpful, peaceful, and financially important, but they fell outside the community" (Benedict 1996, 155; citations omitted; see also Benedict 2006).[17]

In the city of Salmon, some 30 miles north of the place where the Lemhi "trail of tears" commenced, the Lemhi County museum holds a collection of Indian leatherwork, beadwork, tools, weapons, toys, pictures, and stories that try to keep memories of what happened in the valley, some of it anyway, alive. Books by non-Indian historians bear the visages of nineteenth-century "chiefs" and "braves." The face of Tendoy graces the front of a book that bears his name, and tells of his people's struggle to reserve a place for themselves in the valley. As noted above, for a few years in the late 1800s there was indeed a Lemhi Reservation and Agency, whose buildings are still standing but are now used as a senior center for the valley's aging non-Indian inhabitants. Not far from the agency, a stone monument marks Tendoy's grave, surrounded by 12-foot-high chain-link fencing. Nearby, a large sign commemorates the removal of the "Lemhi Indians" to Fort Hall Indian Reservation between 1905 and 1909, starting just one hundred years after the Jeffersonian "Corps of Discovery" reached this valley in its quest for a water route to the Pacific. Though there is no longer a reservation here, the Lemhi Valley is now struggling to claim its fame as the birthplace of Sacajawea, the young Lemhi Shoshone girl who was brought along with her newborn baby, Pomp, and her French trapper husband, Toussaint Charbonneau, as the Corps left Fort Mandan, then Sioux territory. According to the scant mention of her in the journals of the corps' commanders Meriwether Lewis and William Clark, Sacajawea acted as guide and translator once the corps reached the land and people of her birth.[18]

Two hundred years later, some of Sacajawea's descendants at Fort Hall spearheaded a drive to build an interpretive center near the city of Salmon, while other descendants of the Lemhis say they discovered their "Lemhi" ancestry only by finding a name or names of relatives on the marker memorializing their ancestors' removal to Fort Hall. They remind us that their name for themselves as a people was never "Lemhi." According to descendants of the Lemhi group, their people referred to themselves according to their livelihood with names like *tuku-deka'* (sheep eaters) or *agai-deka'* (fish eaters), which varied depending on the time of the year and the place. "Lemhi" (pronounced "lem-high") is an appellation that seems to have stuck, but it was inherited from the Mormon missionaries who spent several years (1855–58) trying to "civilize" and convert the people they found in what would become the Lemhi Valley.[19]

Breaking Silence

The only time Walter Nevada ever spoke more than two words to me in English, it was to describe what lay beneath the whispering grasses of a hill somewhere near what used to be the Lemhi Valley Indian Reservation. "Indians were buried all through here," he said as he swept his long arm across the gray-green scene in front of us. This is where Indians used to bring their dead a long time ago, even before the plagues that preceded Lewis and Clark's intrepid adventure across the Continental Divide into this very valley.

Walter Nevada was three when the "bluecoats," the United States Army, removed his family, and ultimately his entire community, from the Indian reservation that had been established for them in Idaho's mountainous southeast. His parents had come from Nevada. Hence the family name, given to them during the census that established the original rolls at Fort Hall. Before they were removed along with the other "Lemhis," they traveled between the Lemhi Valley, the Salmon River Valley to which the Lemhi River is tributary, and the Lost River Valley to the west, near the town of Challis, where hot springs spill into the Salmon River. In the Lemhi Valley, on the ground where the reservation used to be, a wooden memorial marker has been erected by the U.S. Department of the Interior, Bureau of Land Management. It reads, in white block lettering on a shiny brown background, now cracked and fading on the side that faces the sun:

MEMORIAL 1905–1909 DEDICATED TO THE LEMHI INDIANS WHO WERE FORCED TO MOVE FROM THEIR HOMELAND IN THE LEMHI VALLEY TO THE FORT HALL RESERVATION.

Below the dedication are lists of names, ages, and kinship designations: "son," "dau," "wif," "hus," "orphan." The sign is large, and it takes both sides to complete the lists. Walter searches for his name, finds it midway down on the left, points to it and taps with a weathered knuckle on the white number indicating his age at the time of removal. "Three," he says, and raises the other hand, three fingers extended upward in silent echo.

Of the 561 names listed on the sign, Walter is the only one still living. He likes the idea of reestablishing a Lemhi Indian presence in the valley, even if it is a conflicted memorial to the famous woman (Sacajawea) who helped lead the first whites into the valley. But for Walter, the century that has passed between his birth and the sound of his knuckle knocking against a token of official regret has failed to dissuade him of his desire for more than a memorial. He owns land allotments at Fort Hall, and he respects the value of that land in the way that it "still takes care of the people." But he does not speak of Fort Hall as his *home*. This designation he reserves for the valleys from which his family was removed when he was yet too young to know what was happening.

After removal, Walter says that his family traveled around awhile before relinquishing their freedom to the reservation and to the General Allotment Act—Congress's imposition of private land ownership, the magic tool of "civilization." As a result of what he refers to as his parents' love for travel and their lack of understanding about what was happening during the Allotment era (1887–1934), he says they ended up with land that "was not too good," the leftovers. As a child, Walter himself was allotted land, as was every enrolled tribal member during those years. In fact, it was all bound up together, enrollment in a "tribe," settlement on a "home reservation," sometimes U.S. citizenship. Sons, daughters, wives, husbands, and orphans. They were given 40, 80, or 160 acres of grazing land and 20 acres of irrigable land for pasture.

"Given"

Of the ground that had been reserved to the tribal members' forebears in perpetuity under treaty with the United States, enough was surveyed and parceled out to match every enrolled Indian with a plot of his or her "own" land. Then, "once they ran out of Indians" (as today's heirs and

FIGURE 6.1. The back of a Bureau of Land Management memorial marker listing the names, ages, and kinship of the 561 Lemhi (Shoshone and Northern Bannock) Indians who were forcibly removed from their reservation in the Lemhi Valley of southeastern Idaho to the Fort Hall Indian Reservation some 150 miles to the southwest between 1905 and 1909. Descendants of some of those memorialized on the marker are working to regain a presence in the Lemhi Valley. In 1995 the Fort Lemhi Indian Community was formed to begin the long process of petitioning for formal federal recognition of the Lemhi as a tribe. (Courtesy of Jack Waller)

allottees say with a wry sense of humor) the "surplus" was ceded to the United States, and "opened up" to homesteaders. Historical photographs of the "opening" of reservations are all dust and flying horses' hooves, spinning wheels and whips unfurled, faceless men on foot, on horse, in wagons; and Indian people standing by, watching.

A tremendous quiet tends to grow up around Western cities and towns of dubious extraction, like Pocatello, like Salmon. It is not that there aren't histories and stories and artifacts around to remind you of the places' multiple pasts: of the first settlers, the miners, the explorers, and of the people who lived here prior to Europe's and the United States' drawn-out invasion of the Americas. It is just that there is relative silence about how the places were precipitated in the first place; and more to the point, there is a silence about how multiple places may persist in the same space. Like the discordant neighboring that happens from time to time, as described above, between residents of Pocatello and Fort Hall, or the Lemhi Valley and the Lemhi Reservation, these places harbor multiple histories that have scant opportunity to find one another in meaningful ways, in what Heidegger referred to as "face-to-face encounters."

The "Indian problem" of previous centuries referred to the United States' predicament in dealing with the persistence of distinctive Native presences in an otherwise "indivisible" national image (see "Imagining the Nation Indivisible" in chapter 1). The "white problem" to which I refer in this chapter is an equally persistent disconnect between that national image as it is played out locally—in non-Indian histories, stories, and treatment of artifacts of a frontier past (including disestablished reservations) in which "conquest" is represented as an accomplished fact—and the loaded silences of a resilient, resistant frontier present. The "white problem," whether carried forth by non-Indians or Indians, consists in its studious ignorance of what Simon Ortiz refers to as "continuance," which is not only "something more than survival and saving ourselves" (Ortiz 1992, 32), but also, I suggest, an attentiveness to the failures and fissures of colonialism, those spaces, like Indian land itself, where no "conquest" was accomplished, where true neighboring can begin to take—to remake—place.

On Being Encountered

> It is not a matter, then, of a search for form as it is superficially and
> customarily understood, but rather a problem of the spirit, of the culture,
> in those countries in which alien currents meet and for centuries do not
> blend, but instead form narrow zones of confluences, while in the deep-
> est and widest places the main currents flow on, unyielding, incredibly.
> —José María Arguedas, *Yawar Fiesta*

It must have been a late
summer day for all the noise
we heard issuing from the creek
bed as two coyote pups scrambled
up the hill over there
on the other side trampling
dried up and crackling leaves
of arrowleaf balsamroot under paw

We stopped to
watch as the two low-tailed it
up over the crest of the hill followed
seconds later by the mother
who loped easily up behind them
reached the top of the hill. And stopped

There she turned to look
at us and then
sat down

We stood captive
quite some time
just looking
and being looked at

Just west of Pocatello, the hills rise abruptly, and the desert grasses,
sunflowers, and sagebrush give way to mahogany and maple, Russian
olives and cottonwood, chokecherries and juniper, the occasional colony

of aspen and forests of Douglas fir. Getting there from here, from where I lived in south Pocatello, is a 10-minute journey. In that small amount of time, you can be without reminder—and (if you try) without memory—of traffic, dust, railroads, and the early morning odors that drift heavily down from Simplot, the fertilizer plant to the north. The stink isn't nearly as bad as it used to be, though. Last time I moved away from here, I vowed never to come back because the air was so bad, especially in the mornings. It was enough to make your eyes water and your throat sting. That was before the phosphate plant next door to Simplot, on the Fort Hall Indian Reservation, shut down. A lot of people lost their jobs. The air got cleaner. Tribal members were paid a per capita to make up for—make up for?—the Superfund site that was left behind on the reservation. It's supposed to get cleaned up someday, but you never know.

Except when a coyote's holding you captive with her gaze. Then, you know.

> Laugh.
> Laughter is immeasurable. Be joyful
> though you have considered all the facts.
> —Wendell Berry, "Manifesto"

I have come and gone from Pocatello a number of times, for school, for jobs, for friendship. When I first came here, some dozen years ago, I wanted to be an ethnobotanist, to live in a kind of timeless place where all that matters is finding the right plant, at just the right stage of growth or maturation to feed the hungry stomach, or soothe the aching tooth, or appease the restive spirit. I wanted to find some wise woman who could teach me how to do this. I would become her apprentice. In return, I would make a beautiful book to hold what she taught me so that none of it would be lost upon her passing, even if the youth of this day didn't want to learn. The next generation might. And it didn't matter to me whether my teacher was brown or white or green and covered with roots and soil like the old lady in that episode of *Night Gallery*, where her garden finally grows *her*. I wanted someone to teach me. I wanted to be part of something bigger than myself, to dive into that stream of being where individual identities are liberated into a river of interdependencies, and what the biologists call "emergent qualities": the whole that is more than the sum of its parts. We would all be helping each other to live well, without injury, and it would all be good.

Stop smirking. Somewhere down there in the depths, where your soul smiles in spite of you, and regardless of the facts, even you might still believe that there are generous teachers and willing apprentices: books that are written for good purpose, not just to make money and a name. Even you might believe that there is a confluence where the color of your skin becomes like the color of water—reflective of everything that's around it, echoing sun, wind, darkness, and constantly changing. Not to be pinned down.

Out of the blue
she said that the wind had spoken to her and
told her that it was angry because of all
the injuries being done to the land
being done on the land.

It had told her that the people should pray so that it
the wind would not do to the people what they
the people had done to the land
and left undone on the land.

I am thinking about this as I walk up a path by a creek
that flows through a narrow gulch out west of town
I am hearing what she told me about the wind
and what she said it said to her of its fury.

One foot in front of the other, I walk, and the wind begins to move,
the crescendo of its voice
rising above my thoughts and whirling overhead
I have just decided to turn around when I realize
that the air around me is calm.

I look up from where I stand
in unruffled space
among trees along the creek
and I see the wind-lashed and whipping
branches dancing above the walls of this ravine.

That was over a year ago. Now that time has passed, I need to ask her again what she hears on the wind. But sometimes her answers leave me feeling like I need a different question. You know? Like I have an answer, but I don't know to *what*. I know she hears me. I know she understands what I'm asking. So I suppose I'm either asking the wrong question, or I'm just not seeing the connection yet between what I seek, and what there is. Either this river isn't going there or, if it is, its route is one I am not familiar with. Of *course* its route is one I'm not familiar with. So I try to feel the current of what was under way before me, all around me, regardless of me. This is a different set of facts, one I have not considered.

We talk about plans for a public forum, one on "Indigenous Resources," where all of the invited speakers will be Indigenous. This is for a college graduate or undergraduate-level anthropology class in "indigenous resource management." Some of the students in the class might give presentations, too, but organizing this forum is their class project and they've said that they want to hear what the indigenous people have to say about "indigenous resources." They worry that the academic romance with "conservation," "the environment," and "cultural diversity" is somehow far-removed and abstracted, even contrary to the concerns of indigenous people. So they want to go to the source. I want them to go to the source. I also worry that the forum might end up causing—or just revealing—rifts between "us" and "them." But she says that things are getting better between this place and that, that hearts are beginning to open, and that we shouldn't be afraid of "shaking things up."

"We just have to plant little seeds," she says. I'm not sure who she means by "we," but she goes on: "That's what we do. Because you know, you never know how they'll grow. Some seeds grow faster than others. Some of these people who have a seed planted in their minds now, maybe one day they will become leaders, and they'll always have the memory of what we've talked about."

A path out west of town
leads through chokecherry bushes and Russian olives
that crowd the banks of a creek called Gibson Jack
named after "Gibson [comma] Jack"
"Jack Gibson, his x mark"

He was a Bannock Chief who signed
an agreement to sell
more land to the Americans
so that the railroad at Pocatello Station
could accommodate its mounting population
its expanding girth
its growing, gurgling
anxious gut

Like the other Chiefs at council that day,
Gibson Jack did not want to sign
but decisions had already been made
by men in high ranking positions
before "talks" had even begun

Pocatello was surrounded by Indian land,
you see, isolated from its destiny
The Indians must be convinced of the moral
rightness, indeed the righteousness
of their sacrifice

The Chiefs
they tried to tell themselves that, after all
the rising generation would be paid for this land
and they tried to tell themselves that, after this
perhaps the whites would finally be content
that maybe they would leave the people be

Now, a hundred and sixteen years after this one fact,
and in consideration of some other facts, as well
like how much and how little seems to change
and how easy and how human it is to hope
that things might really be different
than one fears they really are

I think about the chokecherry bushes and the Russian olive trees
that crowd the banks of Gibson Jack, of how someone said
I ought to love the one, because it's been here always and
abhor the other because it has come but lately

And the birds, they flock to the chokecherry bushes and
the birds, they flock to the olive trees in
riotous, hungry, and equal numbers, scoffing and
spreading seeds, right or wrong, without regard to rank

Unlike the birds I
move through a landscape burdened
by barriers erected by our ancestors and enshrined
in laws, glass ceilings and
invisible iron curtains
guaranteed in perpetuity

"Isn't it funny," she says after a while, "that Pocatello is named after an
Indian, and Fort Hall is named after a white guy?" And indeed, she laughs
at this. The peculiar tricks of history. "I bet nobody ever thinks about that,"
she says.

Indeed, she might be right. I had never considered the two facts alongside one another. The colonial inversion or simple quirk of fate that fixed
the Shoshone-Bannock Nation under the moniker of a nineteenth-century
East Coast investor, and Pocatellans under the name of a nineteenth-
century Shoshone leader.

I wish more people would talk about Pocatello the person, about his
family and the others who frequented this valley before being overrun and
run out by railroad entrepreneurs and sagebrush sooners. How patron-
izing (and how conventional) it now seems to have taken the name of the
displaced and applied it to the place. But then, again, the place carried his
name even before the settlers came; "Pocatello's" was part of its description, or so I have been told. On the other hand, the man after whom Fort
Hall was named may never have set foot anywhere near that place, but
money doesn't need to walk. Instead, it hitches a ride with people like
the Bostonian entrepreneur Nathaniel Wyeth, whose 1834 journey west
was financed by a firm in New England. Having built the first Fort Hall,

Wyeth named it after the "oldest gentleman of [that] concern," and then proceeded to lose it two years later to the Hudson's Bay Company at Fort Boise, downriver. Talk about losing your identity into a stream of interdependencies. The "bastions" and everything else associated with Wyeth's original "terror to the skulking Indians" have long since disintegrated (Conley 1982, 509). I wonder if anybody ever thinks about that.

Or are there just more important things to consider. Like the way things do and do not change. Like the realization—the incarnation—of struggles that start and end in the mind, but can "shake things up" on the ground in between. Like war.

She begins to talk about how the tribes' spiritual leaders have asked her to help decipher the reservation's law and order code, to render it in spoken Shoshoni. The code was written many years ago, but now the tribes are revising it to bring it into step with the times, and to make it more accessible, comprehensible to the people. As a fluent speaker and teacher of Shoshoni, she has been asked by the spiritual leaders and elders of the tribes to help explain the hard to understand language of the code, so that they can advise the political leaders and lawyers. The elders are worried over the "controlled substance" provisions of the code. They are overwhelmed by the dense language of the document, and unsure about what provisions apply and do not apply to tribal members' use of peyote. So she feels honored that they have asked her to help. She wants their minds to be at ease during the ceremonies.

"They shouldn't have to be constantly worried, unable to focus because of the negativity—because they have to ask a member to stand at the door and keep a lookout for the cops! They have to have clear minds as they pray because, you know, they are praying for our people. First, they pray for our own Indian people, and then for all tribes, and then for all indigenous people all over the world. And then [she laughs], then they pray for the non-indigenous people."

I find it hard to laugh at this being relegated to the outer edges of the elders' prayers, and think, well, it is what it is. But I wish it were otherwise.

The next day, I ask her how the meeting went. She says it went well. Really well: "We had our tribal attorneys over here on one side, and then there were the attorneys from the city and county all over there on the other side"—she motions with her hands toward her heart "here" and away "over there." And she continues, "It made me think about the Shoshoni word we would use when we were trying to decide in our minds whether to do one thing or another. Somehow, when that word got translated into the English it took on the meaning of "war," like what the United States is doing in the world right now. I don't know when that happened, when it took on that meaning. But this is what I saw last night. Our lawyers, our people were at war. We were fighting for our unwritten Indian laws and our ceremonies. And, you know, we won."

> "We won," she said.
> The ceremonies
> The right to perform them
> not as "performance" but
> as ceremony: as
> prayer that holds the universe
> together for everyone
> The birthright
> The struggle incarnate and
> turned back
> upon itself at its source
> The seat of intelligence
> The seeds of intelligence
> planted
> though the facts are clear
> All things relative
> All things are relatives
> We one

An Acoma friend once asked me why white people want to know, to understand, how Native people relate to and take care of the land. He wondered, sort of rhetorically, whether anyone had ever told them.

I said I thought it was because "we," too, want to belong here, to be in place. I didn't say that I've been told that this is impossible: that we will never belong here. But I asked a "sort of question" (he called it) about whether he thought understanding somehow resides in the blood. You have it if you're Indian. You don't if you are not.

"No," he said. "Understanding resides in the struggle." Which is to say, in the land itself.[20]

In the river
the losing and regaining and
losing again of one's color
in the laughter and forgetting and
remembering and
struggling to remember
and remembering to struggle

in captivity and perpetuity

I am never sure what winning means
until I encounter
and am encountered

Notes

Introduction

1. Ernestine "Ernee" Broncho Werelus, Fort Hall Indian Reservation, Idaho, December 2000. Ernee is cofounder and coordinator of the Fort Hall Landowners Alliance (FHLA), Inc.

2. The term "tribe" is used here in its technical sense as "the fundamental unit of Indian Law [in the absence of which] there is no occasion for [Indian] law to operate" (Canby 2004, 3). Certainly, there are other, more general and historically laden meanings of the term that tend to militate against its unexamined use, such as the colonial and early anthropological one that placed "tribes" toward the "primitive" end of a cultural evolutionary continuum of "progress" that culminated in the "advanced" nature of European civilization. Unfortunately, the term is ubiquitous in any discussion of federal Indian law and "Indian land," and cannot be avoided. Furthermore, it is undergoing a process of reappropriation by many indigenous groups for its connotations of sustainability ("since time immemorial") and place-based community (for examples, see Grim 2001; cf. Carmody 2001).

3. In *Hodel v. Irving*, 481 U.S. 704 (1987), and again in *Babbitt v. Youpee*, 519 U.S. 234 (1997). For a lengthy discussion of these cases, the court opinions, and scholarly discussion surrounding them, see "Serial Experiments" in chapter 2.

4. To this end, I have followed writers like Nicholas Thomas down a middle path, "which amounts to an ethnography of colonial projects: that presupposes the effect of larger objective ideologies, yet notes their adaptation in practice, their moments of effective implementation and confidence as well as those of failure and wishful thinking" (Thomas 1994, 60).

5. Private land ownership and civil and religious education were thought to be the magic bullets that would, as one "friend of the Indian" put it, "kill the Indian and save the man" (*Official Report of the Nineteenth Annual Conference of Charities and Correction* 1892, 46, as reprinted in Prucha 1973, 260).

6. "Structures" are defined here in their Marxian sense: as relations among forces of production, as economic forms rather than processes (Cohen 2000: 37; cf. Bourdieu 1977, 72). The political "superstructure" is characterized as "a set of non-economic institutions, notably the legal system and the state" (Cohen 2000, 216).

7. "Severalty" is the legal term for "having individual or sole control over something" (*Gilbert Law Dictionary*). The term has a telling etymological kinship with "sever" and "separation" (*Oxford English Dictionary*, Compact Edition).

8. The comment was made by a Shoshone-Bannock tribal member during a forum organized for Native American Awareness Week, Idaho State University, Pocatello, April 2001. I describe Pocatello–Fort Hall "community relations" (including the panel mentioned here) in greater detail in chapter 6.

9. The term "anti-place" comes from Edward Casey's philosophical history (1997) of "place" in Western thought. He writes that the endlessly replicable "site" of modernist prisons, architecture, and the like "is an antidote to place, its very antithesis, its pharmakon—the remedy that is its destruction. [. . .] Site is anti-place hovering precariously over the abyss of no-place"(Casey 1997, 186).

10. "Perceptions" and "conceptions" as used here allude to a Peircean semeiotic framework that posits an interface of language between sense-perceptive (pre-linguistic) knowledge and conceptual (post-linguistic) knowledge. I explore that interface with regard to Indian land and fractionation in Ruppel n.d.

11. When I originally wrote this, the Department of the Interior had instituted a new law redefining (yet again) who is "Indian." The measure came up against heated opposition from individual Indian landowners (see chapter 4).

12. Ernestine "Ernee" Broncho Werelus, Fort Hall Indian Reservation, Idaho, January 2003.

13. Thanks to Ernee Werelus for this insight.

The Indian land base is "more or less intact" because many reservations suffer from checkerboard ownership: non-Indian-owned land interests, whether private (fee), county, state, or federal (restricted), are interspersed with Indian-owned land interests, whether individual or tribal (trust).

14. Over 100 reservations were allotted, either during or prior to the General Allotment period (1887 to 1934). However, some reservations that were never formally allotted (like the Navajo Reservation) nevertheless include properties allotted under special agreements and executive orders. Of the 56 million acres of land now included in reservations, some 11 million acres, or 20 percent of the total, are allotted.

15. The quotation comes from a historical description of British-Indian "boundary" negotiations in the southeastern United States between 1763 and 1768. Jones goes on to describe, from primary historical documents, the prevailing Indian "attachment to the land, amounting almost to an identification with it" as "an incalculable but pervasive influence" on these international negotiations (Jones 1982, 54).

Chapter 1. Nations In(di)visible

1. Cf. Derrida 1992.

2. Of Peirce's numerous definitions of the pragmatic maxim, this one is interesting for its inclusion of "desire," and fortuitous in its mirroring of Culhane's description (1998) of the role of abstraction and theory in Western law and culture as allowing the powerful to conjure whatever reality they might "desire" at the moment (see also Derrida 1992). Thanks to Professor E. V. Daniel, Columbia University Anthropology Department, for supplying a well-timed compilation of some of Peirce's various definitions of the pragmatic maxim.

3. As Dara Culhane (1998) and others have argued, there is much to be gained by opening the story of European colonizing exploits with Britain's conquest of the Irish (cf. Stannard 1992, 224–225; Canny 1973).

4. For one such latter-day presentation of *terra nullius*, see Carrillo 2002. As discussed below, one school of thought holds that the entire body of federal Indian property law is

predicated on the doctrine of discovery as incorporated into the reasoning of Chief Justice Marshall in *Johnson v. M'Intosh* (1823).

The doctrine of discovery is also referred to as the "doctrine of occupation" and the "doctrine of settlement" (Culhane 1998, 47).

5. "Calvin's Case" of 1608 codified what became known as the "infidel rule," under which the laws of the vanquished would be abrogated based on their supposed failure to meet the standard set by the Christian king (Culhane 1998, 47; Getches, Wilkinson, and Williams 2005, 54).

6. This process of redefinition continues to bear toxic fruit in federal Indian legal constructions of who qualifies as "Indian." See chapter 2.

7. On the conceptualization of land as an alienable commodity in colonial New England, see Cronon 1983, chap. 4, 187n35.

8. Which is not to suggest that indigenous conceptions have had no effect on Anglo practices, as we will see below.

9. The founding cases are Chief Justice Marshall's "trilogy," the earliest of which is *Johnson v. M'Intosh*, 21 U.S. 543 (1823), discussed below.

10. The scare quotes around "conquest" signify the term's offensiveness to people who do not see themselves as "conquered."

11. I am using "counter-mythology" here much as Williams (1997) does, to refer to something between hegemony and ideology that may be at once felt—the comes without saying, goes without saying of "habit-forming" hegemony—but that also has at least the partially articulated argument of ideology. Cf. Comaroff and Comaroff 1991, 19–32; and Biolsi 1992, 194n68.

12. "Peopled" and "defended places," as opposed to the abstract spaces and replicable sites of modernism (see Arendt 1958; Casey 1997; Foucault 1977; Deleuze and Guattari 1987).

13. For readable pictures of the "Indian Deed" discussed in Cronon 1983, 66–67, see the Hampden County, Massachusetts, "Registry of Deeds" Web site, http://www.registryofdeeds .co.hampden.ma.us/indian.html/.

14. On English colonial assumptions about the superiority of Anglo property rights (ownership) over Indian use rights (sovereignty), see Cronon 1983, 54–58.

15. Although there was obviously no one Indian or white perspective, certain patterns are discernible in these earliest historical sources. As William Cronon notes: "The popular idea that Europeans had private property, while the Indians did not, distorts European notions of property as much as it does Indian ones. The colonists' property systems, like those of the Indians, involved important distinctions between sovereignty and ownership, between possession by communities and possession by individuals. The distinction between sovereignty and ownership is crucial here. When a colony purchased land from Indians, it did so under its own system of sovereignty: whenever ownership rights were deeded and purchased, they were immediately incorporated into English rather than Indian law. Indian land sales, operating as they did at the interface of two different sovereignties, one of which had trouble recognizing that the other existed, thus had a potentially paradoxical quality. Because Indians, at least in the beginning, thought they were selling one thing and the English thought they were buying another, it was possible for an Indian village to convey

what it regarded as identical and nonexclusive usufruct rights to several different English purchasers" (Cronon 1983, 69–70).

16. "Whether denying or defending Indian rights of land tenure, most English colonists displayed a remarkable indifference to what the Indians themselves thought about the matter. As a result, we have very little direct evidence in colonial records of the New England Indian's conceptions of property" (Cronon 1983, 58).

17. On the Age of Jackson (1829–56), see Smith 1997, 200.

18. For a critical discussion of Marshall's "explicit admonition against questioning," see Carrillo 2002, 41–42.

19. On Marshall's acknowledged concomitant departure in *Johnson v. M'Intosh* from "his general adherence to Lockean notions of natural rights and consensual membership" in favor of the positive law of conquest, see Smith 1997, 184–185.

20. As suggested below, invalidation of M'Intosh's deed would also have called into question the tribe's right to cede its lands to the federal government if it had already conveyed a portion of the same to a private individual. Marshall's contention was that the tribe, under its laws, certainly had the right to annul its grant to the individual. Marshall argued that, even if a tribe decided to grant a portion of its land to an individual (Indian or not) in severalty, that portion "derives its efficacy" under the tribe's laws, and thereby remains "Indian."

21. As discussed at the beginning of this chapter, the doctrine of discovery was to be applied only to lands free of humans, and the doctrine of conquest to those where humans were found. But, of course, no "uninhabited" lands were ever "discovered," only invented.

22. For a fascinating account of recent discoveries of corporate records and John Marshall's own property interests that significantly clarify the motivations behind the landmark *Johnson v. M'Intosh* decision, see Robertson 2005.

23. Robert Clinton (2002, 138) also takes due note of this important but seldom highlighted "between sovereign nations" aspect of Marshall's decision. Cf. Getches, Wilkinson, and Williams 2005, 69–70.

24. See *Johnson v. M'Intosh*, 21 U.S. 543 (1823), *Cherokee Nation v. Georgia*, 30 U.S. 1 (1831), and *Worcester v. Georgia*, 31 U.S. 515 (1832).

25. Compare the two Marshall epigraphs in this section. As Philip Frickey (1990, 1227) sees it, "Chief Justice Marshall's opinion in *Worcester* exemplifies an important hermeneutical insight: interpretation requires an encounter with a specific context, which can have a transforming effect. His encounter with the Cherokee context in his second and third opinions seemingly transformed federal Indian law from the largely unilateral colonialism of his first opinion."

26. Article III, Section 2 reads, in part: "The judicial Power shall extend to all Cases, in Law and Equity, arising under this Constitution, the Laws of the United States, and Treaties made [. . .] under their Authority [and] to Controversies between [. . .] a State, or the Citizens thereof, and foreign States, Citizens or Subjects."

27. The seven-member Supreme Court was split 2–2–2, with one of the justices absent. Four concurred with the decision that the Court lacked jurisdiction in the matter, but, of these, two based their opinion on different grounds from Marshall's.

28. As Clinton (2002, 140) suggests, Marshall was also arguing that "the appropriate forum for the resolution of tribal grievances [. . .] was diplomatic negotiations with the

federal government or warfare," as with any international incident; see also *Cherokee Nation v. Georgia*, 18.

29. When Marshall addresses the Crown's understanding of "discovery," he leaves aside its less egalitarian claims as a colonizing aggressor (Frickey 1990, 1226; Smith 1997, 238). However, as Frickey (1990, 1228) notes, Marshall's approach "presumed tribal sovereignty to be substantial as a matter of law even if weak as a matter of fact. This approach has the practical effect of avoiding judicial decisions that find implicit diminishment of tribal sovereignty. Chief Justice Marshall forced the Congress, as the governmental branch politically accountable for the implementation and consequences of colonization, to destroy the sovereignty of the tribes overtly if sovereignty was to be lost at all."

30. Marshall referred to the tribes' powers of self-government no less than eight times in the twenty-eight-page opinion of *Cherokee Nation v. Georgia*.

31. Specific examples abound in the literature, but see Biolsi 1992, 3–33, for how this social and political control system and its particular technologies of power have played out on the Sioux reservations. See also Nickeson 1976.

32. Marshall's assertions that the federal-tribal relationship warrants federal "protections" was upheld even in the nineteenth century, for example, in *United States v. Kagama*, 118 U.S. 375 (1886), as was his contention in *Cherokee Nation v. Georgia* that any diminishment of tribal sovereignty must come expressly from Congress, not the courts, for example, in *United States v. Holliday*, 70 U.S. 407 (1865). In keeping with the tenor of the times, however, both cases were more endorsements of federal domination over tribes than affirmations of Indian national sovereignty.

33. "Liberal" is understood to refer to those political traditions (ideologies and institutions as well as practices) that stress "government by consent, limited by the rule of law protecting individual rights, and a market economy, all officially open to all minimally rational adults" (Smith 1997, 507n5).

34. Exemplary cases include *Johnson v. M'Intosh* (1823); *Cherokee Nation v. Georgia* (1831); *Worcester v. Georgia* (1832); *Talton v. Mayes*, 163 U.S. 376 (1895); and *United States v. Wheeler*, 435 U.S. 313 (1978). See Price and Clinton 1983, 171; Wilkinson 1987, 62; Getches, Wilkinson, and Williams 2005.

35. The "colonial" school of thought still exists, however, claiming that the sovereign powers of tribes are products of recognition by the Crown and, later, by the federal government. For a brief discussion of the competing Indian law and colonial theories of tribal sovereignty, see Prygoski 1995, 1, at the American Bar Association Web site, http://www.abanet.org/genpractice/magazine/1995/fall/marshall.html/.

36. In their discussion of the "reciprocal interdependence" of hegemony and ideology within any "cultural field," Jean and John Comaroff offer the following explication of the "contradictory consciousness" of oppressed peoples and their reactions to the processes of their oppression: "Those reactions, it is said, consisted in a complex admixture of tacit (even uncomprehending) accommodation to the hegemonic order at one level and diverse expressions of symbolic and practical resistance at another, although the latter might have reinforced the former by displacing attention away from, or by actively reproducing, the hidden signs and structures of domination" (Comaroff and Comaroff 1991, 26; cf. Gramsci 1971, 333). The Comaroffs' counterpoint to this statement is that, while accommodation may

perpetuate relations of domination, "it may also be a source of ever more acute, articulate resistance," which, in turn, may create new forms of domination, and so on. "That is why the history of colonialism [. . .] is such a drawn out affair, such an intricate fugue of challenge and riposte, mastery and misery" (Comaroff and Comaroff 26).

37. For concise descriptions of this period, termed "the Gilded Age of ascriptive Americanism" for all nondominant groups, see Smith 1997, 6, 347–409, 508–509n5; see also Hoxie 2001, 12–39.

38. Two years after Allotment, Martí would write passionately against the United States' 1868 betrayal of Red Cloud and the Sioux, having heard Red Cloud speak on tour in New York (Martí 1889/1975, 226–227). Yet, at least insofar as the indigenous people of the Americas are concerned, Martí's writings seem to reflect the standard dichotomous sentiments of his time. As such, his multicultural vision extends, perhaps in a moment of Rosaldo's imperialist nostalgia (1989), to the noble (but extinct) Indian of Red Cloud's lectures but not to the "ignorant, or savage Indians" of his Americas (Martí 1894/1975, 54).

39. The Fort Hall Indian Reservation was first contemplated under an executive order signed by Andrew Johnson on June 14, 1867, and finally established by the Fort Bridger Treaty of July 3, 1868.

40. For example, agents for the tiny, now defunct Lemhi Reservation in southeastern Idaho were forever pleading for government protection of "their Indians" against the depredations of whites who wanted the "mixed Bannock, Shoshone, Tukarika (Sheepeater) [now "Lemhi"] Indians" removed from the Lemhi Valley. In a letter dated February 12, 1868, John S. Ramsey, under sheriff of Idaho County, wrote to S. R. Howlett, secretary and acting governor of Idaho Territory, concerning encroachments on the Lemhi River fishery by whites. The fishery was almost the sole source of food for the Lemhi Indians, confined as they were to a poorly supplied reservation. "Unprincipled whites" were also said to be supplying "an abundance of ammunition and bad whiskey" to the Indians, who "number[ed] nearly three hundred and [were] general peaceable." Microcopy 234, Letters Received by the Office of Indian Affairs, 1824–80, Newberry Library, Ayer Collection, Chicago, 1974. Cf. Madsen 1996, 295–325; Nabokov 1999, 233; McDonnell 1991; Carlson 1981.

41. Rogers Smith (1997, 393) comments that humanitarian groups like the Friends of the Indian, advocating for bestowal of U.S. citizenship upon "competent" Indians "surrendered what should have been a crucial requirement for respecting Native American interests — that allotment and citizenship come only with a tribe's consent. Instead, both were imposed at the President's [and later, the secretary of the interior's] discretion."

42. Theodore Roosevelt, First Annual Message, December 3, 1901.

43. The need to sell and the inability to purchase parcels of Indian land continue to be problems today and are leading reasons for revisions to laws concerning Indian land consolidation that make it impossible for an Indian landowner to sell land to a non-Indian without giving the tribe the right of first refusal. For a discussion of the Indian Land Consolidation Act, its amendments, and the American Indian Probate Reform Act of 2004, see chapter 2.

44. Frederick Hoxie (2001, 180) describes the "last arrow ceremonies" instituted by the Office of Indian Affairs on several reservations, including Fort Hall, by 1916. Indian people declared "competent" would be asked to publicly "shoot their last arrow" upon receiving fee simple title to their land. To this day, at Fort Hall, tribal members whose ancestors "shot

the arrow" are looked upon as "traitors" by some of those whose ancestors' land remained in trust. This situation is described in chapter 5.

45. I am using "habit" here to evoke Pierre Bourdieu's sense of "habitus," as "history turned into nature [but] denied as such" (Bourdieu 1977, 78), as well as Peirce's "habit," as "the tendency that would guide future actions" (Parker 1998, 182).

46. According to Vine Deloria and Clifford Lytle (1984, 46), "As the thirties began, the Bureau of Indian Affairs and the Senate Indian Committee had more information on the conditions of Indians than any previous administration or Congress." They list five major studies that predate the Meriam Report, and two more that came out at the same time or after. Although all but one of these reports (Lindquist 1919/1923) were authorized or commissioned by the Bureau of Indian Affairs itself, the Meriam Report (Brookings Institution 1928) received the most public attention largely because it came out during a national election year and it offered policy recommendations (Deloria and Lytle 1984, 44).

47. In their nuanced treatment of the passage of the Indian Reorganization Act, Deloria and Lytle (1984, 37) note, for example, that, although the studies of the 1920s and 1930s helped to prepare the ground of reform, the "idea of Indian self-government" embodied in the Indian New Deal policies of the 1930s (especially the IRA) was more likely motivated by the radical reform vision of John Collier than by the frank and detailed admission of the problems of Indian administration. "The effect of reform in the field of Indian Affairs," they contend, "with the solitary exception of the Indian Reorganization Act, has had two major thrusts: change in the rate of delivery of federal services and change in the efficiency of administration. Almost all of the suggestions for reform prior to John Collier, and all of the suggestions since Collier, have accepted the federal institutions as a given element in the equation and sought to adjust other factors. Collier alone attempted to transform the institutions themselves" (55).

48. For a recent declaration on the Interior Department's increasing bureaucratization in lieu of management reform, see ILWG 2007.

49. The epigraph statement is from a presentation by Indian law professional Mariana Shulstad at the Eleventh Annual Indian Land Consolidation Symposium, Carlton, Minnesota, October 2001.

This document and others referred to in the main text or notes but *not* listed in "References Cited" (including most governmental documents) are in my files and available on request.

50. Indian Country with a capital *C* refers to all lands over which tribes, the federal government, or both have legal jurisdiction.

51. One of the proposed—and sometimes contested—solutions to the problem of fractionation has been the tribes' use of revenues from gambling and natural resources to buy allotments from their own members. See chapter 3.

52. Part of the continuing problem is that "the Department of Interior (DOI) has unconscionably increased its layers of administration and administrative personnel all the while what it administers for Indians has been drastically reduced" (see ILWG 2007, 1; see also Hughes 2007a, 2007b).

53. The General Allotment Act of 1887 provided for the devise and partition of allotted lands under the probate laws of the state or territory where the lands were located (25 *U.S.*

Code Annotated 331, sec. 5). The Burke Act of 1906 gave the secretary of the interior legal authority to determine legal heirs of allotted trust land interests (34 *U.S. Statutes at Large* 182, amending sec. 6 of the General Allotment Act). This authority was further extended and clarified under the 1910 amendments to the General Allotment Act (36 *U.S. Statutes at Large* 269), which also provided for Indian testamentary disposition (will-making authority). And, in 2004, the American Indian Probate Reform Act (AIPRA) provided the first uniform probate code for owners and heirs of Indian trust properties. See chapter 2 for further discussion of AIPRA and its precursors, few and far between.

54. The 2004 American Indian Probate Reform Act facilitates the partition of highly fractionated parcels, one of its many provisions that are of concern to Indian landowners and their advocates. See chapter 2.

55. Amendments to the Indian Land Consolidation Act and the American Indian Probate Reform Act now guarantee Indian landowners access to names and addresses of their co-owners under the Freedom of Information Act (FOIA). Landowners have routinely had to demand this kind of information from their local BIA offices even though, on some reservations, lists of names and addresses have been supplied to non-Indian farmers interested in leasing Indian land. Later chapters discuss several lawsuits that bear on this problem.

Chapter 2. Appropriating the Trust

1. Servan is listed among the French magistrates who strove to reform criminal law by "generalizing punishment": to "increase its effects while diminishing its economic cost [. . .] by dissociating it from the system of property, of buying and selling [. . .] , and [also diminishing] its political cost" (see Foucault 1977, 80–81). Perhaps not surprisingly, there are eerie similarities between the control apparatus that Michel Foucault describes for eighteenth-century France and the nineteenth- and twentieth-century "humanitarian" reform efforts of the federal Indian trust.

2. As used here, the "type" is a general thing whose particular instantiations, or tokens, are endlessly replicable. Thus, as far as federal governance is concerned, the allottee is the endlessly replicated individual, the token of "the Indian" type.

3. Arendt's "twofold flight" has also been described as a peculiarly Western historical progression from the local particularities of place to the homogeneity of space and the replicability of site. For example, Michel Foucault 1977, 204, 205, identifies "the rule of functional sites whose aim is to bring about a constant 'location of bodies in space.'" The preeminent example of the functional site, first proposed by Jeremy Bentham in 1787, was the Panopticon—the "site of sight" over everything—the paradigm for the prison watchtower (see also Casey 1997, 184–185). Edward Casey (1997) presents a far-reaching narrative of the philosophical history of the concept of place, beginning with a smattering of Western and non-Western creation narratives. The bulk of Casey's work explores place in the Western tradition, from Plato to the present.

4. The term "contradictory consciousness" refers to the dissonance between the world as it is hegemonically constituted and the world as it is actually encountered. Although usually applied to the ambivalences and ambiguities of subaltern resistance to or compliance with dominant social and traditional institutions and ideologies, contradictory consciousness can

also describe the inconsistencies inherent in hegemony itself as it seeks "a certain compromise equilibrium" with the dominated (Gramsci 1971, 161; see also Scott 1985, 335–340). In the case of Indian land, this turns out to be a shifting equilibrium as earlier hegemonies (for example, a settled if qualified belief in Native sovereignty) are joined by or only partially replaced by later hegemonies (for example, a settled belief in assimilation; and later, a settled belief in guardianship). The most successful hegemonies are, on balance, the least irritating to their subordinate subjects, bringing forth relatively more compliance than resistance because their ways of ordering the world come to seem "natural" or "reasonable" regardless of their underlying inconsistencies: the twentieth-century version of "Indian (trust) land" as an index of "authentic" Indianness (and vice versa) may, at times, be one of these. I follow Comaroff and Comaroff (1991, 23–26) in suggesting that hegemony and ideology exist on a continuum between the unconscious and the conscious: thus hegemony is more likely to be felt than thought; and ideology is more likely to be thought than felt. In related terms, hegemony carries the "power of ideals" that "call forth," whereas ideology conveys the "force of existents" that "push against" (Colapietro 1989, 113; see also Daniel 1996, 100–103, 120).

5. For the Comaroffs, the "invisible roots" in this quotation are said to "anchor inequality." Even though, on balance, the federal-Indian relationship has been dominated by the raw power of the United States, as discussed below, the roots of the federal Indian trust are also attached to profound and enduring assertions of tribal sovereignty and Indian personhood.

6. Indian law scholars like Felix Cohen, Robert Williams Jr., Vine Deloria Jr., and David Wilkins, to name but a few (see Cohen 1942a/1971; Williams 1997; Deloria and Wilkins 1999), have been insisting on the deeper significance of the trust relationship for years. My point is that the everyday, on-the-ground practices of that relationship tend, by their very nature, to make its roots invisible, focusing, as they must, on the myriad details of the here and now, in legislation, regulation, litigation, and negotiation. As discussed in chapter 5, education is the one avenue that allows a deeper appreciation and assertion of the trust relationship.

7. Francis Jennings (1975, 119) notes, "Treaty is one of our ambiguous English words that can refer either to a process or product." I would suggest that, rather than being ambiguous, the term aptly describes a both-and reality. If it is to have effect, it is always both process and product.

8. "The basic theory of American constitutional law," declares Robert Clinton (2002, 160), "not only explains the baseline understanding of power and authority in the tribal federal relationship, it also explains why virtually all federal laws enacted prior to 1885 only applied to non-Indians who dealt with Indians, rather than regulating the Indian tribes directly. Since the Indian tribes were not part of the federal union and their citizens (members) were not part of 'We the People of the United States,' they had delegated no authority to the federal government other than through treaty. Federal and state powers simply could not be asserted over them directly without the benefit of their agreement through treaty." Of course, the treaties may be understood as signs of other colonial intentions, as well (for example, "conquest," or Euro-centric hegemonies). But, as discussed in chapter 1, treaties have become more, not less, significant to assertions of indigenous autonomy and self-determination (cf. Jones 1982; Wilkinson 1987; Pommersheim 1995, 40–41; Williams 1997; Getches, Wilkinson and Williams 2005).

9. Robert Williams Jr. (1997, 8–9, 139–140n3) analyzes Indian-European treaty documents

from the seventeenth and eighteenth centuries, but economic and protective alliances (i.e., Indians protecting Europeans) can be traced to the earliest periods of European exploration and colonization. See also Cohen 1942b/1960; Jones 1982, 30; Getches, Wilkinson and Williams 2005, 55–58.

10. See U.S. Supreme Court opinions such as those in *Cherokee Nation v. Georgia*, 30 U.S. 1 (1831), and *Worcester v. Georgia*, 31 U.S. 515 (1832), which first articulated the trust doctrine; *United States v. Mitchell*, 445 U.S. 535 (1980), and *United States v. Mitchell*, 463 U.S. 206 (1983), which further defined and directed enforcement of the United States' trust responsibilities; and District Court opinions in the Indian Trust case, *Cobell v. Norton*, 334 F.3d 1128 (D.C. Cir. 2003; originally *Cobell v. Babbitt*, now *Cobell v. Kempthorne*).

11. The "visions" described in Williams 1997 and elsewhere (Jones 1982; Deloria and Wilkins 1999) are settled beliefs embodied in and acted upon by their holders. That is, though they may remain or have become newly accessible as concepts, they have also been naturalized into the felt perception of how the world ought to be. As such, they can be intensely creative and open to (prepared to take advantage of) transformative or agentive moments. They represent the "mindful mood" of the face-to-face encounter. On "mood, moment, and mind" and on the "agentive moment," see Daniel 1996, 104–105 and 191, respectively.

12. Original allottee, activist, and Chehalis Indian elder Helen Sanders, Lake Quinault Lodge, Washington, June 2002.

13. "Pragmatically" is meant here in the dialectical sense of interpreting the relationship, and the maintenance of it, in light of its bearing on conduct, whether that conduct be in the day-to-day praxis of land ownership, the avenues of resistance, or the development of new policies. New policies, of course, affect and effect new perceptions and enactments of the trust relationship, which, in turn, may serve to generate new policy, and so on and so forth.

14. That is, in part and for some Indians (but by no means all), the trust relationship is a question of identity, although, for many, it is simply a sign of hegemonic domination and the insidious racism of empire (see, for example, Grinde and Johansen 1995). Allottee advocates also recognize this aspect of the trust relationship, but, for them, whether for economic or other reasons, the problem of its colonial heritage has no "simple" resolution. In taking their appropriation of the trust relationship seriously, I seek to acknowledge and explore their counter-discourse as a possible antidote to empire. Transformative forms of agency are as likely to manifest themselves in apparently insignificant moments of habit change (power to) as they are in rather more significant moments of ideological persuasion (power over).

15. For example, Rogers Smith (1997, 505) describes the political tasks of American citizenship in general: "Their patriotism must thus be at once profound and qualified, recognized as something both necessary and dangerous, and thus as an allegiance that is deepest when it harbors searching doubts." Cf. Williams 1997. But see also Bonnie Honig's important discussion of "foreignness," "democratic cosmopolitanism," and democracy itself as "a commitment to generate actions in concert that exceed the institutional conditions that both enable and limit popular agencies" (Honig 2001, 13).

16. While activists litigate, legislate, and try to educate, theorists like Frank Pommersheim (1995, 45) argue for a reconceptualization, "both theoretically and operationally," of the trust relationship itself. In a comparable (post)colonial context, Mahmood Mamdani (1996, 15–16) suggests that institutions inherited from colonial times may be impossible to reform. And

Indian law scholar Robert Clinton (2002, 258) contends that the federal government should return to the "treaty federalism model" of its earliest dealings with Indian tribes.

17. Congressional fiat dates back to the passage of the Major Crimes Act (1885), which extended federal jurisdiction over seven (now fourteen) serious crimes committed in Indian country by an Indian person against the person or property of another person, whether Indian or not (see Clinton 2002, 170–171). Judicial fiat dates back to the U.S. Supreme Court's decision in *United States v. Kagama* (1886), in which the Court defended the constitutionality of the Major Crimes Act by ignoring the theretofore assumed status of tribes as one of the three sovereigns in the United States, and by construing their "domestic dependency" as a consequence of racial and tribal (cultural, political, economic) inferiority rather than pursuant to federal obligations of protection based in the treaties (see Clinton 2002, 175).

18. See Pommersheim 1995, 41: "Treaties not only recognized tribal sovereignty but in many cases also contained affirmative obligations on the part of the U.S. government [which] help to form part of the basis for a unique continuing federal legal duty. This is not a question of federal largesse but rather one of a federal legal obligation."

19. To the extent that the trust relationship is a consequence of the treaties, and to the extent that the treaties are symbolic of indigenous autonomy, the trust relationship may be construed as a ground for agentive action by tribes and tribal members (for example, as when assertions of indigenous fishing rights culminate in increased federal protections for indigenous fishing; see *Washington v. Fishing Vessel Assn.*, 443 U.S. 658 [1974]; but see also Grinde and Johansen 1995, 145–169). Likewise, to the extent that the trust relationship is a consequence of colonial and hegemonic forms of dominance, it reveals grounds for growing dominance (for example, when appeals for federal protection simply result in assertions of congressional "plenary power" over tribes; see *United States v. Kagama*, 118 U.S. 375 [1886] and *Lonewolf v. Hitchcock*, 187 U.S. 553 [1903]). Then again, hegemonic discourse being the dialectical phenomenon that it is, hegemony and counter-hegemony may each appropriate the signs of the other to its own purposes, transforming the grounds of action and reaction in the process. As E. Valentine Daniel (1996, 101) writes: "The conch that sounds for muster sounds for prayer too." See also Daniel 1996, 72–103; Povinelli 2002.

20. U.S. colonial policies of assimilation and separation, though conflicting, are not polar opposites. See, for example, Hoxie 2001, 239–244.

21. Deloria and Lytle (1984, 8–9) distinguish between "nationhood" and "peoplehood" by contending that "the idea of the people is primarily a religious conception [through which] Indians had [developed] a good idea of nationhood, but they had no knowledge of the other attributes of political existence that other people saw as important."

22. "Probate" (from the Latin *probāre*, to prove), the process of determining (proving) a will's legal authenticity, can also refer to the legal administration of wills and estates (Canby 2004; *Oxford English Dictionary*, Compact Edition).

23. See also Hoxie 2001, 159. Probate authority over allotted Indian lands was first enacted in 1910 and is codified under 25 *U.S. Code* 372, 373 (Cohen 1942a/1971, 110). In other words, an Indian person's right to dispose of real property by devise (will) was not formally recognized by the United States until 1910.

24. Helen Sanders, Portland, Oregon, June 2002. Helen Sanders's story is told in greater detail in chapter 3.

25. Although formally titled *The Problem of Indian Administration*, this document is commonly referred to as the "Meriam Report," after its primary author, Lewis Meriam of the Institute for Government Research (now known as the "Brookings Institution").

26. The "Indian Service" referred to the various administrative agencies of the English colonies and later of the United States in their dealings with American indigenous people (see Cohen 1942a/1971, 9).

27. Testimony by John Carver before Senate Subcommittee on Indian Affairs, *Indian Heirship Land Problem: Hearings*, 87th Cong., 1st sess., 1961, p. 29.

28. Michael Lawson originally wrote his report, "Heirship: The Indian Amoeba" (1984), for delivery at the Seventy-fifth Annual Meeting of the Organization of American Historians in 1982. In 1984, the report was inserted in the record of congressional testimony given by Bertram E. Hirsch, general counsel to the Sisseton-Wahpeton Sioux Tribe of Lake Traverse Reservation, North and South Dakota. Hirsch's testimony was in support of a bill proposed by the Sisseton-Wahpeton Sioux Tribe to provide a trust land inheritance code specific to the Lake Traverse Reservation. Much of the testimony on the bill revolved around assertions by the BIA Director of Office of Trust Responsibilities Sidney L. Mills that the bill's provisions duplicated those of the recently passed Indian Land Consolidation Act. The ILCA, Mills said, "was passed to prevent the Congress from having to address, on a yearly basis, these types of problems pursuant to individual bills for individual tribes" (Hearing before the Select Committee on Indian Affairs, U.S. Senate, 98th Cong., 2d sess. on S. 2663, p. 105). In fact, the bill contained several provisions that would have reduced fractionation at Lake Traverse but would not be reflected in the ILCA for another decade or more, including restriction of inheritance to tribal members with life estates for nonmember survivors; an order of intestate succession different from the applicable state law; a method for determination of land use by life tenants and distribution of their lease income; majority (instead of 100 percent) consent to partition; and tribal power of eminent domain over fractionated interests and abandoned or unclaimed property.

29. "Seriously fractionated" in 1937 meant that one extremely fractionated allotment of 160 acres at Lake Traverse Reservation had 150 co-owners. The original allottee had died in 1891 and, by 1937, probate costs for his estate had reached $2,400 and "required more than 250 typewritten pages" (Lawson 1984, 85–86). By 1982, the number of heir co-owners of the same allotment had risen to 439 and "the lowest common denominator (LCD) used to determine fractional interests was 3,394,923,840,000" (Lawson 1984, 86).

30. At the time (1938), that is. The Indian Land Consolidation Act of 1983 contains provisions for both, as does the American Indian Probate Reform Act of 2004.

31. Sally Willett, "An Overview of Allotting and Fractionation," January 2003, p. 3. Judge Willett is a Cherokee Indian legal scholar and activist who served for nearly two decades as an administrative law judge with the BIA. Her advocacy work among Indian landowners consists largely in helping to interpret and analyze proposed legislation for its effects on the day-to-day lives of Indian landowners. For more on Judge Willett, see "On the Whip End of Someone Else's Crazy" in chapter 4.

32. Of the 50,000 questionnaires sent out as part of the study commissioned by Congress, only 9,000 (or 18 percent) were usable returns (Williams 1971, 713n18).

33. Legal reviews and congressional testimony from this period and the 1950s tell stories similar to those in Lawson's report (1984). See, for example, Gilbert and Taylor 1966; Williams 1971; H.R. Rep. no. 2503, 82d Cong., 2d sess., 1952; H.R. Rep. no. 2680, 83d Cong., 2d sess., 1954; H.R. Rep. no. 1044, 89th Cong., 1st sess., 1965; Hearings on H.R. 11113 before the Subcommittee on Indian Affairs of the House Committee on Interior and Insular Affairs, 89th Cong., 2d sess., 1966. "Since the Meriam Report," notes Ethel Williams (1971, 713), "there have been at least a dozen bills introduced in Congress to enable the Indians to halt the fractionation process, but none has been enacted."

34. I contend that the "costly Supreme Court decision" in *United States v. Mitchell* (1983), also called *Mitchell II*, was a significant motivating force for change. See discussion of Helen (Mitchell) Sanders and the Mitchell cases in chapter 3.

35. During his two terms in office, President Clinton issued a series of presidential memoranda and executive orders recognizing and detailing the responsibility of federal departments and agencies to seek tribal consultation and participation in decisions and activities that could affect American Native people, reservation properties, and access to resources guaranteed in the treaties. For cultural resources, the resulting consultation process, or section 106 review, has already grown into an unwieldy bureaucracy, requiring extensive training to gain mastery over its myriad rules. It is also the subject of much consternation among, for example, tribal archaeologists who must respond "in a timely fashion" to consultation requests. If they do not respond in the allotted time, the requesting agency is considered to have fulfilled its section 106 responsibility. According to one severely overworked tribal archaeologist, the sheer number of requests received per month thus makes consultation a farce. Abuse of the consultation process also affects Indian people working within federal agencies. For example, one Native archaeologist working for the Forest Service told me in November 2002 of being approached by agency officials who wanted to discuss proposals with him and then call it "consultation." "Whenever someone asks me what I think of a project," he said, "I tell them that whatever I have to say is just my opinion—they can't call it 'consultation' just because I'm an Indian. I'm not the Tribe, damn it!"

36. Point 10.B. of the American Indian Movement's 1972 "Trail of Broken Treaties 20-Point Position Paper—An Indian Manifesto" reflects the creative and cautious concern being brought to this issue during the revolutionary period leading up to the modern "Wounded Knee." Manifesto author and longtime Native rights activist Hank Adams would write:"For example, the 13.5 million acres of multiple and fractionated heirship lands should not represent a collective denial of beneficial ownership and interests of inheriting individuals, but be considered for plans of collective and consolidated use. (The alternatives and complexities of this subject and its discussion require the issuance of a separate essay at a later date.)." See AIM Web site, at http://www.aimovement.org/archives/. For more on the manifesto and the important work of its author, Hank Adams, see Deloria 1974/1985.

37. According to the 1992 H.R. Report 102-499, p. 2: "Scores of reports over the years by the Interior Department's inspector general, the U.S. General Accounting Office, the Office of Management and Budget, and others have documented significant, habitual problems in BIA's ability to fully and accurately account for trust fund moneys, to properly discharge its fiduciary responsibilities, and to prudently manage the trust funds." The report goes on

to cite GAO audits from 1928, 1952, 1955, and 1982, all of which found essentially the same deficiencies including "disbursements of individual Indian moneys without adequate support, deficiencies in accounting for cash and bonds and in the computation and distribution of interest income, and other weaknesses in internal procedures" (p. 9, citing GAO audit B-114868, November 1955, p. 1).

38. Judge Sally Willett to Kristin T. Ruppel, May 16, 2001.

39. Judge Sally Willett, "An Overview of Allotting and Fractionation," January 2003, p. 3.

40. Judge Sally Willett, "An Overview of Allotting and Fractionation," January 2003. Evidence of Judge Willett's assertion is borne out, most recently, in the Interior Department's ongoing and expensive obstruction of congressionally and court ordered reform of the Indian trust (see discussion of Cobell case in "Individual Indian Money" later in this chapter).

41. "Real property" refers to possessions that are considered permanent and relatively immovable, such as land, buildings, and other "permanent attachments to the land." It is distinguished from "personal property," which refers to movable possessions, such as a vehicle or money in a private checking account. *Gilbert Law Dictionary.*

42. Judge Sally Willett, "An Overview of Allotting and Fractionation," January 2003, p.3.

43. "Restricted lands" are any lands (whether held in trust or fee simple) that have government-imposed restrictions on their use, disposition, or both.

44. Most of the inheritance provisions of the American Indian Probate Reform Act of 2004 became effective June 20, 2006. As of the date of this writing, the real concern among Indian landowners is over proposed regulations implementing the act, and changes to current regulations "in the areas of land acquisitions; leasing; grazing; minerals and energy; rights-of-way; and trust fund accounting and appeals" (*Federal Register* 72, no. 236 [December 10, 2007]: 69860, found online at http://vlex.com/vid/37824856/).

45. Descriptions such as Schmid's—of generalized Indian tribes stereotypically "roaming over territory" and, it is to be assumed, not "really" owning it—have been roundly criticized in anthropological and Indian legal scholarship for decades (see, for example, Fey and McNickle 1959; Cohen 1960; Deloria 1969/1988; Jennings 1975; Berkhofer 1978; Limerick 1987; Wilkinson 1987). However, as the Schmid example illustrates and as Jo Carrillo argues in her discussion of the role of "disabling certitudes" in legal pedagogy, the "symbolic Indian" remains to this day an unexamined "node in the network of a continuous discourse in law about familiar binaries such as the superiority of liberalism over tribalism, of private property over communal property, of the agricultural use of land over other uses" (Carrillo 2002, 37).

46. Indeed, in this instance, Schmid (1989) seems to be a product of the very pedagogical tradition condemned by Carrillo (2002, 42), in which "a student segueing in a property casebook from [uncritical analyses of] *Johnson v. M'Intosh* to economic arguments about productivity [. . .] is primed for what is often (predictably) the next lesson in the property casebook: learning that indigenous rights are presumably only occupancy rights, and accepting that any and all of the violence that flowed from the U.S. dispossession of indigenous communities was a (necessary) cost of both nation-building and the efficient (agricultural) use of land" (citations omitted).

47. A number of Indian law scholars, historians, and advocates have pointed out that there is no constitutional basis for the absolutist version of congressional "plenary power." Frank Pommersheim (1997) suggests that the Constitution should be amended, not to

provide a textual basis for Congress's assumption of plenary power over tribes, but to clarify the federal-Indian relationship. Robert Clinton (2002, 258) argues that, while this might resolve "technical legal defects" regarding the scope of federal authority over tribes, the only way to return constitutional legitimacy to the federal-Indian relationship is to reinstitute a "treaty-like process" that would conform to "America's basic commitments to constitutional delegation of authority by those governed."

Cases exemplifying these two lines are, respectively, *Lone Wolf v. Hitchcock* (1903) and *Shoshone Tribe v. United States* (1937). See Schmid 1989, 749n95, 750n97 for other cases along the same lines. See also Frickey 1990, 1138; Smith 1997, 6, on the cyclic and reactive nature of American citizenship policies in general, and on the "none too coherent compromises" that emerge from an American civic ideology that Rogers Smith asserts is a blend of "liberal, democratic republican, and inegalitarian ascriptive elements in various combinations designed to be politically popular." But see Honig 2001, 11–12, for cogent criticism of Smith's argument as a thesis that "works to direct our critical scrutiny away from the object being defended (in this case, liberal values and institutions), while encouraging a demonizing attitude toward the objects of critique (in this case, more explicitly ascriptive forms of life)."

48. The "consultation" process, newly codified under the Clinton administration, is the subject of ongoing criticism and intense elaboration. Indian landowners rarely feel that they have been "consulted." Not only are they not asked to participate in the drafting of proposed legislation; they are expected to respond to proposed policy changes without being given the time they feel they need to do so thoughtfully and intelligently. See discussion and landowners' congressional testimonies below.

49. A similar, and related, disconnection appears in legal reviews of the Supreme Court's decisions in the ILCA cases. With few exceptions, law scholars (unlike landowners) have tended to read the Court's rejection of the escheat provision and its concomitant protection of the constitutional rights of individuals as economically shortsighted at best, assimilationist at worst (see discussion below).

50. Ernestine "Ernee" Broncho Werelus, Fort Hall Indian Reservation, Idaho, December 2000.

51. Lynn Trozzo, "Notes from the Editor's Desk," *Federal Indian Probate Post* 2, no. 3 (May–June 2000): 3. The *Federal Indian Probate Post* (FIPP) is a desktop-published bulletin whose mission is to "serve Indian heirs and allottees, assist all agencies and tribal governments, and advance the probate process into a fairly efficient system."

52. The majority based its judgment on a takings argument. The argument of Justices John Paul Stevens and Byron White hinged, instead, on the "unwarned impact of the statute on an individual Indian who wants to leave his property to his children" as a due process violation (*Hodel v. Irving*, 481 U.S. 704, 726 [1987]).

53. The original section 207 of the ILCA reads: "No undivided fractional interest in any tract of trust or restricted land within a tribe's reservation or otherwise subjected to a tribe's jurisdiction shall [descend] by intestacy or devise but shall escheat to that tribe if such interest represents 2 per centum or less of the total acreage in such tract and has earned to its owner less than $100 in the preceding year before it is due to escheat" (96 U.S. *Statutes at Large* 2519). "Descent" is defined, legally, as "the transfer of real estate by inheritance and

the operation of law, not by will," whereas "devise" is defined as "a gift by will" (*Gilbert Law Summaries Law Dictionary*).

54. Section 207 as amended can be found in Public Law 101–644, sec. 301, 104 *U.S. Statutes at Large* 4666–4667. It is also reprinted and discussed in detail in *Babbitt v. Youpee*, 519 U.S. 234, 241 (1997).

55. In court case designations, the name of the plaintiff, appellant, or petitioner always comes first; that of the defendant, appellee, or respondent always comes second. Thus the order of parties named in a suit reverses when the party against whom it is brought appeals the decision, as in the case of *Youpee v. Babbitt*, 67 F.3d 200 (9th Cir.; 1995), which, on appeal, became *Babbitt v. Youpee*, 519 U.S. 234 (1997).

56. In his dissent, however, Justice Stevens at least partly understood the pragmatics at issue in the application of Indian law: "During [the more than seven years between the enactment of section 207 and Mr. Youpee's death in 1990] Mr. Youpee could have realized the value of his fractional interests in a variety of ways. [. . .] I assume that he failed to do so because he was not aware of the requirements of §207. This loss is unfortunate. But I believe that Mr. Youpee's failure to pass on his property is the product of inadequate legal advice rather than an unconstitutional defect in the statute" (*Babbitt v. Youpee*, 247).

57. "Testamentary freedom" is defined as "the ability to designate what property will be transferred and to whom" upon one's death (Guzman 2000, 635). Katheleen Guzman notes that, in the case of Irving, the Court "boldly flirts" with grounding testamentary freedom in the Constitution "by recognizing its tradition within Anglo-American jurisprudence and characterizing it as an extraordinarily valuable right over which restraint must be carefully exercised" (636). See *Hodel v. Irving*, 715–716.

58. A common legal metaphor for rights in property is the bundle of sticks, where every stick represents a different right. In *Hodel v. Irving*, the Court saw that because federal trusteeship had already taken the right of disposal (alienation), ILCA's abrogation of the rights of devise (will) and descent (inheritance) constituted a more serious infringement than it would have if levied against the rights "bundle" of a non-Indian, whose right of disposal is assumed to be intact (that is, the government does not hold land in trust for non-Indians).

59. In each of these works, criticism of the ILCA reflects an awareness of its practical effects on individual Indian landowners. Mark Welliver's description (2002) of his own family's allotments is especially compelling in this regard, as is Katheleen Guzman's excellent and ethnographically informed treatment (2000).

60. See also Thompson 1997, 309, where the Court is seen as sending "a strong, clear message to Congress that Native American property rights are to be respected and protected"; and Schwab 1998, 823, where forced escheat is seen as taking "from Native Americans to solve a problem created by the government."

61. See, for example, Chester 1995, 1198, where the Court holdings are seen as "strange and defiant" departures from traditional takings jurisprudence; Heller 1998, 687, where the Court is seen as perpetuating a "tragedy of the allotment anti-commons" by protecting fragmentary ownership interests, and Heller 1999, 1222, where it is seen to do so by undercutting the "economic goals of a private property regime." See also Tsosie 1997, 37, where the *Irving* Court is noted as having sacrificed group property claims to Anglo-American private property norms.

62. Again, it is Justices Stevens and White in their concurring opinion to the *Irving* ruling who point out the potential for conflict of interest between tribal members and tribal government, although their rendering of where the conflict may lie depends, of course, on the tribe in question: "The [escheat] statute takes the disposition of decedent's fractional land interests out of control of the decedent's will or the laws of intestate succession; whether the United States or the tribe retains the property, the landowner's loss is the same. The designation of the tribe as beneficiary is an essential feature, however [. . .] Since the tribe is the beneficiary, its own interests must conflict with its duty to bring the workings of the statute to the attention of the property owner" (*Hodel v. Irving*, 481 U.S. 704, 727 [1987]). The point is, the justices recognize at least that the tribe and tribal members (whether individually or collectively) may have divergent interests, and that the tribe is not the same as the tribal collectivity.

63. "Post–Indian Reorganization Act of 1934" refers to the administrative and bureaucratic constitutional traditions deployed among tribes that agreed to be "organized" under IRA forms of government after 1934. Not all tribes agreed to IRA provisions, and even those that did usually retained some form of traditional tribal (sometimes called a "cultural") council alongside the "organized" government. At Fort Hall, for example, the tribal council takes its authority from the IRA but also from a "general council" of the voting tribal membership. It also receives advice from a "cultural council" of respected elders.

There is also no discussion in Clinton 2002 of the fact that the Indian Land Consolidation Act deployed, to put it mildly, an idiosyncratic form of escheat (as discussed above).

64. Michael Heller (1998, 678) describes the emergence of anti-commons property "both in [post-socialist] transition and in developed market economies, whenever governments define new property rights." He defines "anti-commons property" as a "property regime in which multiple owners hold effective rights of exclusion in a scarce resource" (668); and he locates anti-commons property in a triumvirate of property relations that includes commons property (in which multiple owners hold privileges of inclusion) and private property (in which one owner holds a bundle of rights in an object such that he or she can exclude all others from its use; 668–673). In a concluding footnote, Heller speculates that because "the government might have created a legal regime that inadvertently preserves Native American conceptions of trusteeship over nature, not ownership, use, and exploitation, [. . .] the idea of 'underuse' may assume the values of a pre-existing market economy," and therefore "need not be viewed as tragic" (687n319).

In a follow-up article, Heller (1999, 1223) seems to take up this possibility again by concluding with a challenge to the Court that "if protecting fragments serves competing values, then the Court should make these values explicit and confront the tradeoffs they engender."

65. For example, as part of a running tragicomedy of landowner advocacy, Indian probate expert and former administrative law judge Sally Willett provides allottees with a sample of a "Plain Language Indian Will." See end of "Staying Power" in chapter 5.

66. For example, at Colville Reservation in Washington State, lease terms were so inequitable that landowners finally revolted, refusing to lease their land at all and letting it lie fallow until the non-Indian lessors agreed to pay fair lease rates.

67. Ross Racine's 1999 testimony before the Senate Committee on Indian Affairs is especially instructive with regard to Heller's contention. That is, "underutilization" does not

necessarily mean "lying fallow": "Under existing administration, which is generally limited to open market leasing of surface and sub-surface estates, fractionated lands are not and cannot be developed to their potential. Most remain in an undeveloped, grazing state, which generates the least possible return to the landowners, and does nothing to improve the equity in the land. There is a strong economic disincentive for lessees to develop these lands because they cannot retain ownership of the improvements and the lease cost will increase in subsequent years under the current management. Best case economic management for a lessee is to conduct the absolute minimum maintenance required by the terms of the lease, in order to avoid attracting competition during the next open market bidding process" (Testimony of the Intertribal Agriculture Council before the U.S. Senate Committee on Indian Affairs S. 1586, *Indian Land Consolidation Act Amendments of 1999*, p. 8).

68. Jessica Shoemaker (2003) echoes Guzman's concerns in passing, citing Guzman 2000.

69. Empowering allottees to overcome these hurdles is the primary preoccupation of grassroots landowner advocates, as we will see in chapters 3 and 4.

70. The "experimental" nature of federal Indian policy is especially apparent in allotment (which Congress tried to "fix" with the Indian Reorganization Act), and termination (which Congress tried to "fix" by reinstating many of the terminated tribes), to name just two of the grander episodes of federal experimentation with Indian peoples' lives. ILCA's 2 percent provision is just one of the more recent examples, as Supreme Court Justices Stevens and White bluntly observed in their concurring opinion in *Hodel v. Irving*: "An examination of the circumstances surrounding Congress's enactment of 207 discloses the abruptness and lack of explanation with which Congress added the escheat section to the other provisions of the Indian Land Consolidation Act that it enacted in 1983. When the Senate bill was considered by the House Committee on Indian Affairs, the Committee [. . .] added 207—the escheat provision at issue in this case—to the bill. [legal citation omitted] The Report on the House Amendments does not specifically discuss 207. The House returned the amended bill to the Senate, which accepted the House addition without hearings and without any floor discussion of 207. The text of the Act does not explain why Congress omitted a grace period for consolidation of fractional interests that were to escheat to the tribe pursuant to that section. The statute was signed into law [. . .] and became effective immediately. [. . .]" (*Hodel v. Irving*, 481 U.S. 704, 720–722 [1987]).

71. Judge Sally Willett, "An Overview of Allotting and Fractionation," January 2003, p. 3.

72. Delmar "Poncho" Bigby, chairman of the Indian Land Working Group, testimony before the U.S. Senate Committee on Indian Affairs on S. 1586, *Indian Land Consolidation Act Amendments of 1999*, p. 2. Bigby was chairman of the Indian Land Working Group from 1999 to 2002. He succumbed to cancer, after a long fight, in April 2003.

73. Judge Sally Willett, "An Overview of Allotting and Fractionation," January 2003, p. 3.

74. Delmar "Poncho" Bigby, *Indian Land Consolidation Act Amendments of 1999*, p. 4.

75. Austin Nuñez, chairman of the Indian Land Working Group and chairman of the San Xavier District of the Tohono O'odham Nation, testimony before the Senate Committee on Indian Affairs on S. 1340, a bill to amend the Indian Land Consolidation Act, May 22, 2002, p. 7.

76. Judge Sally Willett is fond of quoting humorist and fellow Cherokee Will Rogers, who was fond of saying, "If it weren't for reformers, Indians wouldn't need saving."

77. The ILCA amendments of 2000 were the product of compromise legislation (S. 1586) crafted by Department of the Interior representatives and a single staff person from the Senate Committee on Indian Affairs "with minimal input from the tribes or individual landowners" (Carmody 2002, 10).

78. Congress's amendments to the ILCA over Indian objections call to mind the Department of the Interior's fast-track promulgation of new regulations during the "heritage building" days of Secretary of the Interior Bruce Babbitt (and President Clinton), viewed by tribes and individual landowners alike as a steamrolling process (Poncho Bigby, InterTribal Monitoring Association (ITMA) Conference, Las Vegas, Nevada, October 2000). Ironically, among the reasons conveniently cited by Interior for its fast-track approach were the reforms demanded in ongoing *Cobell* litigation, as well as timely incidentals, such as an order issued by an Idaho District Court requiring Interior to promulgate long-overdue regulations in regard to an Indian land trespass case brought by the Fort Hall Landowners Alliance. See chapter 4.

79. Helen Sanders, Portland, Oregon, June 2002.

80. The original (1983 and 1984) versions of the Indian Land Consolidation Act defined as "Indian" anyone for whom the United States holds land in trust, and anyone who could demonstrate Indian blood. The ILCA as amended in 2000 defined as "Indian" the members of federally recognized tribes, persons eligible for enrollment in federally recognized tribes, or any person who has been found to meet such a definition under a provision of federal law that is consistent with the purposes of the ILCA. Judge Willett points out that there are no other general federal provisions dealing with the consolidation of Indian land. And Indian Land Working Group Director Theresa Carmody, in her report to the First Nations Development Institute in April 2002, notes that the new definition (as interpreted in BIA training guides) excludes other federal definitions of Indian, such as those contained in the Indian Reorganization Act or the Indian Child Welfare Act. Thus the interpretation excludes "persons with multiple tribal ancestors who are not enrolled or eligible to be enrolled at any one tribe, even though they have Indian lineage from several different tribes. It also excluded heirs who are from non-federally recognized tribes and terminated tribes" (p. 11).

81. John Sledd is a longtime advocate for individual Indian landowners. In 2004, he received the Pierce-Hickerson Award from the National Legal Aid and Defenders Association, for outstanding contributions to the protection of Native American rights.

82. The bills were S. 1340 (summer 2001), S. 550 (spring 2003), and S. 1721 (fall 2003), all introduced by Senator Ben Nighthorse Campbell. For a concise and insightful commentary on the legislative history of the American Indian Probate Reform Act, see Sledd 2005.

83. This information was gleaned from videotaped presentations given by administrative law judges Patricia McDonald-Dan and James Yellowtail, both of whom were employed by the Department of the Interior's Office of Hearings and Appeals. The presentations were given at a symposium I organized at Montana State University, called "Inheriting Indian Land: Indian Land Tenure in the Wake of the American Indian Probate Reform Act." Copies of the videotaped presentations are available at www.montana.edu/indianland/ and through the Montana State Bar. I've heard similar comments by Judge Sally Willett (see chapter 3) and others.

84. In a footnote, Sledd records the following: "Senator Campbell asked DOI for such facts as the typical number and range of owners per parcel, and the typical and range of share sizes in different areas. DOI attempted a response, but felt so insecure about the quality of its data that the information was never released. [. . .]"(Sledd 2005, 16n8).

85. Originally *Cobell v. Babbitt* (1996), then *Cobell v. Norton* (2001), then *Cobell v. Kempthorne* (2006). Bruce Babbitt was secretary of interior under President Clinton; until she resigned in 2006 and was replaced by Dirk Kempthorne, Gale Norton was secretary of interior under President Bush. Eloise Cobell is a member of the Blackfeet Tribe in Montana, where she was instrumental in starting the first American Indian–owned bank on a reservation, for which she received a MacArthur "genius grant."

86. In fact, because many records have been lost or destroyed by the Department of the Interior, the number of account holders is unknown. The plaintiffs insist that the number of account holders they represent is greater than 500,000.

87. In *Cobell v. Norton*, 334 F.3d 1128 (D.C. Cir. 2003), the Court of Appeals vacated the contempt citations against Secretary Norton and her Assistant Secretary Neal McCaleb on a technicality.

88. Austin Nuñez, testimony before the Senate Committee on Indian Affairs on S. 550, May 7, 2003, p. 108.

89. Reply brief was in response to Trustee-Delegates' brief in opposition to Plaintiff-Beneficiaries' petition for U.S. Supreme Court review of the removal of Judge Lamberth. Available at http://www.indiantrust.com/_pdfs/20070305ReplyreReassignment.pdf/.

90. A copy of the letter and "Key Facets of Acceptable Indian Trust Reform and Settlement Legislation" can be found online, at http://indian.senate.gov/public/_files/letterfromkempthorne.pdf/.

91. Statement of Alberto R. Gonzales, attorney general of the United States, before the U.S. House of Representatives, Committee on Appropriations, Subcommittee on Science, the Departments of State, Justice, and Commerce, and Related Agencies, March 1, 2005.

Chapter 3. Ambivalent Allottees

1. My computer's English-language thesaurus lists the following synonyms of "ambivalent": "unsure," "undecided," "in two minds," "of two minds," "hesitant." The antonym given is "decisive," whose synonyms, in turn, include "strong-minded," "clear-thinking," "resolute," "earnest," "positive," "determined." The implied association of weakness with "ambivalence" is noteworthy in its blatant value-laden-ness.

2. *Oxford English Dictionary*, Compact Edition, Supplement.

3. The "social purposes of production" identified by Marx are "use value" and "exchange value" (see Cohen 2000, 80–81). To these, we can usefully add a third: "sentimental value." If, as in Peircean thought, "sentiments" are differentiated from "emotions," and understood as a "stable system of emotional attitudes, [or] fundamental values which govern the instinctive responses which guide [our] reasoning and inquiries" (Hookway 2000, 241), then "sentimental value" refers to the viscerally felt attitudes that tell us—at the affective level—whether something is "good" or "bad," thereby eliciting emotional responses like attraction or revulsion that, in turn, motivate actions. Sentimental value is thus a culturally

imbued gut reaction that helps to align production — use and exchange values — with societal norms. If societal norms are primarily capitalist in both principle and mentality (cf. Cohen 2000, 300–301), then sentimental value gets subordinated, like use value, to the insatiable demands of exchange value. In capitalist production, endlessly increasing productive activity is assessed only in "terms of its extrinsic value," that is, in terms of its ability to increase exchange value: "Its meaning for the producer is irrelevant" (Cohen 2000, 311). If, on the other hand, societal norms are something other than capitalist in either principle or mentality, then sentimental and use values can emerge in their endless variety.

4. Helen Sanders, Chehalis Indian Reservation, Washington, May 2002.

5. I am referring to tribes "organized" under the Indian Reorganization Act of 1934 (IRA). My fieldwork did not address whether such tribes are more or less receptive to the concerns of individual tribal members than tribes not so organized.

6. The presence of tribal interests in an undivided allotment should protect all of the interests from condemnation. As Ernee Werelus puts it: "A tribe's undivided interest in an allotment is like a drop of dye in a pool of water; it colors the whole pool."

7. For example, Elmer Rusco (2000, 56) writes: "When the proposal that became the IRA was sent to Congress, some of the strongest opponents were Indians who objected to the sections designed to end the issuance of allotments and return allotted lands to the control of Indian governments."

8. Delmar "Poncho" Bigby, InterTribal Monitoring Association Conference, Las Vegas, Nevada, November 2000.

9. That is, two families with interests in each other's allotments might agree to exchange interests in order to consolidate their respective ownership rights in a particular allotment, without actually reducing the total number of owners. Under such an arrangement, however, land use decisions would (at least theoretically) become less problematic.

10. Examples of such regulatory provisions include the 2 percent escheat rule (twice struck down as unconstitutional) and, more recently, the intestate joint tenancy provision (P.L. 106-462, 25 *U.S. Code*, sec 2206(c)) of the Indian Land Consolidation Act (ILCA) as amended in 2000; and the single heir and forced-sale rules for interests of less than 5 percent (P.L. 108-374, 25 *U.S. Code*, sec. 2206[a][2][D][iii] and sec. 2206[o][5][A]) of the American Indian Probate Reform Act of 2004 (AIPRA). See discussion under "Negotiation" in chapter 4.

11. Indian Land Working Group (ILWG) Inventory (Carmody 2001, I-47). Information on the Tribal Land Enterprise (TLE) was also gleaned from writings of the past executive director of the organization, Ben Black Bear (Ben Black Bear to Senator Ben Nighthorse Campbell, November 4, 1999, letter supplementing oral testimony before the Senate Committee on Indian Affairs on S. 1586).

12. In his November 4, 1999, letter to Senator Ben Nighthorse Campbell (urging the Indian Affairs Committee to find "alternative ways to deal fairly with owners of fractionated heirship interests [by] roll[ing] up its sleeves and work[ing] with tribes"), Ben Black Bear wrote: "Between November 1996 and October 1999, Tribal Land Enterprise assisted the Rosebud Sioux Tribe, in 841 transactions, acquire 9,335.19 acres of trust and restricted land. Four hundred eighty-nine (58 percent) of those transactions involved interests in heirship land of 2 percent or less. Yet, the value of those 2 percent or less acquisitions was $76,968.21, five percent of $1,674,478.97 in total trust land purchases during that period. Tribal Land

Enterprise now purchases between $40,000 and $70,000 in fractionated heirship interests per month."

13. Theresa Carmody, telephone interview, July 2007.

14. Fern Bordeaux, Carlton, Minnesota, October 2001.

15. Helen Sanders, Carlton, Minnesota, October 2001.

16. Ernee Werelus, telephone conversation, July 2007. For examples of Indian-owned banks and revolving loan funds, see the Rural Development and Finance Corporation Web site, at http://www.rdfc.org/mnadfi_members.htm/.

17. Ben Black Bear to Senator Ben Nighthorse Campbell, November 4, 1999, letter supplementing oral testimony before the Senate Committee on Indian Affairs on S. 1586.

18. The two Supreme Court cases, *United States v. Mitchell* (1980) and *United States v. Mitchell* (1983), referred to in the legal scholarly literature as *Mitchell I* and *Mitchell II*, are described below. Helen Sanders's married name at the time of the lawsuits was Mitchell.

19. Helen Sanders, Pendleton, Oregon, October 2000. The history, progress, and products of the Indian Land Consolidation Symposia and their founding advocacy organization, the Indian Land Working Group, are discussed in chapters 4 and 5.

20. The National Congress of American Indians is the largest and oldest of the national intertribal associations.

21. Helen Sanders, Eleventh Annual Indian Land Consolidation Symposium, Carlton, Minnesota, October 2001.

22. The Quinault Indian Reservation, initially established at 10,000 acres under the 1855–56 Treaty of Olympia, eventually "consolidated" eight "fish-eating" tribes on 220,000 acres of dense timber under President Grant's 1873 executive order. The original "affiliated" tribes are the Quinault, Quileute, Chinook, Cowlitz, Chehalis, Quit (Queet), and Ozette (Makah). Later arrangements provided separate reservations for the Quileute, the Chehalis, and the Makah, but under special legislation all of the affiliated tribes were allowed to apply for allotments on the much larger, timber-rich but living site–poor Quinault Reservation. The Office of Indian Affairs had discontinued allotment at Quinault in 1912. Its chief supervisor of forests, J. P. Kinney, argued strenuously that Indian timberlands could not be properly managed "for forest production and slope protection" if divided among individuals (Kinney 1927, 431; Professor Alan McQuillan, personal communication, July 2007). In an instance of early allottee activism, it was Quileute tribal member Thomas Payne's lawsuit that resulted in a Supreme Court decision forcing the Office of Indian Affairs to resume allotment at Quinault (*United States v. Payne*, 264 U.S. 446 [1924]). In light of the *Mitchell* decisions described later in this chapter, it is ironic that both J. P. Kinney (1937, 267–268) and Janet McDonnell (1991, 12) focus upon the disparity in the values of individual landholdings as a result of the *Payne* case, and not on the equally (if not more) serious problem of landless and (with fractionation) virtually landless Indians.

23. Helen Sanders, Lake Quinault Lodge, Washington, June 2002.

24. The other common arbiter of tribal membership is blood quantum. About two-thirds of federally recognized tribes followed federal urgings and use blood quantum as a criterion for tribal membership.

25. The Quinault and Quileute were the only signatories to the 1855–1856 Treaty of Olympia and, although post-treaty language (executive order of 1873) provides for the "other

tribes of fish-eating Indians of the Pacific Coast" on the Quinault Reservation, several law-
suits attest to the divisive relations between the Quinault Tribe and the other seven tribes.
See *United States v. Payne* (1924); *Halbert v. United States* (1931); *Quinaielt Tribe v. United
States* (1945); *Wahkiakum Band of Chinook Indians v. Bateman* (9th Circ. 1981). See also
Dennis Whittlesey's "History of the Quinault Reservation."

26. Helen Sanders, Portland, Oregon, June 2002.

27. Helen Sanders, Portland, Oregon, June 2002.

28. Alan Graham McQuillan to Kristin T. Ruppel, July 6, 2007. Professor McQuillan
was an expert witness during the *Mitchell* trials. He has also been an expert witness in the
Individual Indian Money (*Cobell*) case. He says that an estimated 5 percent of the billions
of dollars of Indian money lost or left uncollected by the BIA comes from the sale of timber
on Indian trust lands.

29. U.S. Department of the Interior, Bureau of Indian Affairs, timber contract no. I-101-
IND-1766 (341), executed September 26, 1960.

30. Alan Graham McQuillan, telephone interview, July 2003.

31. By today's standards, the BIA's 1916 "cruise" (timber estimate) significantly underestimated the amount of timber at Quinault by counting only certain species and, of those,
only trees that could produce logs of 12-inch minimum diameter at the small end. Given
mill technologies of the day, the 1916 cruise represented common practice, and, according
to McQuillan, was characteristic of the first inventories done by the Indian Service under
J. P. Kinney. "The problem," says McQuillan, "was that, although the 1916 cruise was known
to be largely underestimated (because Quinault timber sales of the 1930s had cut out at much
higher volumes) the BIA nonetheless used the 1916 cruise, unadjusted, as the basis for the
huge Taholah and Crane Creek sales in 1948 and '50." "Re-cruises," continues McQuillan,
"weren't done until 1950s, the 1960s at Quinault" (telephone interview, July 2003; McQuillan to Ruppel, July 6, 2007).

According to McQuillan, the value of timber as well as the costs of logging were based
on industry averages. "But the client is not average," he exclaims, "he's the guy who is willing
to pay the most!" (Or to build a road for the least.) "Which is why you expect competitive
bidding to raise the price above the appraised price (which is based on averages)." "So," he
continues, "say you estimate that it's going to cost a million dollars to build a road and pull
off an estimated million board feet of timber: that's a dollar per board foot that the contractor
is going to subtract from the gross value of the timber. But, say there's actually two million
board feet of timber that gets cut. If you fail, as the BIA did, to reappraise the volume of
timber coming out of the forest, then the contractor ends up with twice the value, but his
costs haven't changed. He's still going to subtract a dollar per board foot even though his
actual costs per board foot are only fifty cents" (telephone interview, July 2003; McQuillan
to Ruppel, July 6, 2007).

32. A 1975 "pickup scale" inventory done by Alan McQuillan and Nelson Terry found
that between 10,000 and 15,000 board feet per acre of merchantable logs had been left on
the ground by the two logging companies. "They left more timber laying on the ground than
there is standing timber in the average forest in Montana," says McQuillan. There are two
things going on here, he explains: "(1) West Coast contracts usually included provision for
pickup scale, and the Taholah and Crane Creek contracts did. So BIA scales were supposed

to go out on the ground before the loggers moved their equipment to another unit, measure what had not been removed and charge the logger for these logs regardless of whether the logger then chose to remove the logs or not. The BIA either did pickup scale too late or underestimated the volume remaining, or (frequently) didn't do it at all. And (2) a common practice in West Coast contracts is to issue a separate salvage contract (under competitive bidding) to a salvage (especially cedar shake or shingle) contractor after termination of the primary logging contract. Thus," he concludes, "because (1) the original contractors also got the salvage rights and (2) they knew the BIA could be relied on to not do adequate pickup scale, the contractors could abuse the system by leaving logs lying on the ground and then taking the valuable cedar (that does not rot) out later at salvage prices. The logs of other species would rot and never have to be paid for. This was fine with the contractors because they left smaller logs of the non-cedar species—logs which were worth less than (a properly set) selling price because prices are always based on the average size within a grade and species" (telephone interview, July 2003; McQuillan to Ruppel, July 6, 2007).

33. Helen Sanders, Portland, Oregon, June 2002.

Two of the five panelists were Phileo Nash and Jim Officer, who would become secretary and assistant secretary of the interior, respectively.

34. Helen Sanders, Portland, Oregon, and Lake Quinault Lodge, Washington, June 2002.

35. Nelson D. Terry would later become an expert witness during *Mitchell I* (1980).

36. Helen Sanders, Lake Quinault Lodge, Washington, June 2002.

37. For example, in a report presented for the Indian Land Working Group at the Twelfth Annual Indian Land Consolidation Symposium, Albuquerque, New Mexico, November 2002, Helen wrote: "My request to log a portion of my original allotment has been denied [by the BIA]. A part was logged in 1950. The rest of 40 acres was logged in 1968, eighteen years' difference in growth. The reason stated in [the BIA's] letter is that I should wait until the trees logged in 1968 are of merchantable size. Their plan would clear-cut 40 acres at once. My plan is sustained yield management which is the law" (Item 3, ILWG Response to Legislative Considerations, Fractionation Meeting, Washington, D.C., August 14–15, 2002, p. 46 of Symposium Handbook, Day 2).

38. Even though it was superseded by the Indian Reorganization Act of 1934, the courts had decided elsewhere that the General Allotment Act of 1887 would remain "the starting point for all statutory interpretation" involving Indian trust resources (*United States v. Mitchell*, 547 [1980]).

39. The majority opinion in *Mitchell I* (1980) was delivered by Justice Thurgood Marshall, joined by Justices Potter Stewart, Harry Blackmun, Lewis Powell, and William Rehnquist. Dissenting were Justices Byron White, William Brennan, and John Paul Stevens. Chief Justice Warren Burger did not take part in the decision.

40. The allottees had invoked jurisdiction of the Court of Claims under the Tucker Act of 1887, which provides (in part) that "[t]he Court of Claims shall have jurisdiction to render judgment upon any claim against the United States founded either upon the Constitution, or any Act of Congress, or any regulation of an executive department, or upon any express or implied contract with the United States, or for liquidated or unliquidated damages in cases not sounding in tort." In *Mitchell II* (1983), the Court would go on to "resolve [the]

confusion" created by its own terminology in prior decisions "as to whether the Tucker Act constitutes a waiver of sovereign immunity." In considering the history of the Act and its amendments in the Indian Tucker Act, and after explaining how its provisions have been applied, the Court concluded that "[i]f a claim falls within the terms of the Tucker Act, the United States has presumptively consented to suit" (*United States v. Mitchell*, 463 U.S. 206, 212, 216 [1983]).

41. The *Irving* case was filed in March 1983; the Indian Land Consolidation Act was passed on January 12, 1983.

42. Before the *Mitchell* cases, there are only a handful of instances (excepting the nineteenth-century cases referred to as the Marshall Trilogy; see chapter 2) in which the Court has been asked to deliberate over the pragmatic meanings (the consequences) of the United States' trusteeship, and it has done so primarily through the language of "guardianship" and "dependency" (see Canby 2004, 38–49).

43. Congress began its regulation of timber management in 1910, when it authorized the interior secretary to sell timber on Indian lands for the benefit of allottees; regulations for the 1910 act were promulgated in "Regulations and Instructions for Officers in Charge of Forests on Indian Reservations" (1911); mismanagement of timber on Indian lands was addressed in the Indian Reorganization Act of 1934, codified at 25 *U.S. Code* 466; an act of April 30, 1964, amended the 1910 act to provide comprehensive regulations for the management of Indian timber, codified at 25 *U.S. Code* 406, 407, 466. It is interesting to note that regulations for the 1964 Act were not promulgated until 1983 (under 25 *Code of Federal Regulations*, pt. 163)—almost 20 years after the act was passed—and the same year *Mitchell II* was decided. See *United States v. Mitchell*, 463 U.S. 206, 219–222 (1983). The delay in promulgation of regulations under which a statute can be applied was also a factor in the Fort Hall case *Papse v. BIA* (U.S.D.C. Idaho, 2001); see chapter 4.

44. The majority opinion in *Mitchell II (1983)* was delivered by Justice Marshall, joined by Chief Justice Burger, and Justices Brennan, White, Blackmun, and Stevens. Dissenting were Justices Powell, Rehnquist, and O'Connor. In the ongoing *Cobell* litigation, the District Court has harkened more than once to Justice Marshall's rendering of the United States' fiduciary responsibilities in *Mitchell II*. See chapter 2.

45. Helen Sanders, Lake Quinault Lodge, Washington, June 2002.

46. The Court's use of "alleged," Alan McQuillan points out, was as it should be since the Court wasn't ruling on the case itself but, rather, on whether and under what authority the federal government can be held liable for mismanagement claims and alleged breaches of trust.

47. Helen Sanders, Lake Quinault Lodge, Washington, June 2002.

48. Statement of Helen Sanders concerning H.R. 2743 before the House Committee on Resources, July 29, 1998.

49. Walter Nevada, Fort Hall, Idaho, April 2001.

50. Ernestine "Ernee" Broncho Werelus, Fort Hall Indian Reservation, Idaho, October 2000. Ernee is referring to a right-of-way case in which she represented a number of landowners in litigation and negotiations with a utility company. The case involved the BIA's illegal agreement to renew a 50-year right-of-way to which the landowners never consented and for which they were never paid fair compensation. It took seven years to resolve the case. Fifteen

of the affected landowners passed away before seeing more than a trifling benefit from the utility company's lucrative use of their land. See chapter 5.

51. To linguists, Shoshone and Bannock both belong to the Numic branch of the Ute-Aztecan language family. They are distinct languages, however, Bannock being more closely related to Northern Paiute than to Shoshone.

52. Most of the allotments at Fort Hall were assigned between 1911 and 1916, some fifteen years before Ernee was born (Liljeblad 1972, 60).

53. The spread of sprinklers, as opposed to flood irrigation, affected the whole region of southeastern Idaho, not just Fort Hall. Elderly non-Indian residents also remember a massive shift during the 1950s. As one acquaintance from the small town of Mackay, Idaho, in the aptly named Lost River Valley, once told me: "When the hand lines [sprinkler pipes movable by hand] came in, everybody started drilling wells. They spread that water way up onto the benches where, before, even the sagebrush had trouble finding water. Now these farmers are growing alfalfa up there, but the river's drying up." The labor-intensive hand lines have now largely been replaced by the more capital-intensive wheel lines: massive, mechanized sprinkler systems that slowly roll through a field, spraying millions of gallons of water (with dissolved pesticides, herbicides, and fertilizer) as they go.

54. This farmer, a representative of a large local potato grower, later returned — twice — to the Werelus residence, each time protesting their right to reject his lease. Finally, he capitulated, agreeing to pay the rate requested.

55. As one study funded by the Department of Housing and Urban Development documented: "The total cost of producing an acre of potatoes in 1973 was approximately $500.00 (labor, fuel, pesticides, fertilizers, water, power and interest) including inflationary trends. The only added cost was an average $15.00 fixed lease rate paid to the landowner — the Indian allottee or the Tribe. Thus, one (1) acre of potatoes worth $1,700.00 gross was worth $1,185.00 net in May, 1974 ($1,700.00 - $515.00 = $1,185.00): Since the Indian owner receives only $15.00 fixed net return (the lease income) on a return to the non-Indian farmer of $1,185.00, something is amiss — unconscionably amiss — at Fort Hall" (Peterson & Associates 1976, Agriculture, p. 2).

56. U.S. Congress, Senate, Subcommittee on Indian Education of the Committee on Labor and Public Welfare, "The Education of American Indians: Field Investigation and Research Reports" (Washington, D.C,. Government Printing Office, 1969), p. 132.

57. The Fort Hall Business Council Chairman at the time the GAO report was requested was a man named Frank Papse. Twenty-three years later, Papse would become the director for the Fort Hall Landowners Alliance, and the primary plaintiff in *Papse v. BIA*. See chapter 4.

58. The refutations in the 1976 Peterson report point out the GAO's absurd and the "categorically false" claims. For example: the reservation's capital-intensive "circular sprinkler systems" (blamed by the GAO for supposedly higher power and irrigation costs) are the same "wheel lines" referred to earlier (see note 53) as having gained popularity throughout the region, not just at Fort Hall. The sandy soils that characterize the reservation's agricultural lands (and account, according to the GAO, for supposedly substandard crops) are actually preferred by farmers for growing root crops like potatoes, the most lucrative crop grown at Fort Hall. As for the supposedly higher winds suffered by the reservation, "High winds are not

unique to Fort Hall—there are no special 'High Winds' caused by Indians. Occasional high winds, especially in winter, are a meteorological and climatological fact for the entire Snake River Basin" (Peterson & Associates 1976, 12). Finally, in reference to the GAO's identification of the reservation's "heirship problems" as an intangible factor in mitigating income disparities between whites and Indians, the Peterson report points out that, as the Kennedy subcommittee also found, "the BIA solves this problem for the lessees by walking their lease application through for them [. . .] the BIA [does] the legwork for the non-Indian lessees" (13). For more on this last point, see discussion of the Freedom of Information Act and FHLA's lawsuit against the Fort Hall Agency BIA under "Proof of Suffering" in chapter 4.

59. Technically, at Fort Hall, an "elder" is anyone over the age of 55. Informally, the term also refers to those who are thought of as leaders, regardless of age.

60. The Shoshone-Bannock Tribes' Land Use Department is responsible only for management of the tribes' allotments, not for those of individual tribal members.

61. Memo on file at Fort Hall Landowners Alliance office.

62. Because of intermarriage among Indians from different tribes, many people have inherited undivided interests on more than one reservation.

63. It is the Treasury Department's responsibility to invest Individual Indian Money funds at the direction of the Interior Department. The Office of Trust Funds Management is supposed to maintain the records of individual Indian landowners, but it relies on the Treasury Department's accounting and financial management of IIM funds to reconcile its own IIM records (*Cobell v. Norton*, 240 F.3d 1081 [D.C. Cir. 2001]: Part I.B. Federal IIM Trust Responsibilities).

64. One of the many injustices noted in the *Cobell* IIM trials is the amount of money lost to landowners during this process. Writing for the D.C. Circuit Court of Appeals in 2001, Judge David Sentelle notes: "[W]hen OTFM issues a check to an IIM trust beneficiary, the amount is deducted from the relevant fund, even though the money remains in the Treasury's general account. Thus, the IIM beneficiary loses any interest that would be accrued between issuance and cashing of the check. The district court found that while 'this time lapse may be short in the private sector, it can be much longer in the IIM trust context because OTFM often has incorrect addresses for the recipients.' [*Cobell V*, 91 F. Supp. 2d at 12]" (*Cobell v. Norton*, 240 F.3d 1081 (D.C. Cir. 2001): Part I.B. Federal IIM Trust Responsibilities).

65. IIM account holders tend to "disappear," too, as Judge Sentelle notes: "The federal government does not know the precise number of IIM trust accounts that it is to administer and protect. At present, the Interior Department's system contains over 300,000 accounts covering an estimated 11 million acres, but the Department is unsure whether this is the proper number of accounts. Plaintiffs claim that the actual number of accounts is far higher, exceeding 500,000 trust accounts" (*Cobell v. Norton*, 240 F.3d 1081 [D.C. Cir. 2001]: Part I.B. Federal IIM Trust Responsibilities; legal citations omitted). See also chapter 2.

66. These kinds of statements were elicited from BIA Agency Realty officials at Fort Hall, where illegal practices unearthed by the Alliance have resulted in lawsuits, brought by FHLA against the Fort Hall Agency. Illegal practices have included: providing non-Indian farmers with confidential appraisals of Indian land before opening lease negotiations with the same farmers; basing appraisals on incomplete, inaccurate, or outdated information, or any com-

bination of these; leasing out allotments without the owners' consents; failing to advertise lease negotiations; failing to require lessees to comply with contractual obligations of their leases, including timely payments. Two of the Alliance's landmark cases are described under "Litigation" in chapter 4. Some, though by no means all of the BIA officials at Fort Hall blame the FHLA, and Ernee Werelus in particular, for the "troubles" that began to surface when the Alliance became active in fall 2000.

67. Walter Nevada, Fort Hall, April 2001. Walter is featured, among other elderly allottees, in an educational video produced during my fieldwork. The video and its production are described under "Staying Power" in chapter 5.

68. The environmental degradation associated with fractionation and the BIA's leasing practices, so evident anecdotally, has also been well documented. It includes instances of deforestation (as in *Mitchell I* [1980]); overexploitation of farm and grazing lands (one of Ernee's pet peeves: "If the farmers don't want to pay fair rates, then tell them that's fine! These fields need to rest anyway."); water pollution from agricultural runoff (of pesticides and fertilizers as well as soils); and erosion (as in the Peterson report: "There is disparity in land use and conservation practices between Indian and non-Indian lands. Sheet and gully erosion wash thousands of tons of this valuable topsoil into Fort Hall's once glimmering streams. The serious question regarding the commitment of 27,000 acres to dryland [farming] is that no substantive research has ever been conducted to assure that the depletion of the land by drylanding on fragile soils at high elevations is not irreversibly damaging to the land resource base. All available evidence indicates it is irreversibly destructive to the land" [Peterson & Associates 1976, 14]). Moreover, the high correlation of nuclear test sites, uranium mines, nuclear waste storage centers, and the like with reservations produces its own brand of environmental degradation and "ecocide," all of which is exacerbated by the poverty, disempowerment, and virtual landlessness associated with fractionation (see Grinde and Johansen 1995; Kickingbird and Ducheneaux 1973).

69. On this note, G. A. Cohen (2000, 312) writes: "The basis of the argument is the incontrovertible proposition that, *in Marxian terms*, capitalist production is production for exchange-value. Alfred P. Sloan (one-time head of General Motors) recognized [this] truth when he said that it was the business of the automobile industry to make money, not cars. That, indeed, is why it makes so many cars."

70. Blackfeet tribal member and executive director of the Intertribal Agriculture Council (located in Billings, Montana) Ross Racine illustrates this same problem, from a tribal perspective: "The ideals of a homeland wherein the Tribes continue to reign in their traditional role is completely undercut when the Tribe and its members can only react to federal nonmanagement of their dwindling assets because there are no true owners, and they cannot make direct or beneficial use of their assets" (Testimony of the Intertribal Agriculture Council before the U.S. Senate Committee on Indian Affairs on S. 1586, *Indian Land Consolidation Act Amendments of 1999*, p. 8).

71. See, for example, Tsosie 2001, 1298, and accompanying footnote, in which the Supreme Court's decision in *Hodel v. Irving* (1987) (protecting the Indian allottee's right to devise fractionated interests in land) is characterized as giving undue priority to individual property rights (to "minute fractionated heirship interests") over interests of the tribe. The *Hodel* decision is used to support the argument that, in recent jurisprudence, the Supreme

Court has tended to side with private property interests over (here conflated) common or tribal interests: the mistaken assumption being that tribes, themselves, were fully in favor of a federal mandate that unconstitutionally divested tribal members of their private property rights. Rebecca Tsosie goes on to argue that it is "important to ensure that [the Anglo-American property structure] is not being used to unfairly suppress and disregard Native peoples' interests" (1308): the implication being that those "interests" do not include the "minute" properties of individual Indian landowners. See also discussion of the *Hodel* decision under "'Serial Experiments'" in chapter 2.

72. Citations omitted. Nadasdy is quoting Richard Handler (1991, 71).

73. "The Indian [that is, the "simulated Indian"] is an occidental invention," writes Vizenor (1994, 11), "that became a bankable simulation; the word has no referent in tribal languages or cultures. The postindian is the absence of the invention [. . .] the closure of that evasive melancholy of dominance."

74. For example, Liisa Malkki (1992, 30) has argued that "it is a consequence of the nation-state's ideological need for rootedness that, in some discourses, the 'natives' are [spatially] incarcerated in primordial bioregions and thereby retrospectively recolonized."

75. On one reservation, in March 2001, a BIA staffer who tried to support allottee efforts to manage their own land (for example, by helping them gain access to their records when other staffers wouldn't, by providing allottees with material evidence of improper appraisal procedures, and the like) toned down his advocacy after being called upon by the agency superintendent to account for his activities. He later explained to me, "I'm only a few years away from retirement, you know. I can't go getting myself fired." In the Individual Indian Money (*Cobell*) case, in March 2000, a whistleblower named Mona Infield had her job scaled back to nothing—though the BIA continued to pay her $80,000 annual salary—after she filed affidavits with the *Cobell* court regarding her concerns that trust account records were being improperly handled, and that the Interior Department's new Trust Asset and Accounting Management System (TAAMS) didn't work. On the BIA's self-perpetuating bureaucratic structure, see, for example, Nickeson 1976; Prucha 1984, 250–251; Biolsi 1992, 176–181.

76. Case in point: an illegal sharecropping arrangement at Fort Hall, where the non-Indian farmer and longtime lessee John McNabb was receiving a federal subsidy that totaled more than $2 million in "wheat deficiency payments" (calculated per bushel) through the Farm Service Agency while paying Indian landowners just $15 per acre for the use of their land. When the state Farm Service Agency (FSA) discovered in 1995 that the Fort Hall Agency had no record of its subsidy payments to McNabb, state FSA Director Dick Rush cancelled further payments to McNabb and ordered an investigation. A 1992 letter from a Fort Hall Realty officer to the FSA revealed the BIA's and McNabb's rationale for paying pittance sums to landowners while McNabb received the federal subsidy: "We have been paying a $15 per acre rate to the landowners, since they have been *used to* receiving this amount under the previous program" (emphasis added).

77. In an analogous example, Richard Perry (2002, 140) notes that, in Canada, "what is most instructive [. . .] is what is not necessarily legally distinctive to Native peoples, for [Canada's new Inuit indigenous territory of Nunavut] came into being as the outcome of a Native reappropriation or re-envisioning of the foundation myths of federalism and majority rule."

Chapter 4. Continuance

1. Judge Sally Willett, "Identity Crisis in Indian Country," unpublished essay presented at the Oklahoma Supreme Court Sovereignty Symposium, Oklahoma City, March 2003, p. 6.

2. The Federation of Southern Cooperatives has a 35-year history of helping low-income black families develop cooperatives and credit unions, protect and expand landholdings, and advocate for public policies that benefit black and other small farmers and rural communities. The federation merged with the Emergency Land Fund in 1985 to form the Federation of Southern Cooperatives / Land Assistance Fund. The new organization provides comprehensive legal, educational, and financial support for black landowners and other rural smallholders. It also acquires land for development into agricultural cooperatives. See its Web site, at http://www.federationsoutherncoop.com/.

3. "Landowners Association Meet Land Officials," *Sho-Ban News* (Fort Hall, Idaho), February 7, 1997, 8.

4. Gus, also known as Alvin James, is a Paiute from the Pyramid Lake Reservation in western Nevada. He has served in tribal government and in BIA realty services for Pyramid Lake. LaNada [Boyer] War Jack is a Shoshone-Bannock, has a doctor of arts in political science from Idaho State University, and is currently executive director for the Shoshone-Bannock Tribes. When I first got to know LaNada, she was serving as director of education, employment, and training at Fort Hall. She is the youngest woman to have held a council seat at Fort Hall (1976–78). And she was part of the original Native student occupation of Alcatraz Island in 1969. She remained on the island for the students' entire 19-month occupation. In 1985, Gus and LaNada worked together on contesting the Pyramid Lake Water Settlement. Gus later became the chairman of the Pyramid Lake Tribe and worked on a significantly improved water settlement for the tribe. Gus and LaNada have served on other projects together including the Youth Indian Land Symposium, sponsored by the Federation of Southern Cooperatives in Alabama and held at the James Ranch on the Pyramid Lake Reservation.

5. For the same reasons, others may find the term "minority" objectionable "because it implies a certain delegitimacy in a majoritarian system; and if one adds up all the shades of yellow, red, and brown swept over by the term, we are in fact not [minorities]" (Williams 1991, 257). Williams frequently qualifies "minorities" by using terms like "black" and "white," she explains, "in order to accentuate the unshaded monolithism of color itself as a social force" (257). For better and worse, American Indians are the only minority distinguished by the Founding Fathers in the Constitution, which sets "the Indian Tribes" on a par with "the several States" and "foreign Nations" (Article I, Section 8: the Indian commerce clause) and which excludes "Indians not taxed" from the "Enumeration" of state populations to be represented in Congress (Article I, Section 2).

6. Allotment, large reservations, and the huge expanses of mostly arid public lands managed by the Bureau of Land Management, the National Forest Service, and the National Parks Service are western phenomena. One well-known activist at a land tenure conference at Madison, Wisconsin, shocked some in his audience by calling for a "new Homestead Act" under which all of the "empty [public] land" in the West could be parceled out in

reparation to black farmers. He specifically mentioned national parks (like Yellowstone) without, apparently, realizing their significance as ceded aboriginal territories to which Indian treaty rights still apply.

7. The "Who Owns America?" Conference is hosted by the University of Wisconsin–Madison. I attended its third annual incarnation, whose focus was "Minority Land and Community Security," again in Ernee's stead, in the spring of 2001.

8. The Confederated Tribes of the Colville Indian Reservation (CTCIR) are in northern Washington. CTCIR's comprehensive Land Use Policy has been in effect since 1976, facilitating the sale and exchange of fractionated trust land interests among tribal members, and between tribal members and the tribes. In 1986, the tribes entered into a Cooperative Agreement with the BIA (under the Indian Self-Determination and Education Assistance Act of 1975), where all BIA functions—including forestry, realty, range, roads, and land operations—were to fall under the supervision of the Colville Confederated Tribes. In 1996, CTCIR entered into a self-governance "compact" with the federal government, under which it was able to gain control of the reservation's titles and records and appraisals functions from the BIA's Portland Area Office. According to an inventory of landowner organizations carried out by the Indian Land Working Group (ILWG) in 1999, when CTCIR retrieved its land title records from the Portland Area Office, "12 years' worth of documents needed updating. Since appraisals and title verification are now done locally, real estate transactions can be done within hours, instead of [the] days, weeks, or months [required by] the Portland Area Office" (Indian Land Working Group [ILWG] Inventory of Landowner Organizations, 1999, I-18, I-19). The Indian Land Working Group and related organizations are discussed in chapter 5.

9. Like the Land Retention Summit at Epes, Alabama, the "Who Owns America?" Conference at Madison, Wisconsin, concerns land tenure issues among American minorities (including some of those south of the U.S. border). Unlike the Land Retention Summit, the Madison conference is large and attended mostly by academics, although grassroots activists also attend. In comparison, the Summit at Epes is, first and foremost, a personal and impassioned gathering of people whose lives might be characterized by their struggles to gain or maintain tenure over land that is, by their own estimations, indicative and symbolic of who they *are*.

10. Basing their report on the USDA's Agricultural Economics and Land Ownership Survey of 1999 (AELOS), its 1997 Census of Agriculture, and a 1993 report from the Intertribal Agricultural Council on Indian land ownership, Jess Gilbert, Spencer Wood, and Gwen Sharp (2002) find that individual American Indians hold just 3.4 million acres of agricultural land, worth $5.3 billion, as compared to black landowners with 7.8 million acres, valued at $14.4 billion, and "Spanish-Origin" landowners with 13 million acres, worth more than $18 billion. The only "racial minority group" reported to hold less agricultural land than Native Americans is "Asians," with less than 1 million acres of the most valuable land in the United States (mostly in California and Hawaii), worth $6.9 billion. Here the authors make a critical point: that census figures for American Indian agricultural lands are highly suspect. "The 1997 Census of Agriculture [tables 17, 19 and appendix B] reports that 18,495 Indian farmers operate 52 million acres, for an average Indian farm size of 2,812 acres—almost seven times the average farm size for all U.S. farms. This measure is highly unlikely; it results from the Census's counting each reservation as a single farm. The 46 million acres on Indian

reservations is included [. . .] in the total for Indian agricultural land. Thus it is difficult to compare census of agriculture data on Indians with data on other groups, for whom individually held land is the dominant type of ownership" (Gilbert, Wood, and Sharp 2002, 58–59; cf. Lubowski et al. 2002: 35–36).

11. The Bureau of Indian Affairs estimates that 55.7 million acres are now held in the federal Indian trust, of which approximately 11 million acres are owned by individuals (see http://www.doi.gov/bureau-indian-affairs.html/; see also the U.S. Forest Service's link to and fact sheet on "Indian Nations" at http://www.fs.fed.us/people/tribal/tribexd.pdf/; cf. Frantz 1999, 39; Pevar 2004, 70; Lubowski et al. 2002, 36)

12. Interestingly, advocates of Indian land tenure insist that current levels of fractionation are still "manageable [. . .] if a concentrated effort is made to educate, facilitate, and assist individual owners and tribes to avoid further fractionation." They cite statistics from a 1992 GAO Report, identifying "34,006 parcels of fractionated Indian land on eleven reservations in Montana, South Dakota, North Dakota, and Washington. Of those parcels, 78 percent of tracts had fewer than 25 owners and 51 percent had fewer than ten owners. In the non-Indian world of real estate," they argue, "parcels of land are owned and managed by a corresponding number of individuals who personally own the land. Surely similar mechanisms can work in Indian country" (Carmody 2001, 16).

13. The landowners had proof that the Bureau of Indian Affairs had given names and addresses to the Idaho Power Company, "as evidenced by the consent to lease forms they [had] already mailed, by certified mail, to the landowners" (1998 letter from FHLA Chairman Frank Papse to BIA Superintendent Eric LaPointe, quoted in Memorandum Decision and Order of March 17, 2003 [Docket no. 219, p. 5], United States District Court for the District of Idaho, Case no. CV-99-52-E-BLW).

14. The BIA also eventually claimed Freedom of Information Act protection under 5 *U.S. Code*, sec. 552b (6), which permits withholding of information when disclosure "would constitute a clearly unwarranted invasion of personal privacy."

15. The original complaint named Secretary of the Interior Bruce Babbitt as defendant. This was later amended to include the Bureau of Indian Affairs and, in 2000, defendant Babbitt was replaced by Bush's first interior secretary, Gale Norton.

16. Memorandum Decision and Order, March 28, 2001 (Docket no. 166, p. 12), U.S.D.C. for the District of Idaho, Case no. CV-99-52-E-BLW.

17. The U.S. District Court would eventually agree, stating that neither the government's "single statement" that it would not contest the plaintiffs' claims nor the "interim relief" provided by the ILCA Amendments (nor a "guidance memorandum" issued by the BIA Portland office subsequent to the suit) were sufficient to "completely and irrevocably eradicate the effects of the alleged violation" (Memorandum Decision and Order, March 28, 2001 [Docket no. 166, p. 9], U.S.D.C. for the District of Idaho, Case no. CV-99-52-E-BLW).

18. Plaintiff's Memorandum in Support of Cross Motion for Summary Judgment, December 2000, U.S.D.C. for the District of Idaho, Case no. CV-99-52-E-BLW.

19. Complaint, February 5, 1999 (Docket no. 1, para. 47, p. 12), U.S.D.C. for the District of Idaho, Case no. CV-99-52-E-BLW.

20. This and the following quotations are taken directly from my notes of telephone conversations and e-mail correspondence with Ernee Werelus, December 2001.

21. Memorandum Decision and Order, August 20, 2002 (Docket no. 204, p. 11), U.S.D.C. for the District of Idaho, Case no. CV-99-52-E-BLW.

22. According to court records, the superintendent of Fort Hall Indian Reservation gave permission to Idaho Power Company (IPC) to construct an electrical transmission line across the Reservation in November 1942. IPC completed the line in March 1943, without receiving prior consent of the landowners, and without ever having formally applied for a right-of-way. Although the government was required by law to seek easement deeds from tribal and individual allottees, there is no evidence that it did, that individual allottees ever consented to the construction of the line across their lands, nor that they ever received any annual payments for Idaho Power Company's use of their land. Instead, as per "custom," the Fort Hall Superintendent levied estimated lump-sum damages against the power company and waived any annual rental charges. For a 50-year lease, landowners were paid a total of $628.50, or less than $13 per year, and the Shoshone-Bannock Tribes were paid $193.00. Only one individual's allotment appears to have been appraised for damage, and was assessed at $10. In 1946, the Idaho Power Company applied for and received a right-of-way more than 21 miles long and 40 feet wide across the reservation, to accommodate the electrical transmission lines it had built four years earlier (Second Amended Complaint, January 23, 2002 [Docket no. 183, pp. 8–11], U.S.D.C. for the District of Idaho, Case no. CV-99-52-E-BLW).

23. At that time, however, the government disputed two of the four requirements for finding a Privacy Act violation: namely, that the disclosure of information have an "adverse effect" on the plaintiffs, and that the disclosures be "willful and intentional" (Memorandum Decision and Order, March 28, 2001 [Docket no. 166, p. 12], U.S.D.C. for the District of Idaho, Case no. CV-99-52-E-BLW). The other two requirements are that the information disclosed be covered by the act as a "record" in a "system of records" and that the "agency" in question have in fact "disclose[d]" the information in question (5 *U.S. Code* sec. 552a[b]).

24. Memorandum Decision and Order, March 28, 2001 (Docket no. 166, p. 12), U.S.D.C. for the District of Idaho, Case no. CV-99-52-E-BLW.

25. Patricia Williams (1991, 8–9) characterizes Anglo-American jurisprudence as involving "at least three features of thought and rhetoric: (1) the hypostatization of exclusive categories and definitional polarities [such as] rights/needs, moral/immoral, public/private, white/black [;] (2) the existence of transcendent, acontextual, universal legal truths or pure procedures, [an] essentialized world view [that tends] to disparage anything that is nontranscendent (temporal, historical), or contextual (socially constructed), or nonuniversal (specific) as 'emotional,' 'literary,' 'personal,' or just Not True[; and](3) the existence of objective, 'unmediated' voices by which those transcendent, universal truths find their expression [such as] 'the courts,' 'the judge.'[. . .]"

26.In the *Mitchell* cases (1980 and 1983), even a favorable decision ended up essentially blaming Indian allottees for their own powerlessness. It is appropriate to compare the *Mitchell* and FHLA cases since *Mitchell II* is a precedent for all decisions involving breach of trust, and FHLA's Privacy Act case is no exception. See discussion of the *Mitchell* cases under "Ambivalent Judgment" on pages 84–89.

27. The feeling of having been bought off by the federal government is not confined to Indian landowners and their advocates. At the 2001 "Who Owns America?" Conference in Madison, Wisconsin, mentioned above, one panel discussion involved the class-action

lawsuit brought against the USDA (*Pigford v. Glickman*, no. 97–1978 [D.D.C. 1997]) for its discriminatory treatment of African American farmers and landowners. A plaintiff who had been intimately involved in bringing the suit responded disapprovingly to the $50,000 reparation payments to individuals. "Fifty thousand dollars is nothing," he growled. "A guy can barely buy a tractor with that. How's he supposed to farm if he's got a tractor but still can't afford to buy land? Where's his goddamn forty acres?"

28. As Felix Cohen (1942a and b) and others have labored to demonstrate, Europe's "conquest" of what would become the United States, early on, comprised international negotiation and business transactions more often than it did military operations, giving ample legal and historical precedence to the ideal of the sovereign-to-sovereign relationship between tribal and federal governments (see "From Treaties to Trust" in chapter 1). Yet "every American schoolboy is taught to believe that the lands of the United States were acquired by purchase or treaty from Britain, Spain, France, Mexico, and Russia, and that for all the continental lands so purchased we paid about 50 million dollars out of the federal treasury. As for the original Indian owners of the continent, the common impression is that we took the land from them by force and proceeded to lock them up in concentration camps called 'reservations.'

"Notwithstanding this prevailing mythology, the historic fact is that practically all of the real estate acquired by the United States since 1776 was purchased not from Napoleon or any other emperor or czar but from its original Indian owners" (Cohen 1942a, 34–35).

Cohen points out that, for example, the United States paid 15 million dollars to Napoleon for the "power to govern and tax" the lands making up the Louisiana Territory, but that it would eventually pay twenty times that amount to tribes in its effort to extinguish "Indian title" over these same lands. The point is, the myth that "the Indians lost" and must therefore capitulate to everything "American" and "join the culture" (or "the nation" or "civilization" or whatever idealization is used to legitimate domination) is as popular a fantasy now as it was in Cohen's day.

29. At the Eleventh Annual Indian Land Consolidation Symposium in Carlton, Minnesota, in October 2001, I sat with several women from different allotted reservations and wrote down a list of responses from some BIA employees—they called them "lies"—that they all had heard repeatedly as allottees. Besides the warning quoted in the main text, striking in its similarity to ones I heard while working at Fort Hall, other responses seemed common to bureaucracies in general, like "We'll have to get back to you on that," and "No problem! We'll take care of that," or the concomitant "Nope, sorry, that can't be done. It's against policy."

30. Another troubling aspect of the *Cobell* (Individual Indian Money) case is that (as of December 31, 2000) 22 percent of the accounts managed by the BIA and the Office of Trust Funds Management (OTFM) are "Whereabouts Unknown" accounts. According to Interior Department's Office of Historical Trust Accounting and the OTFM Monthly Statistics Report, more than 60,000 IIM accounts (61,673 in December 2000; 63,071 in May 2002) are listed in the name of individual Indians for whom neither the BIA nor OTFM has a current address. As of December 2000, $65.4 million had been deposited in Whereabouts Unknown accounts. Landowner advocates contend that the Interior has done little to find the owners of these monies. According to its first newsletter, *Indigenous Lands Reporter* 1, no. 1 (Spring 2003): 17, the Indian Land Working Group endorses a "diligent search" process used by the

Indian-owned and -operated firm, Val Tech & Associates. As the judge originally presiding over the *Cobell* case wrote, more generally: "There are over 300,000 IIM trust accounts on Interior's system. Interior cannot provide the exact number of IIM trust accounts that should be on this system. Plaintiffs contend that there should be approximately 500,000 IIM trust accounts. While the overall number is quite large, it is important to note that OTFM has identified 16,700 IIM trust accounts with a stated balance of below one dollar and no activity for at least eighteen months. Of course, it is a farce to say that these accounts actually contain any given amount. Although the United States freely gives out 'balances' to plaintiffs, it admits that currently these balances cannot be supported by adequate transactional documentation" (*Cobell v. Babbitt*, 91 F. Supp. 2d 15 [D.D.C. 1999]; legal citations omitted).

31. "Accidentally" because the landowners did not set out to "change the system" except inasmuch as it affected their ability to manage their own lands. They couldn't have predicted that the Bureau of Indian Affairs would so efficiently catch itself in its own manipulations of the law that its actions would resonate up through its own ranks and beyond, into the corridors of legislative power at just the right moment in history.

32. Frank Papse Sr., Fort Hall, Idaho, April 2000.

33. Howard Belodoff, Pocatello, Idaho, January 2001.

34. Information in this section was gleaned from the following sources: Title 25 *Code of Federal Regulations* Part 15, "Proposed Rules"; reports and correspondence produced by the Joint Workgroup on Trust Policies and Procedures of the National Congress of American Indians (NCAI) and the InterTribal Monitoring Association on Indian Trust Funds (ITMA); notes and interviews from the NCAI–ITMA Joint Workgroup meetings, Las Vegas, Nevada, September–October 2000, which I attended with Ernee and Steve Werelus; reports and testimony of the Indian Land Working Group (ILWG). The NCAI–ITMA Joint Workgroup was formed at the request of then Assistant Secretary of Interior Kevin Gover (former director of the BIA) specifically to review the draft and proposed regulations discussed here.

35. A fifth part, 114, "Special Deposits," was also revised for inclusion in part 115.

36. Greg Bourland, Tenth Annual Conference of the InterTribal Monitoring Association, Las Vegas, Nevada, October 2000.

37. John Dossett, Tenth Annual Conference of the InterTribal Monitoring Association, Las Vegas, Nevada, October 2000.

38. In their September 22, 2000, letter, the eighteen senators echoed the NCAI's and ITMA's argument that "the proposed regulations for leasing, grazing, and trust account management are inconsistent with the letter and spirit of a number of Federal statutes and policies including the American Indian Trust Fund Management Reform Act of 1994, the American Indian Agricultural Resources Management Act of 1993, and the President's Executive Order on Consultation and Coordination with Indian Tribal Governments (Executive Order 13084), to name a few."

39. Senator Ben Nighthorse Campbell and Senator Daniel K. Inouye to Secretary of the Interior Bruce Babbitt, September 22, 2000.

40. Judge Sally Willett to Kristin T. Ruppel, May 21, 2001.

41. Judge Sally Willett, Tenth Annual Indian Land Consolidation Symposium, Pendleton, Oregon, October 2000. The conference was hosted by the Confederated Tribes of the Umatilla Indian Reservation.

42. ICC (Indian Country Consultants) Indian Enterprises offers realty training and consulting services to tribal governments and associated federal organizations. They also provide services to private companies that conduct business with Indian tribes and the Bureau of Indian Affairs.

43. Most of Judge Willett's essays are published under a nom de guerre in the *Federal Indian Probate Post* (FIPP; see note 51, chapter 2). Her less acerbic essays are reserved for Indian Land Working Group literature, congressional testimony before the Senate Committee on Indian Affairs, and educational and training materials.

44. Judge Sally Willett to Kristin T. Ruppel, May 21, 2001.

45. Judge Sally Willett, Tenth Annual Indian Land Consolidation Symposium, Pendleton, Oregon, October 2000.

46. When I was first writing this section, the joint tenancy with right of survivorship (JTWROS) provision was awaiting certification by the secretary of the interior that the department "ha[d] the capacity, including policies and procedures, to track and manage interest in trust or restricted land held as joint tenants with the right of survivorship." Indian landowner advocates called for its repeal under S. 1340 (the Senate bill that became the Indian Probate Reform Act of 2001), and again under a resurrected version of that bill, S. 550, called the "American Indian Probate Reform Act of 2003," and yet again under another substitute bill, S. 1721, a version of which was finally accepted. On October 27, 2004, the American Indian Probate Reform Act of 2004 was signed into law, canceling the JTWROS provision—never certified because impracticable.

47. "BIA Northwest Region—ILCA Amendments—Training—April 2001."

48. *Indian Land Consolidation Symposium Handbook,* November 2002, Day 2, p. 47.

49. In fact, Judge Willett argues that she finds no instance in either state or international law in which joint tenancy with right of survivorship has been used in intestate inheritance. Thus its use in Indian probate is, she insists, simply another experiment.

50. Austin Nuñez, chairman of the Indian Land Working Group and chairman of the San Xavier District of the Tohono O'odham Nation, testimony before the Senate Committee on Indian Affairs on S. 1340, a bill to amend the Indian Land Consolidation Act, May 22, 2002.

51. According to testimony in *Cobell* litigation, the BIA's then-current system already showed a probate backlog of some 15,000 cases ("Indian Probate Reinvention Lab—Phase II, December 1999—Background"). More recent statements by Ross Swimmer, the Special Trustee for American Indians, indicate that the probate backlog is at least double that number (see Carmody n.d., 3).

52. Delmar "Poncho" Bigby, Tenth Annual Indian Land Consolidation Symposium, Pendleton, Oregon, October 2000. Poncho Bigby was chairman of the Indian Land Working Group from 1999 to 2002. He died in the spring of 2003.

53. Judge Sally Willett, *ILWG Newsletter,* Spring 2003, 11.

54. Another advocate known for his irreverent wit, David Harrison has faulted proposed fractionation legislation and regulations for, among other things, emanating out of a mistaken assumption that the fundamental historical role of the BIA was to preserve Indian assets and trust resources. To the contrary, says Harrison, the BIA's purpose was to "preside over the orderly liquidation of Indian trust estates . . . to keep records of what white guy got

what rights to what used to be ours." (Tenth Annual Indian Land Consolidation Symposium, Pendleton, Oregon, October 2000).

55. Judge Sally Willett, Tenth Annual Indian Land Consolidation Symposium, Pendleton, Oregon, October 2000.

56. Judge Sally Willett, "Special Issue: Indian Country Fires Back—'The Plots and the Plotters: A Familiar and Constant Menace to Indian Country,'" p. 14.

57. Judge Sally Willett, "The Full Court Press: Termination by Adjudication," November 2001 (draft), p. 7.

58. For example, NCAI General Counsel John Dossett held a conference call with representatives of the Allottee Association and of the Indian Land Working Group in July 2002 to discuss the concerns of individual landowners in regard to S. 1340's proposed amendments to the ILCA. The NCAI has formally stated that it supports the involvement of allottees and landowner advocates in legislative negotiations, increased education and funding for landowner education, and individual and tribal land consolidation. Nevertheless, the NCAI represents the concerns of tribal governments first and foremost, and of individual allottees only insofar as these do not conflict with tribal governance and economic interests.

59. Terms like "troublemakers" and "militants" are common currency wherever the activities of landowner associations have helped to increase lease rates and engender new-found BIA adherence to federal regulations (requiring, among other things, the advertisement of lease renewals and a competitive bidding process). In one case, an association of non-Indian farmers—leaseholders—was formed in response to the rumor that the tribe and BIA were instituting changes that would drive up land rents on the reservation. The BIA superintendent was provided with leaseholder association correspondence in which a certain BIA official was referred to as being part of a "militant faction." The superintendent's immediate response was to write a detailed letter to the leaseholder association president. He took great pains to describe the regulatory and economic reasons for the changes (rumored and otherwise), and the actions of "some of his more energetic and concerned staff members." He countered the leaseholder's use of the term "militant" with the following retort: "First of all, it is somewhat disturbing that you have referred to some of my staff as being party [to] some militant faction. I don't believe that there is anyone on my staff that has any militant involvement, and for you to use that type of language is unacceptable. Implying that there is some comparison to our review process and the actions displayed by nationally prominent extremists is grossly inaccurate."

60. And my favorite several-liner: "Two guys are seated next to each other on a small plane, one Indian and one white. The white guy is looking out the window as the plane takes off. Once the plane is in the air, he turns to the Indian, and says, 'So, do you own land down there?' The Indian says, 'Yep, 640 acres on the Rez.' The white guy sniffs, and says, 'Huh, well, it takes me all day to drive across my ranch in my pickup.' To which the Indian replies, 'Yeah, I used to have a truck just like that.'"

61. The reference, of course, is to the landmark 1983 Supreme Court ruling that recognized a federal fiduciary responsibility to Indian individuals as well as tribes, namely, *United States v. Mitchell*, 463 U.S. 206 (1983). For extended discussion of this decision, see under *Mitchell I* and *Mitchell II* in chapter 3.

62. The amended Indian Land Consolidation Act defined an "Indian" as "anyone who is a member of a tribe or is eligible to become a member of any tribe."

63. Section 509(b) of "Uniform Indian Probate Code" proposed by the Indian Land Working Group, May 7, 2003.

64. The National Congress of American Indians and congressional sponsors of the ILCA amendments insisted that the amended definition was meant to include, not exclude. As the amendments' main sponsor, Senator Ben Nighthorse Campbell, wrote in regard to S. 1340, the first in a series of bills proposing amendments to the ILCA: "The [amended] definition of 'Indian' tracks existing definitions employed in other statutes. For example, under the Indian Child Welfare Act of 1978, an unmarried person under 18 years of age is considered an 'Indian child' if he or she is 'eligible for membership in the tribe' and the biological child of a member of a tribe (25 U.S. Code, sec. [2] 1903[4]). For example, a number of tribes recognize membership based on lineal descendancy. Since these individuals are 'eligible for membership' upon their birth, they are to be treated as Indians for purposes of this Act. The definition recognizes that in many instances a person may be eligible for membership or enrollment in a tribe before official action is taken to memorialize their membership or enrollment.[. . .]" (S. Rep. 106-361).

65. I use the term "genetically" with some trepidation, simply to refer to "lineal descent" within families. Likewise, the term "real" is meant as a prod to think more deeply about the effects of its imposed relation to the "ideal." Cf. Deborah Jackson's discussion of identity, ethnicity, and community among urban and rural Anishinaabe tribal members and of the "semiotic self" as an intersubjectively felt (if not understood) process of community (e.g., family), as opposed to the "Cartesian self" as an objectively understood (if not felt) product of regulation (e.g., blood quantum; Jackson 2002, 3–18).

66. Regarding the real possibility that the redefinition of "Indian" would result in massive — and capricious — disinheritance, Sally Willett writes: "In some areas according to GAO and Interior's Heirship Task Force as many as 1/7 of the existing landowners are unenrolled. In Nevada (Western Nevada Agency) 95 percent of the landowners are listed as unenrolled; however, the extent of NE [unenrolled] landowners there may be idiosyncratic to the area due to specific practices of BIA" (Willett to Ruppel, March 6, 2003).

67. For instance, in *Montana v. United States*, 450 U.S. 544 (1981), the Court ignored canons of construction requiring that treaty language be interpreted in the tribe's favor. Instead, the Court decided that the Crow Tribe's sovereignty did not extend to the regulation of non-Indian fishing rights in a riverbed running through fee land owned by non-Indians within the reservation, even though the Second Treaty of Fort Laramie (1868) expressly states that "the Indians" retain "absolute and undisturbed use and occupation" of their reserved lands (15 U.S. *Statutes at Large* 649, art. 2). In another infamous case from the same period, *Oliphant v. Suquamish Indian Tribe*, 435 U.S. 191 (1978), the Court held that tribes do not have criminal jurisdiction over non-Indians on a reservation without express delegated authority from Congress.

68. In place of the passive trust provision, though with a different function, is a new "owner-managed" status in which living landowners may, with unanimous agreement of all co-owners in a parcel, agree to enter into 10-year agricultural leases without the approval or

oversight of the secretary of the interior (American Indian Probate Reform Act, *U.S. Code* 25, chap. 24, sec. 2220). Landowner advocates see this as a step toward the federal government's termination of its trust responsibilities.

69. Ernestine Broncho Werelus to Senator Ben Nighthorse Campbell, May, 19, 2003.

Chapter 5. One More Arrow

1. Ernestine "Ernee" Broncho Werelus, "Landowners Association Meet Land Officials," *Sho-Ban News* (Fort Hall, Idaho), February 7, 1997, 8.

2. Conservation Reserve Program (CRP) Information Meeting Minutes, Fort Hall, November 21, 1997, p. 1.

According to its Web site, the Farm Service Agency (FSA) of the U.S. Department of Agriculture (USDA) "administers and manages farm commodity, credit, conservation, disaster and loan programs as laid out by Congress through a network of federal, state and county offices." See http://www. fsa.usda.gov/FSA/ webapp?area= about&subject=landing&topic= landing/. Idaho's FSA is one of those state offices in the national FSA network.

3. Ernestine "Ernee" Broncho Werelus and Frank Papse Sr. to Dick Rush, October 30, 1997.

4. Rush made this clear in his final statement to those gathered for his visit: "I would like to express the direction . . . I am under the President and Secretary of Agriculture. They have not been pleased with the performance of the USDA in the civil rights area, dealings with the tribes . . . . We have a huge problem in the southeast of the United States. It's not a tribal issue. It is a civil rights issue. I can tell you that we are directed to, as far as tribes . . . to deal with the tribes government to government to do everything possible to do what you want us to do, to sit down and negotiate." Conservation Reserve Program (CRP) Information Meeting Minutes, Fort Hall, November 21, 1997, pp. 6–7. See also note 27, chapter 4, on the class-action lawsuit brought by black farmers against the USDA.

5. Federal law stipulates that no more than 25 percent of a county's agricultural acreage can be in the Conservation Reserve Program in any given year.

6. In testimony before the House Committee on Resources, Elouise Cobell identified a similar dynamic in the Individual Indian Money (IIM) litigation. With reference to section 137 of the House Interior Appropriations bill ("Mandatory Account Adjustment Directive" or MAAD), she states: "A central stated justification for Section 137, the appropriators' MAAD proposal, is the mistaken notion that there is no end in sight to the *Cobell v. Norton* lawsuit. That is simply not true" (July 9, 2003). And Native American Rights Fund (NARF) attorney Richard Guest writes with regard to section 137: "The truth is that it is precisely because the Court is reaching resolution [. . .] that the Department of the Interior was desperate for Congress to pass Section 137. The truth is that a credible alternative has been presented which will bring real reform to the Indian trust and resolution to the *Cobell v. Norton* lawsuit. Both parties have agreed to engage in mediated settlement." "Section 137: Reality and Myth," *Indigenous Lands Reporter* 1, no. 2 (Summer 2003). Congress did not pass section 137.

7. The 2001 *Indian Land Tenure Partnership Plan* reports: "Generally, all colleges teach and support programs based on general concepts of 'Indian land.' However, all of these

curriculums generally focus on the ecological and environmental qualities of land and land management. In every college [in the eight state region surveyed] there are complete course programs resulting in degrees or certificates and/or entire departments devoted to land subjects such as 'Environmental Science,' and/or 'Natural Resource Management,' or land/water programs like 'Agriculture,' and 'Fisheries Management,' that are geared toward specific economic activities on the land" (Carmody 2001, app. E, p. 12). The eight states surveyed are Washington, Oregon, Idaho, Montana, North Dakota, South Dakota, Minnesota, and Iowa. The partnership plan proposed the development of a nonprofit Indian Land Tenure Foundation (see below in this chapter).

8. Judge Sally Willett, "Plain Language Indian Will" (Phoenix: 1994), 1–3.

9. Delmar "Poncho" Bigby, Pendleton, Oregon, October 2000. The late Poncho Bigby was chairman of the Indian Land Working Group when I first began attending the Indian Land Consolidation symposia in 2000.

10. Austin Nuñez, *Indigenous Lands Reporter*, 1, no. 2 (Summer 2003).

11. Theresa Carmody, personal communication, July 2007. The *Estate Planning and Probate Manual* (Carmody 2006) also includes a "Resource Document" CD with the relevant laws (ILCA and AIPRA) and forms; and DVD with interviews of tribal representatives and landowners talking about fractionation, estate planning, the probate process, and the importance of tribal probate codes.

12. Simon Ortiz to Kristin T. Ruppel, March 25, 2002.

13. Heidegger wrote: "The achieving of phenomenological access to the beings which we encounter, consists rather in thrusting aside our interpretive tendencies, which keep thrusting themselves upon us and running along with us, and which conceal not only the phenomenon of such 'concern,' but even more those beings themselves *as* encountered of their own accord *in* our concern with them" (see Dreyfus 1990, 47).

Chapter 6. Encounters

1. "Chiefs May Hang Up Headdresses: Chamber Group Pressed to Change," *Idaho State Journal*, April 19, 2001, 1.

2. Aside from the immigrants from east and west who came to prospect, homestead, and speculate after the end of the Civil War, thousands upon thousands of families and millions of head of livestock followed the Oregon Trail through this area during the Gold Rush decade following 1848. The transient crowds and herds devastated plant and animal life for miles either side of the trail, making Native subsistence (already tenuous because of pressure from other displaced tribes) untenable. Wagon train ruts are still discernible along sections of the trail west of Pocatello.

3. In another of many examples of its assumed "plenary power" over American Indian affairs, Congress unilaterally ended the executive's power to make treaties with Indian nations in 1871.

4. I use the term "inhabitants" instead of "owners" not to belittle or deny Native territorial claims (as does federal Indian law, which recognizes "aboriginal title" as a right of occupancy, alienable only to the United States or, originally, the Crown), but to acknowledge the

possibility and presence of various other, indigenous forms of land tenure (that is, those not necessarily based in assumptions about the essential alienability of land).

5. Brigham Madsen (1983/1996, 242) recounts: "[In] 1887, the Indian Commissioner reviewed the entire case [and] pointed out that in their application for land at Pocatello, the two railways requested a plot of 1,600 acres to add to the 80 acres already granted the Utah Northern at that place. The commissioner considered that amount of land an "unreasonably large quantity [. . .] to be required for railroad purposes alone at any single point," and added that "within the experience of this office no railroad company has hitherto required such an extent of land for railway purposes on an Indian reservation as is here asked for."

6. The foregoing history of Pocatello's founding is related in detail in a number of Brigham Madsen's works, including *The Northern Shoshoni* (1980/2000), *The Bannock* (1983/1996), and to a lesser extent in *The Lemhi: Sacajawea's People* (1979/1990).

7. The Fort Hall Indian Reservation is shaped something like an elephant head, with the trunk extending down a valley to the west and south of Pocatello, and the chin and neck resting to the city's north and east. My thanks to Ernee Werelus for the image.

8. Madsen's historical works rely heavily on newspaper accounts and editorials to give a flavor of the attitudes of the time.

9. "Chiefs May Hang Up Headdresses: Chamber Group Pressed to Change," *Idaho State Journal*, April 19, 2001, 1.

10. Excavated by ISU archaeologists under the auspices and blessings of tribal officials and spiritual leaders, the "Wahmuza" site has helped the Shoshone-Bannock Tribes to gain legal ground in the ongoing fight for control of waters flowing through Shoshone-Bannock treaty lands.

11. All unattributed poetry is by the author.

12. The railroad also transported people, as it switchbacked its way up to a tunnel burrowing under the Continental Divide at Bannock Pass, east of Leadore. The trip up to the divide took eight to nine hours to complete, during which time travelers could disembark and walk alongside the slowly advancing train. In existence for only a short time (1910–39), the G&P is still remembered locally as the "Get Off and Push" railroad. Or, occasionally (according to one historical treatise), as the "Grunt and Puff" (Waite 2002, v).

13. The population sign at Leadore read 111 throughout the 1970s. The town's population had dropped to 73 by the 1990s but rose to 90 in the most recent census.

14. The Lemhi Reservation owed its "marginal sufficiency" to the white clamor for their land and water—which left them with a reserve too small to sustain their essentially captive population—compounded by a miserly federal bureaucracy and manipulative, "mostly incompetent and sometimes dishonest" Indian agents (Benedict 1996, 137, 151; Madsen 1979/1990, 160–161). Madsen (1979/1990, 161) writes: "The end of the century found the tribe striving for a living on an overpopulated speck of land hidden away from the notice of the Office of Indian Affairs, whose officials wondered why the Lemhi would not agree to move to Fort Hall."

The period of Nez Perce resistance to removal from their ancestral homelands, when the United States' unilaterally abrogated their 1863 treaty, was referred to as the "Nez Perce Wars." In an 1880 report to Congress, Senator Henry Moore Teller (a vociferous opponent of allotment policies) quoted "a chief" who said: "They asked us to divide the land, to divide our mother upon whose bosom we had been born, upon whose lap we had been reared" (see Cohen 1942a/1971, 208).

15. Shoup later represented Idaho as a U.S. senator (Madsen 1979/1990, 139, 145).

16. The Cheyenne and Arapaho estimated that fewer than 200 Indians were killed, whereas Colonel Chivington and other participants in the massacre reported much higher numbers, between 350 and 600. See http://www.coloradohistoricnewspapers.org/ for an archive of newspaper accounts (including reprints of letters from Chivington and Shoup) and editorials from the period. See also Ortiz 1981.

From Denver's *Rocky Mountain News*, December 22, 1864: "Headed by the First Regiment band and by Colonels Chivington and Shoup, the rank and file of the 'bloody Thirdsters' made a most imposing procession. Although covered o'er with dust, the boys looked bully." And: "Cheyenne scalps are getting as thick here as toads in Egypt. Everybody has got one, and is anxious to get another to send to the east."

17. Hope Benedict (1996) contends that the assumption that Western mining settlements were inherently prone to disintegrate oversimplifies and overlooks those places, like the city of Salmon and Lemhi County, where community formation did in fact occur and has endured. Although Benedict's discussion of the Lemhi Indians is hardly central to her study, I am indebted to her for the observation that the Lemhi County "sense of place" excluded non-Anglo participation.

18. By most accounts, Sacajawea was taken from the Lemhis as a small child during a raid by another tribe. However, the spelling and meaning of her name as well as her tribal or ethnic affiliation—including the place of her birth—are all topics of contention. She has long been claimed by and capitalized upon by the Mandan Sioux. In fact, some of the goods marketed under her name and personage, like the "Sacajawea Chocolate" bars for sale in Salmon, Idaho, are produced in Mandan, North Dakota.

19. The Mormon missionaries originally named the region and its inhabitants after "Limhi," the son of "King Noah in the Land of Nephi" (South America). Limhi is said to have battled mightily against the "Lamanites," the unbelievers who, according to the *Book of Mormon*, are "the principal ancestors of the American Indians" (*Book of Mormon*, "Introduction"; see, for example, Mosiah 20, 21; see also Conley 1982, 214).

20. Thanks to poet and professor Roger Dunsmore for reviewing this chapter and suggesting this, in keeping with the arguments of the late Vine Deloria Jr. and the experiences of many indigenous people for whom "understanding resides in the spirits, in the soil itself."

References Cited

Arendt, Hannah. 1958. *The Human Condition*. Chicago: University of Chicago Press.

Arguedas, José María. 1950/1985. The Novel and the Problem of Literary Expression in Peru. In *Yawar Fiesta*. Austin: University of Texas Press.

Axtell, James. 1992. *Beyond 1492: Encounters in Colonial North America*. New York: Oxford University Press.

Benedict, Hope Ann. 1996. Place and Community in the Mining West of Lemhi County, Idaho, 1866–1929. Ph.D. diss., University of Oregon.

———. 2006. *Lemhi County, Idaho*. San Francisco: Arcadia.

Berkes, Fikret. 1999. *Sacred Ecology: Traditional Ecological Knowledge and Resource Management*. Philadelphia: Taylor & Francis.

Berkhofer, Robert F., Jr. 1978. *The White Man's Indian: Images of the American Indian from Columbus to the Present*. New York: Knopf.

Berry, Wendell. 1985. *Collected Poems*. San Francisco: North Point Press.

Biolsi, Thomas. 1992. *Organizing the Lakota: The Political Economy of the New Deal on the Pine Ridge and Rosebud Reservations*. Tucson: University of Arizona Press.

Bobroff, Kenneth H. 2001. Retelling Allotment: Indian Property Rights and the Myth of Common Ownership. *Vanderbilt Law Review* 54, no 4:1559–1623.

Boland, Eavan. 2000. The Last Year. Sesquicentennial edition. *Harper's Magazine*, June, 119–122.

Bordewich, Fergus. 1996. *Killing the White Man's Indian*. New York: Doubleday.

Bourdieu, Pierre. 1977. *Outline of a Theory of Practice*. Translated by Richard Nice. Cambridge: Cambridge University Press.

Brookings Institution. 1928. *The Problem of Indian Administration*. Baltimore: Johns Hopkins Press.

Canby, William C. 2004. *American Indian Law in a Nutshell*. 4th ed. Saint Paul, Minn.: West.

Canny, Nicholas P. 1973. The Ideology of Colonization: From Ireland to America. *William and Mary Quarterly*, 575 (October 30): 575–598.

Carlson, Leonard A. 1981. *Indians, Bureaucrats, and the Land: The Dawes Act and the Decline of Indian Farming*. Westport, Conn.: Greenwood Press.

Carmody, Theresa. n.d. *The American Indian Probate Reform Act Is Not All Reform*. Albuquerque, N.M.: Indian Land Working Group.

———. 1998. *Indian Land Consolidation Manual*. Albuquerque, N.M.: Indian Land Working Group.

———. 2001. *Indian Land Tenure Partnership Plan*. Albuquerque, N.M.: Indian Land Working Group.

———. 2002 The ILCA Amendments: More Potential Mismanagement of Alotted Lands. *First Nations Development Institute Business Alert* 17, no. 2: 1, 5, 10–15.

———. 2006. *Estate Planning and Probate Manual.* Albuquerque, New Mexico: Indian Land Working Group.

Carrillo, Jo. 2002. Getting to Survivance: An Essay about the Role of Mythologies in Law. *PoLAR* 25, no. 1:37–47.

Casey, Edward S. 1997. *The Fate of Place: A Philosophical History.* Berkeley: University of California Press.

Chester, Ronald. 1995. Is the Right to Devise Property Constitutionally Protected?—The Strange Case of *Hodel v. Irving. Southwestern University Law Review* 24:1195–1213.

Chomsky, Noam. 1993. *Year 501: The Conquest Continues.* Boston: South End Press.

Clinton, Robert N. 2002. There Is No Federal Supremacy Clause for Indian Tribes. *Arizona State Law Journal* 34:113–260.

Cohen, Felix S. 1942a/1971. *Handbook of Federal Indian Law.* Albuquerque, N.M.: University of New Mexico Press.

———. 1942b/1960. The Spanish Origin of Indian Rights in the Law of the United States. In *The Legal Conscience: Selected Papers of Felix S. Cohen,* 230–252. Edited by Lucy Kramer Cohen. New Haven, Conn.: Yale University Press.

———. 1945/1960. Indian Claims. In *The Legal Conscience: Selected Papers of Felix S. Cohen,* 264–272. Edited by Lucy Kramer Cohen. New Haven, Conn.: Yale University Press.

———. 1953/1960. Indian Wardship: The Twilight of a Myth. In *The Legal Conscience: Selected Papers of Felix S. Cohen,* 328–334. Edited by Lucy Kramer Cohen. New Haven, Conn.: Yale University Press.

———. 1960. *The Legal Conscience: Selected Papers of Felix S. Cohen.* Edited by Lucy Kramer Cohen. New Haven, Conn.: Yale University Press.

Cohen, G. A. 2000. *Karl Marx's Theory of History: A Defence.* Expanded ed. Princeton, N.J.: Princeton University Press.

Colapietro, Vincent. 1989. *Peirce's Approach to the Self: A Semiotic Perspective on Human Society.* Albany: State University of New York Press.

Comaroff, Jean, and John L. Comaroff 1991. *Of Revelation and Revolution.* Vol. 1: *Christianity, Colonialism, and Consciousness in South Africa.* Chicago: University of Chicago Press.

Conley, Cort. 1982. *Idaho for the Curious: A Guide.* Cambridge, Idaho: Backeddy Books.

Coutin, S. B. 2000. *Legalizing Moves: Salvadoran Immigrants' Struggle for U.S. Residency.* Ann Arbor: University of Michigan Press.

Cronon, William. 1983. *Changes in the Land: Indians, Colonists and the Ecology of New England.* New York: Hill and Wang.

Culhane, Dara. 1998. *The Pleasure of the Crown: Anthropology, Law and First Nations.* Burnaby, B.C.: Talon Books.

Daniel, E. Valentine. 1996. *Charred Lullabies: Chapters in an Anthropography of Violence.* Princeton, N.J.: Princeton University Press.

Debo, Angie. 1985. *A History of the Indians of the United States.* Norman: University of Oklahoma Press.

De Genova, Nicholas P. 2002. Migrant "Illegality" and Deportability in Everyday Life. *Annual Review of Anthropology* 31:419–447.

Deleuze, Gilles, and Félix Guatarri. 1987. *A Thousand Plateaus: Capitalism and Schizophrenia.* Translated by B Massumi. Minneapolis: University of Minnesota Press.

Deloria, Vine Jr. 1969/1988. *Custer Died for Your Sins: An Indian Manifesto.* Norman: University of Oklahoma Press.

———. 1974/1985. *Behind the Trail of Broken Treaties: An Indian Declaration of Independence.* Rev. ed. Austin: University of Texas Press.

Deloria, Vine, Jr., and Clifford M. Lytle. 1984. *The Nations Within: The Past and Future of American Indian Sovereignty.* Austin: University of Texas Press.

Deloria, Vine, Jr., and David E. Wilkins. 1999. *Tribes, Treaties, and Constitutional Tribulations.* Austin: University of Texas Press.

Derrida, Jacques. 1992. Force of Law: The "Mystical Foundation of Authority." In *Deconstruction and the Possibility of Justice,* 3–67. Edited by Drucilla Cornell, Michael Rosenfeld, and David G. Carlson. New York: Routledge.

Dreyfus, Hubert L. 1990. *Being-in-the-World: A Commentary on Heidegger's "Being and Time," Division I.* Cambridge, Mass.: MIT Press.

Economics Research Associates. 1973. *Economic Study and Plan of the Fort Hall Indian Reservation.* Los Angeles.

Fey, Harold E., and D'Arcy McNickle. 1959. *Indians and Other Americans: Two Ways of Life Meet.* New York: Harper.

Fort Hall Landowners Alliance (FHLA). 2001. *Trust Land: Landowner Organization Handbook.* Fort Hall and Pocatello, Idaho: Fort Hall Landowners Alliance and Idaho State University.

Foucault, Michel. 1977. *Discipline and Punish: The Birth of the Prison.* Translated by A. Sheridan. New York: Pantheon.

———. 1980. The Eye of Power. In *Power/Knowledge: Selected Interviews and Other Writings, 1972–1977.* Edited by Colin Gordon. New York: Pantheon Books.

Frantz, Klaus. 1999. *Indian Reservations in the United States: Territory, Sovereignty, and Socioeconomic Change.* Chicago: University of Chicago Press.

Frickey, Philip P. 1990. Congressional Intent, Practical Reasoning, and the Dynamic Nature of Federal Indian Law. *California Law Review* 78:1137–1240.

General Accounting Office (GAO). 1974. *Land Leases on the Fort Hall Indian Reservation in Idaho.* B-114868. Report to the Subcommittee on Indian Affairs, Committee on Interior and Insular Affairs, U.S. Senate. Washington, D.C.: U.S. Government Printing Office.

———. 1992. *Profile of Land Ownership at 12 Reservations.* B-246894. Briefing Report to the Chairman, Select Committee on Indian Affairs, U.S. Senate. Washington, D.C.: U.S. Government Printing Office.

Getches, David H., Charles F. Wilkinson, and Robert A. Williams Jr. 2005. *Cases and Materials on Federal Indian Law.* 4th ed. American Casebook Series. Saint Paul, Minn.: West Group.

Gilbert, Jess, Spencer D. Wood, and Gwen Sharp. 2002. Who Owns the Land? Agricultural Land Ownership by Race/Ethnicity. *Rural America* 17, no. 4: 55–62.

Gilbert, William H., and John L. Taylor. 1966. Indian Land Questions. *Arizona Law Review* 8:102–131.

Gingold, Dennis, and Keith Harper. 2001. Plaintiffs' consolidated motion to amend [. . .] for defrauding this Court in connection with Trial One. Submitted by NARF attorneys, October 19, 2001. D.C. District Court, Washington, D.C.

Gramsci, Antonio. 1971. *Selections from Prison Notebooks.* London: Lawrence and Wisehart.

Greenhouse, Carol J. 1989. Just in Time: Temporality and the Cultural Legitimation of Law. *Yale Law Journal* 98:1631–1644.

Grim, John A. (ed.). 2001. *Indigenous Traditions and Ecology: The Interbeing of Cosmology and Community.* Cambridge, Mass.: Harvard University Press.

Grinde, Donald A., and Bruce E. Johansen. 1995. *Ecocide of Native America: Environmental Destruction of Indian Lands and Peoples.* Santa Fe: Clear Light.

Guzman, Katheleen R. 2000. Give or Take an Acre: Property Norms and the Indian Land Consolidation Act. *Iowa Law Review* 85:595–662.

Hakansson, Carl G. 1997. Allotment at Pine Ridge Reservation: Its Consequences and Alternative Remedies. *North Dakota Law Review* 73:231–261.

Handler, Richard. 1991. Who Owns the Past? History, Cultural Property, and the Logic of Possessive Individualism. In Brett Williams (ed.), *The Politics of Culture,* 63–74. Washington, D.C.: Smithsonian Institution.

Hanscom, Greg. 1998. Tribes Reclaim Stolen Lands. *High Country News* 30, no. 14:1, 8–11.

Hartshorne, Charles, and Paul Weiss (eds.). 1931–35. *The Collected Papers of Charles Sanders Peirce.* Bloomington: Indiana University Press.

Heidegger, Martin. 1971. *Poetry, Language, Thought.* Translated by Albert Hofstadter. New York: Harper & Row.

Heller, Michael A. 1998. The Tragedy of the Anticommons: Property in the Transition from Marx to Markets. *Harvard Law Review* 111:621–688.

———. 1999. The Boundaries of Private Property. *Yale Law Journal* 108:1163–1223.

Hone, Emily. 1998. Landowners Want More Money for Reservation Farming. *Blackfoot Morning News* (Blackfoot, Idaho), March 4, 1–2.

Honig, Bonnie. 2001. *Democracy and the Foreigner.* Princeton, N.J.: Princeton University Press.

Hookway, Christopher. 2000. *Truth, Rationality, and Pragmatism: Themes from Peirce.* Oxford: Clarendon Press.

Houser, Nathan, and Christian Kloesel, eds. 1992. *The Essential Peirce: Selected Philosophical Writings.* Vol. 1 (1867–93). Bloomington: Indiana University Press.

Hoxie, Frederick E. 2001. *A Final Promise: The Campaign to Assimilate the Indians, 1880–1920.* Lincoln: University of Nebraska Press.

Hughes, Michael D. 2007a. The History of Federal Funding for Indian Trust Restructuring, 1996–2004. In *Proceedings of the Seventeenth Annual Indian Land Consolidation Symposium,* 243–266. Green Bay, Wis.: Indian Land Working Group.

———. 2007b. Bureau of Indian Affairs Natural Resources and Trust Services Fiscal Year 2007 and 2008 Funding. In *Proceedings of the Seventeenth Annual Indian Land Consolidation Symposium,* 267–280. Green Bay, Wis.: Indian Land Working Group.

Indian Land Working Group (ILWG). 2007. Recommendations Related to Specific Deficits in Allotted Land Administration Impacting Orderly Use and Administration of Allotments. Resolution no. 02-07. Available online at Indian Land Working Group Web site, http://www.ilwg.org/policy_projects.html/.

Jackson, Deborah Davis. 2002. *Our Elders Lived It: American Indian Identity in the City.* De Kalb: Northern Illinois University Press.

Jennings, Francis. 1975. *The Invasion of America: Indians, Colonialism and the Cant of Conquest.* Chapel Hill: University of North Carolina Press.

Johansen, Bruce E. 2000. *Shapers of the Great Debate on Native Americans—Land, Spirit, and Power: A Biographical Dictionary.* Westport, Conn.: Greenwood Press.

Jones, Dorothy V. 1982. *License for Empire: Colonialism by Treaty in Early America.* Chicago: University of Chicago Press.

Kickingbird, Kirke, and Karen Ducheneaux. 1973. *One Hundred Million Acres.* New York: Macmillan.

Kinney, J. P. 1927. Forest Policy on Indian Timberlands. *Journal of Forestry* 25, no. 4 (April 1): 430–436.

———. 1937. *A Continent Lost, a Civilization Won: Indian Land Tenure in America.* Baltimore: Johns Hopkins University Press.

Laidlaw, Sally Jean. 1960. Federal Indian Policy and the Fort Hall Indians. Master's thesis, Idaho State University.

Lawson, Michael. 1984. Heirship: The Indian Amoeba. Reprinted in Hearing on S. 2480 and S. 2663 before the Senate Select Committee on Indian Affairs, 98th Cong., 2d sess. Washington, D.C.: U.S. Government Printing Office.

Leavitt, John H. 1988. *Hodel v. Irving*: The Supreme Court's Emerging Takings Analysis— A Question of How Many Pumpkin Seeds Per Acre. *Environmental Law* 18:597–634.

Leupp, Francis. 1910. *The Indian and His Problem.* New York: Scribner's.

Liljeblad, Sven. 1957. Indian Peoples in Idaho. Anthropology Department, Idaho State University, Pocatello, Idaho.

———. 1972. *The Idaho Indians in Transition, 1805–1960.* Pocatello: Idaho State University Museum.

Limerick, Patricia N. 1987. *The Legacy of Conquest: The Unbroken Past of the American West.* New York: Norton.

Lindo, Michelle M. 1997. *Youpee v. Babbitt*—The Indian Land Inheritance Problem Revisited. *American Indian Law Review* 22, no.1: 223–246.

Lindquist, G.E.E. 1919/1923. *The Red Man in the United States.* New York: George H. Doran.

Lorde, Audre. 1981. The Master's Tools Will Never Dismantle the Master's House. In *This Bridge Called My Back: Writings by Radical Women of Color.* Edited by Cherrie Moraga and Gloria Anzaldua. Watertown, Mass.: Persephone Press.

Lubowski, Ruben N., Marlow Vesterby, Shawn Bucholtz, Alba Baez, and Michael J. Roberts. 2002/2006. *Major Uses of Land in the United States.* Economic Information Bulletin no. 14. Washington, D.C.: U.S. Department of Agriculture.

Madsen, Brigham D. 1979/1990. *The Lemhi: Sacajawea's People.* Caldwell, Idaho: Caxton Printers.

———. 1980/2000. *The Northern Shoshoni*. Caldwell, Idaho: Caxton Press.

———. 1996. *The Bannock of Idaho*. Moscow: University of Idaho Press.

Malkki, Liisa. 1992. National Geographic: The Rooting of Peoples and the Territorialization of National Identity among Scholars and Refugees. *Cultural Anthropology* 7, no. 1:24–43.

Mamdani, Mahmood. 1996. *Citizen and Subject: Contemporary Africa and the Legacy of Late Colonialism*. Princeton, N.J.: Princeton University Press.

Martí, José. 1885, 1889, 1894/1975. *Inside the Monster: Writings on the United States and American Imperialism*. Translated by Elinor Randall et al. Edited by Philip S. Foner. New York: Monthly Review Press.

McDonnell, Janet A. 1991. *The Dispossession of the American Indian, 1887–1934*. Bloomington: Indiana University Press.

Nabokov, Peter (ed.). 1999. *Native American Testimony: A Chronicle of Indian-White Relations from Prophecy to the Present, 1492–2000*. Rev. ed. New York: Penguin Books.

Nadasdy, Paul. 2002. "Property" and Aboriginal Land Claims in the Canadian Subarctic: Some Theoretical Considerations. *American Anthropologist* 104, no. 1:247–261.

Nickeson, Steve. 1976. The Structure of the Bureau of Indian Affairs. In *American Indians and the Law*, 61–76. Edited by Lawrence Rosen. New Brunswick, N.J.: Transaction Books.

Ortiz, Simon J. 1981. *From Sand Creek*. New York: Thunder's Mouth Press.

———. 1992. *Woven Stone*. Tucson: University of Arizona Press.

———. 2002. *Out There Somewhere*. Tucson: University of Arizona Press.

Otis, Delos Sacket. 1934/1973. *The Dawes Act and the Allotment of Indian Lands*. Edited by Francis Paul Prucha. Norman: University of Oklahoma Press.

Parker, Kelly. 1998. *The Continuity of Peirce's Thought*. Nashville: Vanderbilt University Press.

Perry, Richard Warren. 2002. Remapping the Legal Landscapes of Native North America: Layered Identities in Comparative Perspective. *PoLAR* 25, no. 1:129–150.

Peterson & Associates. 1976. *Futures: A Comprehensive Plan for the Shoshone-Bannock Tribes*. Boise.

Pevar, Stephen L. 2004. *The Rights of Indians and Tribes*. New York: New York University Press.

Pommersheim, Frank. 1995. *Braid of Feathers: American Indian Law and Contemporary Tribal Life*. Berkeley: University of California Press.

———. 1997. Democracy, Citizenship, and Indian Law Literacy: Some Initial Thoughts. *T. M. Cooley Law Review* 14:457–461.

Povinelli, Elizabeth A. 1993. *Labor's Lot: The Power, History, and Culture of Aboriginal Action*. Chicago: University of Chicago Press.

———. 2002. *The Cunning of Recognition: Indigenous Alterities and the Making of Australian Multiculturalism*. Durham, N.C.: Duke University Press.

Price, Monroe E., and Robert N. Clinton. 1983. *Law and the American Indian: Readings, Notes and Cases*. 2nd ed. Charlottesville, Va.: Michie.

Prucha, Francis (ed.). 1973. *Americanizing the American Indians: Writings by the "Friends of the Indian" 1880–1900*. Cambridge, Mass.: Harvard University Press.

———. 1984. *The Great Father: The United States Government and the American Indians.* Abridged ed. Lincoln: University of Nebraska Press.

Prygoski, Philip J. 1995. From Marshall to Marshall: The Supreme Court's Changing Stance on Tribal Sovereignty. *GPSolo Magazine* 12, no. 4.

Robertson, Lindsay. 2005. *Conquest by Law: How the Discovery of America Dispossessed Indigenous Peoples of Their Lands.* New York: Oxford University Press.

Rosaldo, Renato. 1989. *Culture and Truth: The Remaking of Social Analysis.* Boston: Beacon Press.

Royster, Judith V. 1995. The Legacy of Allotment. *Arizona State Law Journal* 27:1–78.

Ruppel, Kristin T. n.d. Dis-Covering Indian Land.

———. 2004. Nations Undivided: The Dis-Ownership of the U.S. Federal Indian Trust. Ph.D. diss., Columbia University.

Rusco, Elmer R. 2000. *A Fateful Time: The Background and Legislative History of the Indian Reorganization Act.* Reno: University of Nevada Press.

Schmid, Suzanne S. 1989. Escheat of Indian Land as a Fifth Amendment Taking in *Hodel v. Irving*: A New Approach to Inheritance? *University of Miami Law Review* 43:739–763.

Schwab, Chris. 1998. Constitutional Law — Fifth Amendment Just Compensation Clause — Escheat of Indian Trust Lands. *Tennessee Law Review* 65:805–827.

Scott, James C. 1985. *Weapons of the Weak: Everyday Forms of Peasant Resistance.* New Haven, Conn.: Yale University Press.

Sells, Cato. 1917. Declaration of Policy in the Administration of Indian Affairs. In *Annual Report of the Commissioner of Indian Affairs*, 3–5. Washington, D.C.: U.S. Government Printing Office.

Shoemaker, Jessica. 2003. Like Snow in the Spring Time: Allotment, Fractionation, and the Indian Land Tenure Problem. *Wisconsin Law Review*, 729–788.

Sledd, John. 2005. Events Leading to the American Indian Probate Reform Act of 2004 (AIPRA). http://www.montana.edu/indianland/symposium/lawsandregulations.html/.

Smith, Rogers M. 1997. *Civic Ideals: Conflicting Visions of Citizenship in U.S. History.* New Haven, Conn.: Yale University Press.

Stannard, David E. 1992. *American Holocaust: Columbus and the Conquest of the New World.* New York: Oxford University Press.

Thomas, Nicholas. 1994. *Colonialism's Culture: Anthropology, Travel and Government.* Princeton, N.J.: Princeton University Press.

Thompson, Elizabeth A. C. 1997. *Babbitt v. Youpee*: Allotment and the Continuing Loss of Native American Property and Rights to Devise. *University of Hawaii Law Review* 19:265–310.

Tsosie, Rebecca. 1997. American Indians and the Politics of Recognition: Soifer on Law, Pluralism, and Group Identity. *Law and Social Inquiry* 22, no. 2: 359–388.

———. 2001. Land, Culture, and Community: Reflections on Native Sovereignty and Property in America. *Indiana Law Review* 34:1291–1312.

U.S. House Committee on Interior and Insular Affairs. 1961. *Indian Heirship Land Study.* Pts. 1 and 2. 86th Cong., 2d sess. Washington, D.C.: U.S. Government Printing Office.

Vattel, Emmerich de. 1758/2005. *The Law of Nations.* Translated by Joseph Chitty. Livonia, Mich.: Lonang Institute. http://www.lonang.com/exlibris/vattel/.

Vizenor, Gerald. 1994. *Manifest Manners: Postindian Warriors of Survivance*. Hanover, N.H.: Wesleyan University Press.

Waite, Thornton. 2002. *"Get Off and Push": The Story of the Gilmore & Pittsburgh Railroad*. Columbia, Mo., and Idaho Falls, Idaho: Brueggenjohann/Reese and Thornton Waite.

Welliver, Mark. 2002. CP 87 and CP 100: Allotment and Fractionation within the Citizen Potawatomi Nation. *Tribal Law Journal* 2:2–43.

Wilkinson, Charles F. 1987. *American Indians, Time, and the Law: Native Societies in a Modern Constitutional Democracy*. New Haven, Conn.: Yale University Press.

Williams, Ethel J. 1971. Too Little Land, Too Many Heirs—The Indian Heirship Land Problem. *Washington Law Review* 46, no. 4 (July): 709–744.

Williams, Patricia. 1991. *The Alchemy of Race and Rights: Diary of a Law Professor*. Cambridge, Mass.: Harvard University Press.

Williams, Robert A, Jr. 1990. *The American Indian in Western Legal Thought: The Discourses of Conquest*. New York: Oxford University Press.

———. 1997. *Linking Arms Together: American Indian Treaty Visions of Law and Peace, 1600–1800*. New York: Oxford University Press.

Index